MAYA OR MESTIZO?

MAYA OR MESTIZO?

Nationalism,
Modernity,
and its
Discontents

Ronald Loewe

Teaching Culture: UTP Ethnographies for the Classroom

UTP

University of Toronto Press

LIBRARY AND ARCHIVES CANADA CATALOGUING IN PUBLICATION

Loewe, Ronald
    Maya or mestizo? : nationalism, modernity, and its discontents / Ronald Loewe.

(Teaching culture : UTP ethnographies for the classroom)
Includes bibliographical references and index.
Issued also in electronic format.

ISBN 978-1-4426-0142-0

    1. Mayas—Ethnic identity. 2. Mayas—Social life and customs. 3. Maxcanú (Mexico)—Social life and customs. 4. Maxcanú (Mexico)—Religious life and customs. 5. Social classes—Mexico—Maxcanú. 6. Maxcanú (Mexico)—Social conditions. 7. Maxcanú (Mexico)—Economic conditions. I. Title. II. Series: Teaching culture

F1435.3.E72L64 2010   305.897'42   C2010-903667-0

We welcome comments and suggestions regarding any aspect of our publications—please feel free to contact us at news@utphighereducation.com or visit our Internet site at www.utphighereducation.com.

North America
5201 Dufferin Street
North York, Ontario, Canada, M3H 5T8

2250 Military Road
Tonawanda, New York, USA, 14150
ORDERS PHONE: 1-800-565-9523
ORDERS FAX: 1-800-221-9985
ORDERS E-MAIL: utpbooks@utpress.utoronto.ca

UK, Ireland, and continental Europe
Plymbridge Distributors Ltd.
Estover Road, Plymouth, PL6 7PY, UK
TEL: 44 (0) 1752 202301
FAX ORDER LINE: 44 (0) 1752 202333
enquiries@nbninternational.com

The University of Toronto Press acknowledges the financial support for its publishing activities of the Government of Canada through the Book Publishing Industry Development Program (BPIDP).

Cover design and interior by Em Dash Design

Printed in Canada

For Maya and Brandon, the light of my life.

CONTENTS

FIGURES AND TABLES

FIGURES

TABLES

PREFACE

In my first draft, I described this book as "the endpoint of a long journey."
However, in retrospect, though it's been almost 25 years since I began conducting fieldwork in Yucatán, I really don't view this as an endpoint but as a
midpoint or an academic rite of passage, since I intend to continue visiting
the area, corresponding with friends, and writing about this part of the world
until I drop dead. I returned to Yucatán in spring 2010 for the Society for
Applied Anthropology meetings and revisited Maxcanú, the town I lived in
for two years in the late 1980s and have revisited many times.

My first foray into Yucatán occurred during the summer of 1985 when
I was a third-year graduate student at the University of Chicago. I had
spent the previous two years studying Yucatec Mayan in the basement of the
Regenstein Library and was anxious to get into the field. With a dazzler—a
letter of introduction on university letterhead with an embossed gold seal—
and a contact I had been given by my advisor, I headed off in search of Juan
Ramón Bastarrachea Manzano, a physician, ethnographer, and Mayan lin-
guist. Juan, I was told, would help me find a field site where I could spend
the summer and improve my mastery of the language.

Sure enough, Juan greeted me cordially over the phone in Yucatec
Mayan, though when he realized that I wasn't ready for the big leagues, he
switched into Spanish, asked me what hotel I was staying in, told me to pick
up a bottle of rum—*ron añejo* in particular—and be ready the next morning
at eight o'clock. When we met, he told me we had two options in terms of
field sites, but it was clear from his presentation that he had already decided
which one he thought was appropriate; thus, we headed off toward Maxcanú
near the border with Campeche. I'm sure the conversation was lively, because
conversations with Juan are always lively, but I actually remember very little
about it. What I do remember was feeling like a 12-year-old being sent off
to summer camp against my better judgment.

Once we arrived in Maxcanú, Juan began making inquiries about his *compadre*, Pedro *el chaparito* (the short one). I quickly learned that everyone—every male at least—has a nickname, and if you use someone's given name or surname, you're likely to get a blank stare. A couple of people said that they had seen him in a cantina earlier in the morning but thought he had gone back to Calcehtok. So after two glasses of *horchata de arroz* (rice water), we headed out to Calcehtok, a village of approximately 900 people, five kilometers outside Maxcanú. En route, Juan warned me to let him handle the discussion and not to let on that I knew Spanish if I wanted to learn Mayan.

When we arrived, Pedro was nowhere to be found. His wife, Elsy, welcomed us into the house, unrolled hammocks for us to sit in, and sent the five-year-old child, Gorilla, to find his father. A few minutes later Pedro showed up, welcomed his compadre, greeted me, and then sat down for what I thought would be a difficult negotiation. I was waiting for Juan to say something like "how much do you want to house and feed this gringo for two months," but, in fact, nothing that formal ever occurred, at least to my understanding. Despite the fact that there were already two adults, five children, and six dogs living in the two-room, cement-block house, Pedro readily agreed to let me stay there and scoffed at the idea that I should pay him anything. He said there was room in the back, pointing to a hammock hook under a portrait of Jesus and an electric candle that burned continuously. After discussing the latest events in Calcehtok, Juan nodded in my direction, and I pulled out the bottle and handed it to Pedro. I assumed that we would open the bottle and have a toast, but instead the host thanked me in Mayan, asked me to repeat what he said—my first test—smiled, and put the bottle in a wooden chest.

Pedro was the *escribiente* (scribe) for the *ejido* (community farm), a position reserved for someone literate enough to keep track of the different tasks that *ejidatarios* (farmer workers) were assigned and the amount of money they were due. Although this was an elective office with a three-year limit, he had held the position for 17 years, my first indication that local governance was not much different than national governance.

Shortly after the meeting ended and Juan headed back to Mérida, Pedro went to meet a business associate and I was left trying to talk to Elsy in broken Mayan. I really needed to go to the bathroom, but that was one of the things I hadn't learned how to say in the University of Chicago language lab, and I didn't want to try to communicate the concept through a series of vulgar gestures. So, after figuring out that there was no indoor plumbing, I told Elsy that I was going for a walk.

It did not take long to reach the city limits. Once I was a safe distance from any human habitation, I took a sharp left into an overgrown field and

FIGURE 0.1 My home in Maxcanú, Yucatán during the summer of 2007

took care of business. On my way back, I noticed three women balancing baskets on their heads about 100 yards off and thought this would be a good opportunity to practice Mayan. As I approached, I started reviewing Mayan greetings and questions in my head so that I could make a good impression. When the moment arrived, I greeted them and introduced myself in flawless Mayan, announcing that I had just come from Chicago. The oldest of the three looked at me with a toothless smile and replied in Spanish, "Yes, we just met you, you're the gringo who took a dump in the cemetery."

This, unfortunately, was not the only embarrassing experience I had that summer. A few weeks later, Lencho, one of my co-workers in the local orange grove, insisted that I come by for *buul y k'ek'en* (beans with pig), a popular working-class dish. I obliged one afternoon and entered his small, thatched-roof, stick hut, most of which was blackened with soot from cooking fires. The air quality in such homes is not very good, but since the smoke tends to keep insects from nesting in the thatched roof it has its advantages. Exhausted from six hours of work in the hot sun, I sat down on the 18-inch, three-legged stool Lencho had put out for me and continued our conversation about the Chicago Cubs in a mixture of Spanish and Mayan. At this point, the secret was out: everybody realized that I spoke Spanish and actually preferred to speak Spanish when I was tired or irritated. Anyway, after a long 15 minutes, Lencho's wife emerged from the "kitchen" with a large pot, eyed her husband, and waited for him to respond to her look. Lencho grinned at me sheepishly and said, "Maestro, could you please get off the table." He then brought out a couple of tiny wooden stools, approximately six inches in height, which helped me put everything in perspective. It was not until I found out that the Maya, in good humor, refer to chairs as *kis che* (fart wood) that I realized the extent of my error.

As far as I can tell, nothing serious ever came of my *faux pas.* Readers of Jean Brigg's *Never in Anger* (1970) and other introductory texts may feel that anthropologists are easily sidelined or placed in "time out" for inadvertently insulting their hosts, but this was not my experience. I was, at times, considered an affable idiot, perhaps even the village fool, but nobody tried to run me out of town for desecrating the cemetery or the dining-room table, and nobody, as far as I can recall, refused to talk to me. In fact, once I made it clear that my objective was to learn how to speak Mayan, residents of Calcehtok helped me out in large and small ways. People handed me Bibles and other printed tracts written in Mayan, they struck up conversations with me in Mayan, and they patiently corrected my poor pronunciation. Unlike English, vowel length and pitch distinguish otherwise similar words in Mayan, so mastering the spoken language is challenging. Some people questioned how much I could learn in a summer, but guided by the widespread assumption that Mayan and English have a similar sound system, they continually reassured me that I would eventually learn.

Admittedly, much of the summer was tiresome and boring. To build rapport and experience the rhythm of village life, I trudged off to work in the fields every day, mostly in the local ejido, which was dedicated to the cultivation of *naranja agría* (bitter oranges). Every day started out with a bowl of *posole* (corn gruel), which was consumed with chile and salt, along with a healthy dose of dirty jokes. After this we worked for five hours, clearing brush, digging trenches, building lattice wood structures to shade the oranges seedlings from the unrelenting sun, watering the orange plants, and listening to the "*técnicos*" (high school graduates) who had some formal training in agronomy. Most of the ejidatarios despised the "técnicos" whom they considered city kids with a little book-learning but no real knowledge of agriculture.

By 11:00 or 12:00 everyone was back in the village, dispersed among their houses, lying in their hammocks, and waiting for lunch. In my case it was always black beans with scrambled eggs, tortillas, and watermelon juice. I was convinced that my cholesterol had climbed 200 points and swore that I would never eat an egg when I returned to the United States.

In the early afternoon, some of the ejidatarios would begin to gather around a large ceiba tree and drink beer, while others would head out to their own *milpas* (corn fields) to begin the "second shift." I usually tried to sleep, study, or write field notes but was often persuaded to join the men's circle by the sacred ceiba.

After a couple of weeks, I felt I was making progress in my ability to speak Mayan and took some pride in that; however, I felt I should be doing "real anthropology." To me this meant learning more about Maya custom

FIGURE 0.2 Orange seedlings protected from the hot sun in the ejido of Calcehtok

and tradition, visiting with shamans, and witnessing the rituals described in the classic ethnographies of Robert Redfield and Alfonso Villa Rojas, such as the *u hanli kol* (food of the *milpa* ceremony) or the *ch'a cha'ak* (a rain ceremony). However, these, I was told, were rarely done anymore. In fact, I was in a place where nearly everyone, especially the youth, wanted to be modern. Teenagers sported Michael Jackson T-shirts and new punk haircuts and listened to salsa, rock—including heavy metal—and tropical music. Young girls were abandoning the traditional *huipil* (the bulky embroidered folk dress) for tight-fitting blue jeans, if they could afford them, and rushed into their houses at 4:00 p.m. each afternoon to watch the immensely popular soap opera *Tú o Nadie* (You or Nobody) starring the sexy Lucia Méndez.

And just in case I didn't understand the new mindset, one of the drivers who ferried people back and forth between Maxcanú and Calcehtok drove the point home one afternoon by complaining about how the government, specifically the Instituto Nacional Indigenista (the National Indian Institute, or INI), was trying to make them live like poor Indians. "They hate when we wear shirts like this," he said, pointing to an LA Dodgers jersey, "and they don't want us to watch television." The new attitude of INI was a reaction to decades of coercive assimilation and charges by anthropologists in the 1970s that the government was promoting cultural genocide. Therefore, while the dominant goal of INI—now renamed CDI, or Centro de Desarrollo Indigenista—was to modernize the Maya and promote Spanish, consumerism, and assimilation, the message had been recoded, and more attention was being paid to cultural preservation (*rescate cultural*) and tradition. One INI official privately described the new **indigenismo** as a type of "controlled populism"; however, to me it seemed more appropriate to describe the policy in terms of Gregory Bateson's notion of double binds, that is, giving people two contradictory messages and letting them sort them out. Bateson thought that this could lead to schizophrenia.

In any case, I was not going to be prevented from having a real anthropological experience that summer, as noted in the following story, crafted from my field notes after returning to Chicago.

The Summer of 1985

It didn't take long to realize that indigenous conceptions of disease don't hold (nor attract) as much currency in Yucatán as they once did, at least in the sleepy village I was in. I'd been working in the village orange grove for about an hour one morning, my right leg swollen and sore as a result of a fall the day before, and my nose running like a faucet, when Lencho looked over to me and said, "Rolando, you look like a sniveling dog. You should go into Maxcanú and get a shot of penicillin." I was allergic to penicillin so I replied "Nope," in perfect Mayan. "No?" replied Lencho, "what are you going to do?" "I don't know," I responded. My mind had gone blank. I couldn't remember how to say anything else. All that time in the UC language lab, and for what? Switching to Spanish I added, "Well, maybe I'll take some vitamin C." It was all around us, so it seemed the logical thing to say.

I could deal with the fact that my village was not as traditional as Chan Kom [a village which the anthropologist Robert Redfield had studied in the 1930s] but was surprised that penicillin was suggested as a cure. A lot had happened since Redfield's visit, but even some of the tourists I'd met in Mérida had seen shamans. So, after several weeks of moving dirt from one side of the orange grove to the other, my leg aching all the while, I decided to ask about shamans who lived in the area. "Don Calin of Konachen is probably the closest," remarked Lencho, "but you'll have to get a ride from Raj. He's not that close." Not wanting to go alone, I asked Lencho to come along. He agreed, invited his friend Manuel, and set a date for Friday, one of the two days that Don Calin plied his trade. An hour and a few cigarettes later, we were in Konachen. Calin's wife answered the door and told us that, since he wasn't expecting us, he had gone to sleep. Raj was unmoved. "Wake him up," he said authoritatively, "this guy came all the way from Chicago to see him." If a bit blurry-eyed, Don Calin was quite cordial and apologized for being asleep during office hours. He listened carefully as I explained about my leg and told me that although he wasn't a *real* shaman he would try to do something to ease my suffering. "Real shamans," he went on, "know a lot more than I do. You enter their homes and you see medicinal plants all over the walls.

This is all I have." He pointed to a table containing a small altar with a pastel green cross; a pack of Marlboros; a framed picture of a local beauty pageant; an assortment of pills, cough medicine, eye drops, and a dozen glass jars with plants in them; and an issue of *Alarma* featuring a story about murder by decapitation.

As we talked about the differences between real shamans and "strugglers," the term Calin used to describe himself, his wife cleaned out a glass jar and began filling it with a pungent-smelling liquid. Oh no, I thought, he's going to ask me to drink this stuff. What do I do now? Professor Hanks, my thesis advisor in Chicago, hadn't said anything about this. I looked over at Raj, but he wasn't paying attention. He had brought his own copy of *Alarma* and was busy studying one of the pictures. "Don't worry," said Calin, sensing my paranoia, "it's just rubbing alcohol. If your leg is still bothering you tomorrow, you can freeze it with this."

Next, Calin told me to roll up my pant leg; he began to chant in a low monotone as he rhythmically swatted my bared skin with a slender leafy branch. The *santiguadr* (ritual cleansing) was just as Professor Hanks had described it: canted in breath groups and marked by "dense paralinguistic, morphosyntactic, and semantic parallelism." I couldn't have put it better myself. The University of Chicago was vindicated. After about three minutes, Calin began to run out of breath or decided he wanted to go back to bed. "Espíritu Santo," he sighed, and it was all over.

The post-game commentary, however, was much longer. With the formal part of the ceremony concluded, Calin's wife resumed her place in the center of the room and used her husband's performance as a launching pad for a monologue about the good old days when people grew their own food, made their own clothing, and rolled their own cigarettes. "Nowadays," she said, taking one of Calin's Marlboros, "you break a cigarette in half and the tobacco falls out." "Ah," I said, unsurprised, but aware that I had probably missed something important. Understanding her rapid fire Mayan was difficult, but she was on a roll, and I didn't have the heart to tell her that I couldn't understand much of what she was saying. Ten, 15, 20 minutes passed. Finally, Calin returned, pointed to Raj, who was now sound asleep, and said that it was getting late. I thanked him for the cure, and we left.

Back in the pickup Raj lit a Marlboro, making me think of the conversation again. "What did she say about cigarettes anyway?" I asked, hoping he had been awake for that part of the monologue. "Just nonsense," replied Raj, "something about how the tobacco falls out if you break a cigarette in half. What does she expect to happen?" "Ya, pretty sentimental," I muttered.

As a result of this experience, I had to make a decision about what to do next. Should I return to Calcehtok or Maxcanú where I had already established rapport with the locals and learned a fair amount of Mayan? Or should I try to find a field site further to the east where people were supposedly more "authentically" Maya? Two groups of people come to mind when Yucatecans, including Mayan speakers, hear the term "Indian." One is the Lacandon, a group of Mayan speakers in Chiapas who have long hair and, at least in the popular imagination, continue to hunt with bows and arrows. This perception is reinforced by the fact that some Lacandon who now make a living by selling bows and arrows at tourist sites like Palenque know that tourists are more likely to buy their goods if they fit the tourist image of a real Indian. This means wearing a white robe and keeping their hair long. The second group is the Plains Indian seen in old TV westerns, the more feathers the better. However, if one is referring strictly to the Maya of Yucatán, the advice is always to go east of Vallodolid or head into the dense jungles of Quintana Roo.

In the end, my decision was to return to western Yucatán. Rather than searching for a more authentic experience, my life in Calcehtok caused me to reread the classic ethnographies, and some more recent ones, with a different eye, and I began to think that both presented an overly romantic view of the Maya. Ethnographers, it seemed, wanted to see continuity between the present and the past, and, if this was difficult to demonstrate, then at least they would show the residue. Classic and contemporary ethnographies also seemed a little too clean. Where was all the sexual joking I had experienced during the summer of 1985? Where previous writers like Robert Redfield saw the sacred, I saw the profane. I saw no more than a handful of men enter the Catholic church in Calcehtok, and nobody was conducting ancient Maya rituals, but there were always men under the ceiba tree consuming spirits and telling off-color jokes. Women also seemed a lot more irreverent than I expected from my reading, although my ability to access female humor was admittedly limited due to my sex. (For interesting discussions of Maya women, see Elmendorf 1976 and Re Cruz 1996.)

This, I admit, was not just a personal epiphany. Like other graduate students of my generation, I was influenced by books like George Marcus's and James Clifford's *Writing Culture,* which emphasized the way in which the ethnographer's society and culture shaped the narrative he or she produced. Although American ethnographers in the 1940s certainly did not face the same kind of censorship that Soviet writers like Mikhail Bakhtin encountered, they were, undoubtedly, influenced by a different set of literary norms, conventions that in my view resulted in a more orthodox view of religion and a more antiseptic view of social life.

None of us, of course, can step entirely outside of our own culture, and this ethnography is as much a socially constructed narrative as others.

Cultures are complex wholes characterized by rich variation, and the production of cultural knowledge or ethnography is an imperfect science—some
would say an art—in which somebody with certain personal idiosyncracies
ends up interacting with a limited group of informants who have their own
individual quirks. The advantage I have for the time being—and it probably
won't be a long time—is that I am the last dog out of the house and have had
the opportunity to read, learn from, and criticize all who have come before.
I hope I have used this advantage wisely to contribute to a more pluralistic
and somewhat different view of Yucatecan ethnography.

ACKNOWLEDGMENTS

There are many, many people to whom I owe a debt of gratitude, and mentioning their names here is small recompense for the help I received. My parents got me started on this extraordinary journey by taking me to Mexico in 1970 and showing me that you can learn a lot about another culture with a little language ability and a healthy dose of courage. I am also indebted to them for teaching me how to write. Beginning in elementary school they would go over every composition I wrote with a fine-tooth comb and place little red marks in the appropriate spots. This continued until about two years ago—although the red pencil was replaced by a black pen—when my mother developed cataracts and could no longer read my manuscripts. I only wish they were alive to see my first book. Thanks go to my dear sister, Deborah, and my brother-in-law, Pradip, for coming to visit me in the field, buying me a decent meal, and taking me to the beach.

I would also like to acknowledge the help of my dissertation committee at the University of Chicago: Professors Friedrich Katz, William Hanks, and Jean Comaroff. Although this book has moved very far afield from where it was as a dissertation, and I have no idea whether they would like the final version, I learned a lot from their counsel and criticism. Among my friends from the University of Chicago, two stand out for the help and support they gave me during this period, Eve Pinsker and Dan Wolk. We invariably learn more from our peers than from our professors, so thanks to them.

. I am reluctant to list the names of all my friends and informants in Yucatán because I know I will leave some people out and cannot remember the full names of many of them, since I seldom, if ever, used them. Anyway, here goes: Araceli Kab, Roman Ek, Oscar Duran Castillo, Juan Duran Castillo, Janitzio Duran Castillo, Asunción Canul (otherwise known as Don Chon), Norma Canul Rodriguez , Mario Ramón García y Delgado, Carmen Cahum (better known as La Bomba) and her husband Welo, Manuel Dzib Palominos, and Don Calin, the local physician who laughed me through several illnesses. Finally, thanks to my many friends from Calcehtok, including José Barbosa, Daisy and the kids, Don Rogelio, and Lencho and his brothers, who taught me how to wield a machete without cutting off my leg. Special thanks to Juan Ramón Bastarrachea Manzano for helping me get set up in the field.

I would also like to extend my thanks to colleagues and friends who have educated me through their writings and through their criticism. This list would include: Peter Hervik, Allan Burns, Quetzil Casteñada, Alicia Re Cruz, Roby Callahan, Cristina Kray, Mary Elmendorf, Michel Boccara, Domingo Dzul Poot, and the two anonymous peer reviewers who offered many fine suggestions for improving this work. Here, I would also like to thank my former colleague, Rosa Vozzo, of Mississippi State University for helping me with a couple of difficult translations, and my new colleague at California State University (Long Beach), Rita Palacios, for proofing the Spanish. Finally, many thanks to Anne Brackenbury and Betsy Struthers for ushering me through my first book and making it accessible to normal human beings. Thanks also goes to production coordinator Beate Schwirtlich for her diligence and hard work on this book.

I had three fine student assistants who helped proofread, check references, and do other editorial tasks. They are Sarah Taylor, Krystal Kittle, and Rachel Emerine. Special thanks go to Krystal for her fine painting of *Way Kot*, the Eagle Witch, which appears in this book.

My two kids, Maya Loewe and Brandon Loewe, will have to be rewarded for enduring the temporary loss of a father that writing a book involves. I can only imagine what that will cost me. Finally, thanks to my ex-wife, Helene Hoffman. Although we are no longer together, she was there at the time, and that's what acknowledgments are all about.

INTRODUCTION
Nationalism, Mestizaje, and Anthropology

In brief, my objective is to write a scholarly but readable ethnography of Maxcanú, Yucatán (a Maya town of 15,000) that demonstrates both the importance of regional, national, and global influences on community life and the creation of a new, thoroughly modern, and thoroughly Mexican citizen. Since the Mexican Revolution (1915–25)[1] there have been several concerted attempts by federal and state authorities to incorporate Yucatán's Mayan-speaking population into larger administrative structures and to promote identification with the nation-state. Recruitment campaigns by political parties like the Institutional Revolutionary Party (PRI) and its predecessors, the expansion of public education especially since 1935, and the elaboration of a modern political culture—referred to as **mestizo** regional culture—have all played important roles in this process. While I believe the roles of political parties and public schools have been well documented in previous studies, I think a better understanding of the relationship between identity and politics and the construction of the modern Mexican citizen, the mestizo, is needed.

The creation of a national subject, often referred to as **mestizaje**, is part of a long historical process that has roots in colonial Mexico and requires some understanding of the theological or religious underpinnings of Mexican nationalism. Each year on December 12 Mexicans pay homage to the Virgin of **Guadalupe**, their **patron saint**, and for many years this occasion was marked by a sermon on the Guadalupan tradition at the Colegiata de Nuestra Señora de Guadalupe in Mexico City. In 1794 the invited lecturer was a young Dominican friar named Servando Teresa de Mier, a Creole of noble upbringing who was known both for his oratorical abilities and his arrogance. In his sermon, which was attended by the archbishop of Mexico, this *enfant terrible* of colonial society focused on two themes that were a source of pride for New Spain's wealthy Creoles: the pristine evangelization of the New World by the apostle St. Thomas and the miraculous appearance of an olive-skinned virgin, Guadalupe, at Tepeyac, a **pre-Columbian** shrine dedicated to the Aztec goddess **Tonántzin**. The former "proved" that the New World owed no spiritual debt to Spain (or Spanish missionaries), the latter symbolized the incarnation or reincarnation of the Virgin Mary as a *mestiza* (brown woman). While both these themes are important for comprehending the rise of Creole consciousness and the struggle for Mexican Independence, I choose to focus on the latter since it is more closely tied to the creation of a national Mexican subject.

Although the miraculous encounter between the Virgin Mary as Guadalupe and the Indian peasant Juan Diego is said to have occurred in 1531, it was not until the mid-1600s that her cult gained a wide following, and it was not until she saved Mexico City from an epidemic in 1737 that she was recognized as its patroness. Indeed, it is something of a miracle that she was selected at all, given the fact that 40,000 of Mexico City's residents perished while Guadalupe tarried (Lafaye 1976, 246). Moreover, by 1794 when Teresa de Mier gave his famous sermon, the authenticity of the Guadalupan tradition was under attack. Not only had a Spanish historian recently challenged the documents supporting her miracles in front of the Real Academia de la Historia in Madrid, but the leadership of the Guadalupan cult had been taken over by a Spaniard, Archbishop Haro y Nuñez.

In his attempt to reappropriate and reinvigorate the Guadelupan tradition, Teresa de Mier made several amendments to her legend, including the proposition that her image was not painted on a cape belonging to Juan Diego but was impressed in *carne mortal* (in the flesh) on the cloak of the apostle St. Thomas, a sixth-century traveler whom the Indians had recognized as their god Quetzalcoatl. Such a revision not only suggested that the miracle bestowed on Mexico by Guadalupe preceded the arrival of the Spaniards by 1,000 years but circumvented challenges regarding the authenticity of the cape. As O'Gorman writes: " . . . the principal argument against [the Guadalupan tradition] was the physical impossibility of identifying the cloth of the image with a cloak of the kind used by an Indian Juan Diego" (1981, 31).

The corollary to this proposition was that Guadalupe had been worshipped for centuries at Tepeyac, the home of the Aztec deity Tonántzin (Our Mother), a hypothesis that completed the fusion of indigenous deities and Christian saints begun more than two centuries earlier. But if Teresa de Mier was a valiant fighter for Mexican Independence and the rights of his fellow Creoles, his belief in equality did not extend to the lower ranks of Mexican society. In fact, as O'Gorman notes, Teresa de Mier expressed utter contempt for political equality on more than one occasion: "In the Cathedral of Mexico on May 19, 1793 he received much applause for denouncing the decapitation of the [French Monarch] Louis the XVI, maintaining that obedience to the kings was an essential part of Christianity. . . ."(1981, 23–24).

Syncretism

Indeed, implicit in Teresa de Mier's religiously inspired vision of the Mexican nation was a less divine theory of state that reflected the ambiguity inherent in the Creole conception of *el indiano* and, more specifically, the colonial distinction between *el indiano* and *el indio*. In the seventeenth century, the term *indiano* referred generally to native-born inhabitants of the Indies, a group that included Hispanic Creoles as well as pre-Columbian peoples. Victor Ilierosme's 1609 dictionary, *Tesoro de las tres lenguas, francesa, italiana y española,* as well as later sources, define *indiano* simply as "*qui est des Indies, Indiano, huomo delle Indie*" (he who is from the Indies, Indian, person of the Indies) (in Alcides Reissner 1983, 152). In its more restricted sense, however, the term *indiano* referred to the very rich and powerful, a definition that separated the wealthy Creole from the cannibalistic *indio*. In other words, the semantic field inhabited and shaped by thinkers like Teresa de Mier was a hierarchically ordered space where Mexico's pre-Columbian inhabitants could at one moment be included as part of an historic bloc capable of challenging Spanish **hegemony** and, in the next, a group unfit to participate in Mexican society as equals.

In short, from my perspective, there is very little that separates the discursive field of Servando Teresa de Mier and his Creole compatriots and the contemporary ethnic rhetoric I explore in Chapter 3. Both play off the inherent ambiguity of ethnic nomenclature and both conjure up images of friendship between Indians and non-Indians, shared traditions, and a harmonious social order at the same time that they maintain invidious distinctions between groups. While the central metaphors of Teresa de Mier's discourse are rooted in religion as opposed to biology or culture, this is hardly surprising given the fact that the New Spain he inhabited was a theocratic state.

Mexican nationalism and the concept of mestizaje took a distinctly scientific turn following the Mexican Revolution, thanks in no small measure to Manuel Gamio and Mexican anthropology more generally. Although Gamio had been a student of Franz Boas, the father of US anthropology, during the **Porfirio Díaz** dictatorship (1877–1910; also known as the **Porfiriato**), he returned to Mexico following the revolution and held several academic and governmental posts before being named director of anthropology at the Ministry of Agriculture in 1917 (Hewitt de Alcántara 1984, 10). Gamio's work, although extremely diverse, can be seen as an attempt to reformulate the views of such leading nineteenth-century nationalists as Justo Sierra, Vicente Rivas Palacio, and Andrés Molina Enríquez within a framework compatible with his anthropological training.

Intellectual life during the Porfiriato was dominated by the conservative sociology of Comte and Spencer; however, in the work of Molina Enríquez, a teacher of mixed Creole-Otomi ancestry, social Darwinism provided the theoretical armature for a resurgent nationalism that placed the mestizo at the apex of Mexican history. Drawing on the ideas of the German scientist

Haekel, who suggested that hybrid species had greater vitality than either of the strains that produced them, and combining this with the presumption that individuals who lived closer to nature would ultimately adapt better to the exigencies of the national life, Molina Enríquez concluded that the mestizo population would eventually assume political control over Mexican society.

Indeed, from Molina Enríquez's standpoint, the natural laws of evolution actively abetted the growth of nationalism; in his premier work, *Los grandes problemas nacionales* (1909), he insists that *mestizo* is the *only* group capable of uniting Mexico. While the numerous Indian cultures that dotted the landscape were incapable of unifying the country because they lacked a common heritage and a common language, Mexicans of European ancestry were unfit for the task because of their slavish addiction to foreign fashion and their lack of patriotism. The mestizo, on the other hand, was the quintessential bourgeois whose rise to power coincided with the evolution or expansion of individual rights in property, the *sine qua non* of the modern nation-state.

In Gamio's speeches and writings, such as *Forjando patria* (Forging the Nation, 1916), many of these themes reappear. Nationalism not only remains an unquestioned good but is linked to the emergence of a mestizo middle sector and the development of small private property. The main difference, perhaps, is that in place of Molina Enríquez's emphasis on biological miscegenation, Gamio emphasized cultural miscegenation and the need for anthropologists to help the process along.

Describing the Indianist policy (the *política positiva*) at the turn of the twentieth century, Aguirre Beltrán (1992) not only notes that the emphasis on race (i.e., biology) had given way to an emphasis on culture but that the architects of indigenismo, namely Gamio and his colleagues, had constructed a table of values in which indigenous traits could be evaluated in terms such as modern versus archaic, scientific versus superstitious, or simply good versus bad. While Gamio encouraged ethnologists to study indigenous languages as a way to better understand the speakers' mental attitudes, or as a "pathway to their soul," indigenous languages were considered inappropriate for the transmission of scientific knowledge and would have to be replaced by Spanish. Dress, names, and other cultural markers that promoted Indian communal identity were also placed in the category of negative traits that must be made positive if modern industrialism were to succeed.

Speaking at the behest of the Harris Foundation at the University of Chicago in 1926, Gamio explained:

An understanding of their [Indian] mental attitudes, their hopes and aspirations, is essential to an effective substitution of the instruments and institutions of modern civilization, or to a fusion of the modern and the primitive. Unless a substitution or fusion takes place, industrial instruments will have no cultural dynamic influence. . . . (1926, 122)

Ironically, it was in Yucatán, one of the states least affected by the Mexican Revolution at the time of his visit and untouched by the indigenous policy of the national government, that Gamio found the most encouraging signs of nationalism and a model for the rest of the nation. Describing a trip to Mérida sometime prior to 1916, he listed a variety of Yucatecan customs that he considered evidence of the transformation of an ethnically diverse society into a homogenous one:

> . . . all Yucatecans from the most elevated henequén hacienda owner to the lowest cutter of this fiber wear the same white outfit and the same straw hat, items of clothing which are only distinguished by their quality . . . The same can be said of the hammock which is the bed used by everyone in the peninsula. There is also a marked regionalism in music and dance. Cleanliness, the daily purification ritual, is an inherent characteristic of the whole population notwithstanding the shortage of water. (1926, 19)

Gamio considered that these characteristics not only presaged a harmonious convergence between Spaniard and Indian but signified the arrival of a more egalitarian order since he believed the former was impossible without the latter. In short, Gamio's report, which is more an exercise in deductive logic than an ethnographic description, ends up providing a curious legitimacy to the region that most revolutionary leaders considered the last bastion of feudalism in Mexico and that at least one writer, John Kenneth Turner (see *Barbarous Mexico* 1969 [1911]), described as a *de facto* slave state. Indeed, I would argue that Gamio's description also points to the way in which contemporary forms of inequality become submerged within broader notions of culture, custom, and common citizenship.

However, the evolution of Mexican statecraft, and the particular form it has taken in Yucatán, is only half the story. While one of my goals is to show how religion, science, culture, and custom all contribute to the perpetuation of inequality, these same practices are also used to challenge or question the prevailing power. "Power," as Fredrick Douglas noted, "never concedes anything without a fight, it never has, and it never will."[2] However, as recent events in Oaxaca, Chiapas, Mexico City, and other parts of Mexico demonstrate, it also never *exists* without a fight. Therefore, in the second part of this book, I go to considerable length to highlight the resistance to modernization, nationalism (or regionalism), and globalization. In particular, I examine three domains: **spiritist** healing as a critique of modernity, Mayan narrative as a critical commentary on the global economy, and parody and satire as a weapon of the weak.

The Book by Chapters

Chapter 1 provides a general description of Maxcanú beginning with what little is known about its pre-Columbian past. Here, I rely on the *Codice de Calkini,* a book of prophecy, history, and lore written by Maya nobles after the Conquest; several historical sources; and my own observations and archival research, which began in 1985 and continue to the present.

While little can be said about the pre-Columbian past and the early colonial period, there is a good deal of information about the corn and cattle *haciendas* that were established near Maxcanú in the eighteenth century. The advent of the hacienda not only led to a large increase in the local population but to the creation of a multi-ethnic (Creole-Maya) community. Here, in addition to discussing the organization and economy of the hacienda, I briefly describe the *vaquería,* a popular eighteenth-century festival held following the annual cattle branding, which has come to symbolize the confluence of Maya and Hispanic culture. Indeed, performances associated with the vaquería, such as the *jarana* (a popular folk dance), are now staple features not only of the tourist industry but also of regional political campaigns, public dedications, and village fiestas. In short, discussion of the vaquería serves as a way of foreshadowing a more general discussion of the role this event plays in the folklorization of regional culture and the incorporation of Yucatec Maya as citizens and consumers in contemporary Mexico.

Next, I discuss the development of the agro-industrial *henequén* plantation in the late nineteenth and early twentieth centuries, an event that marked the insertion of Mayan speakers into the global economy and the virtual elimination of the independent Maya village. This era, commonly referred to as the *época de esclavitud* (the epoch of slavery), demonstrates, among other things, that the most technologically sophisticated forms of capitalist production can be found in conjunction with the most repressive forms of labor control. In this section I also discuss post-revolutionary federal initiatives aimed at reforming agricultural production, expanding public education, and increasing domestic consumption as a prelude to a more general discussion of consumption, identity, and politics in Chapter 5.

Finally, I conclude by discussing the demise of the henequén industry and agricultural production more generally. While the collapse of henequén production can be tied to the development of synthetic forms of rope and twine in the mid-twentieth century, the collapse of agricultural production more generally (especially the destruction of the communal farm, the *ejido*) is more a result of neoliberal trade policies, including the North American Free Trade Agreement (NAFTA) introduced in the late 1980s and early 1990s and the reform of Article 27 of the Mexican Constitution. In the wake of these changes, a few haciendas have been transformed into luxury hotels and henequén-era museums as local entrepreneurs attempt to attract tourists traveling west from Chichén Itzá or Cancún; however, most lie dormant. The absence of agricultural work has been offset, in part, by the arrival of a small textile plant in Maxcanú; however, as I point out, neither tourism nor light industry has solved the social and economic problems of rural Yucatán.

In Chapter 2 the focus turns towards the social and religious structure of the community, a double helix of sorts, which expresses itself through the **gremio** system, a collection of Catholic confraternities that historically served as mutual aid societies but now generally limit themselves to festive or devotional activities. Focusing on gremio life not only provides a vehicle for discussing competition between clergy and laity, or orthodox and popular versions of Catholicism, but for illustrating the competition that exists between different status groups within the community and the way religious practice is gendered.

To illustrate this point, I offer a brief history of the prestigious *Gremio de Señoras y Señoritas,* an organization started by the wives of prosperous merchants and hacienda owners around 1925. In order to host a celebration worthy of San Miguel Arcángel, the town's patron saint, the *Señoras y Señoritas* invited other, less fortunate women (mestizas) to march in their procession. However, mindful of their place in the community, the señoras always marched at the front of the procession and drank champagne at gremio socials while the mestizas drank lemonade. Not surprisingly, perhaps, the latter eventually tired of their second-class treatment and started their own religious society. The new organization, however, was equally affected by status competition and eventually split into two organizations, a gremio of wealthy mestizas (*mestizas finas)* and one of "devout" mestizas (*mestizas devotas).*

The history of the *Señoras y Señoritas,* however, is not unique. Following the Mexican Revolution, Maxcanú reconstituted its gremio system with nine chapters or sodalities, a logical starting point since the Catholic **novena** is celebrated over a nine-day period. However, factionalism, family feuds, and status competition have led to a series of splits, and Maxcanú now has 18 different gremios, enough for two novenas.

A discussion of the gremio system also provides a unique opportunity to examine the relationship between individual religious obligations, family traditions, and community observance since gremio leadership and paraphernalia are often held by one family or one individual for generations. Indeed, it can be argued that gremio life, though rooted in tradition, is ultimately sustained by the need of individuals to perform public acts of piety or fulfill vows made to the patron saint.

In the second part of the chapter I examine the influence of new religious movements on family and community life. Since the 1960s, Maxcanú residents have witnessed the appearance and growth of several new churches (e.g., Baptist, Presbyterian, Mormon, Church of God, etc.), which have affected the way people worship, their sense of identity, their attitude toward literacy, and how they define family. For example, because members of some of the new churches view their relationship to God as a personal matter rather than a familial or corporate responsibility, they have not only severed their ties to the gremios but also to their *compadres* (spiritual co-parents). In short, while there was little discussion of religion two generations ago—the folk Catholicism of Yucatán was common orthodoxy—religious difference is now a subject of everyday conversation.

The appearance and growth of new churches has also led to the reorganization and increased evangelism by the Catholic Church. In order to stem the tide of the Protestant movement, the parish priest has not only taken religious observance into the street (in violation, according to some, of Mexican federal law) but has initiated a new, more orthodox gremio system. Unlike its predecessor, which was organized by occupation or status, the new *centros de familia* (family centers) are based on a division of the town into nine administrative units. Hence, the new gremio system is not only more closely tied to the clergy but, like the Protestant churches it opposes, is much more egalitarian.

Chapter 3 builds on Chapter 2 by developing a conceptual model of the status hierarchy that exists in Yucatán and in Mexico more generally. While Chapter 2 focuses on devotional societies, formal organizations that contain bylaws and fungible assets, Chapter 3 examines how differences in language, work, and dress, as well as participation in public performances such as the jarana, help create and maintain invidious distinctions between groups. In brief, the goal of this chapter is to explore heterogeneity within the community as well as attempts to subsume such differences within broader notions of shared substance, common ancestry, or common citizenship.

While residents of Maxcanú fall into many different named groups— *Indio, mestizo,* **catrín***, ts'ul*—they are all in one form or fashion considered "mestizos." What does this term mean and how does it unite people who do different types of work, wear different types of clothing, and speak different languages? To answer this question I present a model of ethnic/status relationships that shows how this polysemic category integrates different types of people structurally and symbolically.

Beginning at the lowest level, "mestizo" is really nothing more than a euphemism for the forbidden "indio," and is used to distinguish individuals who engage in agricultural work from people who work indoors or wear urban dress (catrínes). While this distinction is emphasized in certain settings, Maxcanú residents are quick to acknowledge that both groups—mestizos and catríns—share certain biological characteristics (such as pigmentation at the base of their spines, their emotions, etc.) that unite them as a group (mestizo$_2$), and distinguish them from more affluent "white" residents. Much is revealed by the popular saying, "*La mona aunque se vista de seda, mona se queda*" (a monkey dressed in silk is still a monkey).

Similarly, while affluent white residents disdain the term mestizo and emphasize their European ancestry at least privately, they often engage in cultural performances that celebrate the confluence of Maya and Spanish culture (*cultura regional mestiza*) and are emblematic of Yucatecan citizenship. Here, I devote special attention to the jarana, a traditional folk dance that is thought to epitomize the unity of the two cultures and has become an essential feature of major political events as well as regional fiestas. While in theory the jarana is open to individuals from all social classes or ethnic groups, in practice it has become a spectacle in which well-to-do Yucatecans don an elegant version of the folk costume and publicly represent themselves as cultivated mestizos, the first among equals. This analysis also, invariably, leads us back to a discussion of gender relations since the distinction between cultivated and non-cultivated mestizos parallels the distinction between effeminate or gay men and hearty, unquestionably heterosexual men.

While Part I—Chapters 1 to 3—identifies some of the structures of domination that govern life in rural towns like Maxcanú, Part II—Chapters 4 to 6—considers critical perspectives from below. Chapter 4 highlights one of the many ways in which Maya villagers contest religious and political power through parody and burlesque. In the writings of more well-known ethnographers like Robert Redfield and Alfonso Villa Rojas, the **cuch** ceremony is a solemn investiture in which the responsibility for organizing the annual village fiesta is passed from one gremio or religious confraternity to another by delivering a festively decorated pig's head to the incoming religious authority. And in many cases Redfield's description is correct. Redfield, however, failed to acknowledge that in some instances the cuch or the **k'ub pol** (literally, head delivery) is a raucous performance filled with lots of sexual humor and profanity aimed at the clergy, the federal police, and the owner or former owner of the hacienda. The chapter, thus, begins with a conventional description of the cuch, as seen through the eyes of Redfield, before moving on to a less solemn version of the investiture ceremony in San Bernardo, a hacienda about five kilometers from Maxcanú. After all, it is difficult, if not impossible, to understand parody or satire if one doesn't know what the satirist is poking fun at. Finally, I turn to a more artful, bourgeois representation of the k'ub pol in Maxcanú to demonstrate how tourism and the folklorization of regional culture have combined to eliminate political satire and transform the ceremony into an icon of regional and national pride.

Chapter 5 examines another critical commentary on social life and the economy, presented this time through myth rather than ritual. In the tale of *Way Kot* (The Eagle Witch), a popular story throughout the peninsula, and just one of many witch stories that are told there, I look at how commerce and the global economy are represented at the local level. Why is it that unusual consumer goods—such as Singer sewing machines, lingerie, and canned meats—all of a sudden begin to appear on the shelves of local stores?

Why is it that merchants, who sit on their butts all day, amass tremendous wealth while hard-working farm laborers remain poor? What happens to Maya who leave their native communities in search of work?

Way Kot depicts a fantasy world in which human beings become winged beasts and animals betray their natural instincts; however, unlike many studies that explore the intersection of different modes of exchange, I do not view these images as projections of a mystified mind. On the contrary, building on Marx's discussion of money and the aesthetic theory of the Frankfurt School, particularly Adorno's notion of **exact fantasy**, I demonstrate the myth's rigorous logic by showing how it unravels the mysteries of the commodity form. In addition, I highlight the critical function of the tale as rhetorical counterpoint to the commodity aesthetics of the era (ca. 1935). While agents of a rapidly modernizing state were eager to make commodities enchant, *Way Kot* presented commerce as a form of witchcraft and consumption as a form of cannibalism in which unsuspecting Maya consume their relatives. I provide five versions of the tale; Version 1, in alternating lines of Spanish/ Mayan and English, appears in the chapter while the other four versions can be found in the book's Appendix.

Chapter 6 considers another mystery, namely, the virtual disappearance of Maya **shamans** in the western part of the state and the almost unnoted appearance of female spiritists. In the classical ethnographies of Yucatán, mentioned above, shamans and shamanic rituals such as the *u hanli kol* (harvest ceremony) or the *ch'a cha'ak* (rain ceremony) figure prominently; however, by the summer of 1985 when I entered the field for the first time, finding a practicing shaman was much more difficult than finding a diet soft drink or a whole wheat bagel. Although I did eventually make friends with a shaman from Kopomá, a town ten kilometers from Maxcanú, and another in Halacho, ten kilometers in the other direction, they were clearly the last of a dying vocation. Spiritists, on the other hand, are now ubiquitous. While the spiritists of Maxcanú continue some of the medical-magical practices of the latter, such as the **santiguar**, there are a number of elements within the spiritist repertoire (e.g., channeling spirit guides) that attest to the syncretism of Maya and European healing traditions, specifically the spiritist movement associated with Allan Kardec of France (ca. 1870).

In this, admittedly ambitious chapter, I not only provide a brief history of spiritism in Yucatán, tracing it from the drawing rooms of upper-class Mérida families to rural towns and villages, but attempt a synthetic explanation of its growth that addresses recent changes in gender relations and production as well as the nature of healing. In brief, my argument is as follows. The decline of shamanism reflects the decline of **milpa** agriculture and, thus, the need to propitiate the deities for a bountiful maize harvest. Spiritism, in contrast, has never been tied to a particular type of production, so economic changes (e.g., the rise of export-oriented agriculture) has not affected it. In fact, spiritism provides an additional source of income for some households, since spiritists serve as middle-women between novelty stores in Mérida and their clientele in Maxcanú. Secondly, western or allopathic medicine involves many intrusive procedures that violate local norms of modesty, especially since most practitioners who work in the social security clinics are male. However, spiritists, unlike shamans, provide an alternative medical venue in which women can be treated by other women. Thirdly, the rise of spiritism represents a structural adjustment that makes sense in terms of local conceptions of gender. In Yucatán, women have always served as the traditional pole in a symbolic opposition between tradition and modernity, domesticity and public life. They are more likely than men to be monolingual Mayan speakers and to wear the traditional folk costume; therefore, it is hardly surprising that they have finally assumed the traditional role in a dichotomous medical system. Finally, and most importantly, I argue that spiritism is part of a prophetic tradition that honors the Maya past but is highly critical of modern medicine and the modern world more generally. In this sense, Chapter 6 builds on the idea of disenchantment with the modern world that is expressed in Part II.

Finally, I return to the globalization theme once more in the Conclusion by discussing the Maya Diaspora. In particular, I explore the preservation or revitalization of Maya culture in the US—drawing on examples of Guatemalan as well as Yucatec Maya communities—and the relationship between these movements and revitalization movements in Mesoamerica.

PART I

Organizing the Polity: Structures of Coercion and Control

CHAPTER ONE

A TOWN IN YUCATÁN
Maxcanú in Historical and Economic Perspective

In *Tradition and Adaptation* Irwin Press mentions that he decided to do fieldwork in the village of Pustunich, Yucatán because he was offered a drink as soon as he arrived. While this may be as good a reason as any, my decision to work in Maxcanú, a mestizo town of approximately 15,000 people, was based on a different set of considerations, some practical—such as the availability of housing—and some guided by my research objectives. Maxcanú not only has its own archive, a poorly preserved collection of worm-eaten documents dating back to the mid-nineteenth century, but is a short hour's drive southwest of Mérida where there are several regional archives I originally planned to use on a regular basis. Maxcanú is also located within the perimeter of the old henequén zone and was centrally involved in the agrarian struggles of the 1930s, an historical episode I was interested in examining. Thirdly, it is a large, ethnically stratified community, a fact that has obvious relevance for a study of ethnic stratification, my primary objective. Finally, I was offered food and something to drink as soon as I arrived.

Maxcanú is not considered an important center of Maya culture and religion; consequently, the town has largely escaped the attention of ethnographers. It is, nevertheless, a town with a pre-Columbian past. According to the ***Códice de Calkiní,*** a book of history, prophecy, and lore written in Yucatec Mayan following the Conquest, Maxcanú was one of five principal towns founded by the descendants of the Ah Canul lineage after the destruction of Mayapan in 1441. "We know that

FIGURE 1.1 Map of Yucatán

we came from the east [Mayapan], we the descendents of the men, Mayas ... we suffered fatigue ... as we walked the closed roads of Petén Itzá from whence comes the name Canul" (Barrera Vásquez 1980a, 35, 36). Maxcanú, thus, became the northernmost town of the Ah Canul dynasty, one of 19 separate polities that existed on the peninsula in the pre-Columbian era.

What the name Maxcanú means is the subject of friendly, never-ending debate. According to the town "elders," an unofficial group of Mayan-speaking men who gather each evening around the cement benches in the town square, there is general agreement that the second syllable—*canú*—is, in fact, derived from the Mayan patronymic Canul, as Barrera Vásquez suggests in the quote above. Invariably, though, someone suggests parsing the patronym into its constituent morphemes, noting that *kan* is the Yucatec Mayan term for "snake." Others will then jump in and point out that *k'aan* is the Mayan word for "hammock"; that *ka'an* is the Mayan word for heaven; and that *k'an* can mean a variety of things including "yellow," "ripe fruit" and "stone"—in this way listeners are given a lesson on the importance of tonality and glottalization in Mayan. After a few minutes, however, the conversation runs its course, and the group returns to Canul and a discussion about whether a prominent Maxcanú resident with this surname is actually a descendant of the Ah Canul lineage.

What the first morpheme, Max, stands for is anyone's guess. One elder suggests that it derives from the Mayan word *ma'ax,* which means monkey, but no one can remember seeing a monkey around the town so the suggestion seems improbable. A second suggests that the term really comes from the term *me'ex* (beard), but a quick glance around the group reveals that the only bearded individual is the visiting anthropologist. A third thinks that the name may refer to a small but surprisingly hot pepper (*chile max*). The presence of the plant lends plausibility to this suggestion, but the idea of naming an important town after a small pepper strikes the assemblage as rather odd. Thus, the puzzle is abandoned without resolution.

While the conquest of Yucatán was essentially complete by 1542, towns like Maxcanú remained under the jurisdiction of a native nobility for more than two centuries. In 1572, the **batab** or governor of Maxcanú was Juan Canul, a likely descendent of Nahau Canul who had been batab at the time of the Conquest (Roys 1957, 16; Barrera Vásquez 1957, 21). Maxcanú was considerably smaller than the towns in which Spaniards typically settled and, therefore, was probably free of European inhabitants during most of this period. According to the 1549 tax list, Maxcanú had a population of approximately 1,170; however, as Roys comments (1957, 16), the figures probably include two nearby villages, Kopoma and Opichén. A smaller estimate of 500 is given by Fray Alonso Ponce who visited Maxcanú on August 28, 1588 and judged it too small to serve as an ecclesiastical seat despite the "very devout" character of its inhabitants (Ciudad Real 1976, 350). At this point

Maxcanú was still under the guardianship of the town of Calkini, a situation that reflects the pre-colonial system of governance. By 1603, however,
Maxcanú had a convent of its own and, apparently, served as the religious
seat (*cabecera doctrina*) for nearby towns such as Halacho, Kopoma, and
Hopelchén.[1]

It is likely that Maxcanú continued to be an exclusively or almost exclusively Maya settlement throughout the seventeenth century since in 1667 it
was governed by Don Juan Xiu, a descendent of the famous Xiu dynasty.
The governance of Maxcanú by a Xiu descendent is no small irony given the
fact that the Xiu and Ah Canul dynasties were, apparently, bitter enemies
in Mayapan, the last great Maya city; nevertheless, the appointment of Juan
Xiu is consonant with the favoritism the Spaniards showed the Xiu for their
allegiance and with the Spanish strategy of undermining the regional and
dynastic claims of the native nobility by transplanting nobles in new and
unfamiliar terrain.[2]

Throughout the seventeenth and early eighteenth centuries, Maxcanú
was encircled by corn and cattle **estancias** (later referred to as haciendas)
that utilized relatively little indigenous labor and were basically self-sufficient.
While the nature of estancia life has been the subject of some debate over
the last two decades, historians now tend to view the relationship between
patron and client as benevolent or mutually beneficial during this period.
For example, referring to the *criados,* a small cadre of cowboys (**vaqueros**)
and foremen (**mayokoles**) who ran the estancia, Farriss argues that workers received a variety of benefits or protections that villagers lacked and
could leave the estate whenever they liked. The estancia not only covered the
employees' civil and ecclesiastical tax obligations but enabled them to avoid
the personal service that villagers were required to provide. In fact, Farriss
maintains that workers probably held the upper hand: "They demanded
credit as part of the terms of employment and they had the freedom to move
on in search of the best terms as long as (admittedly a big qualification) the
demand for rural labor exceeded the supply" (1984, 215).

The colonial estancia also attracted another category of worker, a **lunero**
(Monday worker), who exchanged one day of service and a small amount of
maize for the opportunity to plant crops on the estancia. In addition, luneros
could be called upon to help at branding time or to do odd jobs. While the
encomendero (landowner) did not cover the tax obligations of these tenant
farmers, luneros had access to water and benefited from the patronage of
the owner. "In effect," Farriss writes, "the tenants exchanged the traditional
patron-client relationship with their own leaders (and to a certain extent
with the parish priest) with the [encomendero], who—until the shift to a
more intensive exploitation of the estates—demanded considerably less in
return for his patronage" (1984, 217).[3]

The colonial estancia also gave rise to Creole cultural forms that figure prominently in Yucatán's well-inventoried "folk" culture and that have come to symbolize the confluence of its two great traditions. For example, the vaquería, a fiesta held following the annual cattle branding, includes syncretic musical and dance performances such as the jarana, a variant of the Spanish *jota* with several regional or Maya embellishments. As discussed in Chapter 4, the jarana not only remains the opening act of the four-day fiesta held to honor San Miguel Arcángel, the patron saint of Maxcanú, but it has become a staple of Yucatán's burgeoning tourist industry. The vaquería also provides a humorous glimpse of hacienda life, as the intrepid John Stephens revealed in his nineteenth-century memoir, *Incidents of Travel in Yucatán:*

> At daylight the next morning the ringing of bells and firing of rockets announced the continuance of the fiesta; high mass was performed in the church and at eight o'clock there was a grand exhibition of lassoing cattle in the plaza by amateur vaqueros. . . . The amateurs rode after [the bulls] like mad, to the great peril of old people, women and children, who scampered out of the way as well as they could, but all as much pleased with the sport as the bull or the vaqueros. . . . This over, all dispersed to prepare for the báyle [sic] de dia. . . . The báyle de dia was intended to give a picture of life at a hacienda, and there were two prominent personages, who did not appear the evening before, called fiscals, being the officers attendant upon the ancient caciques, and representing them in their authority over the Indians. These wore long, loose, dirty *camisas* [shirts] hanging off one shoulder, and with the sleeves below the hands; *calzoncillos,* or drawers, to match, held up by a long cotton sash, the ends of which dangled below the knees; sandals, slouching straw hats, with brims ten or twelve inches wide, and long locks of horse hair hanging behind their ears . . . and each flourished a leather whip with eight or ten lashes. These were the managers and masters of ceremonies, with absolute and unlimited authority over the whole company, and, as they boasted, they had a right to whip the Mestizas [upper class women] if they pleased. As each Mestiza arrived they quietly put aside the gentleman escorting her, and conducted the lady to her seat. If the gentleman did not give way readily, they took him by the shoulders, and walked him to the other end of the floor. A crowd followed wherever they moved, and all the time the company was assembling they threw everything into laughter and confusion by their whimsical efforts to preserve order. (1963 [1843], 64–66)

Toward the middle or end of the eighteenth century the ethnic composition of Maxcanú began to change. The rapid expansion of commercial agriculture in the 1700s encouraged Mérida's Creole population to buy up arable lands and move into towns previously left to the encomendero, the parish priest, and the native nobility. In fact, with access to urban markets and export facilities, the Mérida-Campeche corridor where Maxcanú resides became the site of the greatest *vecino* (non-Indian) concentration and the most intense struggles over land. Parish records show that by 1797, 43 of the 279 children baptized (15 per cent) in the parish of San Miguel de Maxcanú were of Spanish or mestizo ancestry.

TABLE 1.1 Baptisms in Maxcanú 1797

Spaniards/Mestizos		Negros		Mulattos/Indians	
Males	Females	Males	Females	Males	Females
21	22	17	23	89	107

Source: Archivo de la Mitra, Mérida, Estante 1, Libro 3

In another census taken ten years later, but still prior to the dissolution of the semi-autonomous Indian republics, residents of Spanish or mestizo ancestry accounted for more than 17 per cent of the municipal population. Not surprisingly, the overwhelming majority of this group took up residence in the *cabecera*, making the vecinos an even 30 per cent of the town's total population by 1806.[4]

TABLE 1.2 Population of Maxcanú 1806

	Spaniards/Mestizos	Indians	Mulattos	Total
Cabecera	961	1316	917	3,194
Hacienda	25	2416	30	2,471
Total	986	3732	947	5,665

Source: Parish of Maxcanú; see also Farriss, 1984: 397 (Farriss's calculation appears different because the vecino population in her table includes mulattos as well as Spanish and Mestizo hacienda residents.)

It is also likely that Maxcanú's four main *barrios*—Guadalupe, San Patricio, Tres Cruces, and Saragosa—originated during this period (ca. 1780), although arriving at a specific date or dates is not as easy as it might seem. The barrios could very well be remnants of pre-Columbian wards (*cuchteel*) since Maxcanú, as noted above, does have a pre-colonial past. Alternately, they could be artifacts of the early colonial policy of *congregación*, that is, the relocation of small communities within the boundaries of the cabecera in order to facilitate the conversion and surveillance of the local population. Although the inhabitants of these towns were physically relocated, the communities often retained a distinct identity for several generations. Eventually, however, it appears that the barrio became a reservoir for the town's indigenous inhabitants as Spaniards and Creoles began to occupy the town center, one symbol of their authority. In any case, it is doubtful that a cult dedicated to the Virgin of Guadalupe (the patron saint of one barrio) would have been established before the late 1700s since, as González Navarro notes (1970, 24), the Guadalupan movement was not introduced into the peninsula until 1755.[5]

Today, the four barrios not only define the town's perimeter but continue to sponsor their own religious celebrations. Each contains a small chapel in which its patron saint is housed, venerated, and cared for. Although nowadays the annual fiesta is organized by a local entrepreneur who purchases the rights to do so and who subcontracts beer distributors, musical groups, and other vendors, in the past it was a community function planned and paid for by barrio residents as a measure of the neighborhood's worth.

The autonomy of the Indian republic was also weakened by the establishment of the intendant system in Yucatán in the 1770s, an economic reform that placed appointees of the Spanish Crown in charge of tax collection and limited the authority of the batab. As an extension of this policy, the state treasury assumed control over community chests in 1777, leaving many towns and villages impoverished or dependent on the central state. Similarly, **cofradía** estates, a communal resource used primarily for religious celebration, were expropriated in 1780 as the Church undertook its own set of reforms. "As ecclesiastical institutions," writes Farriss, "the *cofradías* were safe from civil authorities. They were not, as it turns out, safe from the church itself, which was pursuing its own fiscal centralization in this period" (1984, 362). In short, the late eighteenth century is now viewed as a period of critical transition in which the control over hacienda labor increased significantly and the independence of Maya communities was greatly diminished.

Nevertheless, there is evidence to indicate that Maya officials continued to play a significant role in local government throughout much of the nineteenth century. For example, *In the Maya World: Yucatec Culture and Society 1550–1850,* Matthew Restall describes an 1851 bill of sale for a residential lot in Maxcanú that not only invokes the office of the batab, but is written in Yucatec Mayan: "*toon batab tente Justicia Regs y escribano uay tu mektan cahil ca cilich yumbil San Miguel Arcangel Patron uay ti cah Maxcanu* ("we the batab, lieutenant, magistrate(s), regidores, and notary, here in the jurisdiction of our holy father San Miguel Arcángel, patron here in the *cah* [town] of Maxcanú") (1997, 308–09). However, what life was like at the end of the nineteenth century is still not well known. As several historians have pointed out (Friedrich Katz: personal communication), we know less about the nineteenth century than about any other period of Mexican history.

The Caste War of Yucatán

While the Caste War of 1848 is certainly one of the most noteworthy historical events of the post-Independence period, the northwestern quadrant of the state, where Maxcanú is located, had little involvement in this epochal clash. The key battles of the Caste War, which resulted in the destruction of numerous sugar plantations and the displacement of Maya rebels to the jungles of Quintana Roo, occurred far to the south and the east. They also, ultimately, resulted in the relocation of Yucatán's planter class to the north-west. In short, then, it could be argued that while Maxcanú played little or no part in the war itself, concerns about security and the unwillingness of the planter class to resurrect the sugar industry in the southeast are directly related to the development of the henequén industry in the region where Maxcanú is located.

An analysis of the Caste War also provides insight into the social con-sciousness that shaped relations between indigenous and non-indigenous populations throughout the peninsula. Whether the term Caste War ade-quately describes this conflict remains a point of contention; in all likeli-hood it was neither caste nor class antagonisms that initiated the war. On the contrary, as Moisés González Navarro points out in *Raza y tierra,* the immediate antecedent to the conflict was a fratricidal struggle between two factions of the peninsular elite. On one side stood Mérida's business leaders who, under the leadership of Miguel Barbachano, bitterly opposed the high tariffs assessed on imports from the US and Cuba and were in favor of seced-ing from Mexico. This sector got its wish on January 1, 1846 when, following a series of skirmishes with the Mexican government, Governor Barbachano declared Yucatán a sovereign republic. On the other side stood the business-men of Campeche who, under the leadership of Santiago Méndez, wished to remain part of Mexico. Their reliance on Mexican port towns, especially those that purchased salt, made such a break impractical.

In the political struggles of the 1840s indigenous leaders, including some who would later play an important role in the Caste War, were recruited on both sides. Manuel Antonio Ay participated in an attack on Vallodolid with the anti-secessionist Méndez forces, and Cecilio Chi fought with the secessionist Barbachano forces on several occasions. Similarly, Jacinto Pat, a wealthy Maya *cacique* (chief), was a loyal Barbachano supporter. Nevertheless, for the Creoles, the motives of indigenous participants were always somewhat in question, especially following bloody conflicts where lower class residents (*vecinos barrianos*) attempted to settle scores with the upper class (vecinos).

By 1847 many Creoles had become convinced that the indigenous popu-lation was conspiring against the white race. As González Navarro notes, the Creoles had not only become avid readers of the **Chilam Balam** (The Maya Book of Prophecy)—which reconfirmed their fears of insurrection—but took actions that would make its prophetic vision of doom a reality. On July 18, 1847, Miguel Gerónimo Rivero, the owner of a hacienda near Tihosuco, informed the district commander that large groups of Indians were storing food at the hacienda of Jacinto Pat and "according to what he had heard" were planning to take over the town. This led to the execution of Manuel Antonio Ay and four Indians for conspiracy, the rape of a young girl, and an attack on indigenous families in Tepich. When Cecilio Chi responded the next day by killing 30 vecino families in the same town, the Caste War began in earnest (González Navarro 1970, 77, 80).

In retrospect, one might say the Yucatán's half-century Caste War was not simply a reaffirmation of Creole notions of Indianness but a result of them as well. This is not to suggest that Creoles viewed all Indians in the same way or that the "Indian" was an unambiguous category. Creoles of nineteenth-century Yucatán, like their forebears, carefully distinguished between at least two types of Indians. Those who lived beyond the pale of Spanish/Creole control, or whose loyalty was in doubt, were referred to as *indio rebeldes* (rebellious Indians) or as *wi'it,* a Mayan term referring to the short pants they traditionally wore. On the other hand, Indians who passively accepted their position as subjects of the Spanish Crown or of the republican governments of independent Mexico were generally referred to by the more respectful term *indígena.* In some cases, as a reward for distinguished military service, including the Caste War, indigenous leaders were even granted the title of *hidalgo* (literally, *hijo de algo* or child of someone important).

In the Creole mind, in short, the distinction between one type of Indian and another was based more on political status than race. The Indian could be civil, but it was the whip (i.e., political subjugation) that made him so. And it was both this attitude and the legacy of the Caste War that helps to explain the unusual brutality of the next epoch.

The Epoch of Slavery

At the beginning of the twentieth century Yucatán was something of an enigma; it was rapidly becoming part of the global economy yet was only tenuously attached to the national capital. As late as 1900, in fact, there were still no major roads or rail lines connecting Yucatán to central Mexico, and trade between the center and the periphery was exceedingly sparse. Cultural and political ties were, if anything, even more tepid as Manuel Gamio, the father of Mexican anthropology, illustrates by means of an anecdote in the introduction to *Forjando Patria* (Forging the Nation):

> A few months ago, after having traveled around the state, I spent some time in Mérida, and on one occasion, while dining in the center of town decided to order a bottle of beer with lunch. "Foreign or national?" asked the waiter. "Foreign," I responded, thinking I would be served an American or German beer. A few minutes later the waiter returned with a gleaming bottle of xx beer from Orizaba [Vera Cruz, Mexico]. (Gamio 1916, 17–18)

As hard as Gamio tried to educate the waiter about Mexican history and geography, the young man insisted that in Yucatán XX was considered a foreign brand. Gamio then goes on to list several characteristics that distinguish Yucatecans from other Mexicans, including the fact that Yucatán is the only state with its own "national anthem."

On the other hand, Yucatán was now tightly linked to the global economy through the sale of henequén or sisal, a type of cactus whose processed fibers were used to produce the binder twine that US farmers were consuming in ever greater quantities. Henequén had been used in limited quantities during the colonial period in the manufacture of cables for seagoing vessels and for certain types of bags (Katz 1962, 103). However, the mass production and export of raw fiber was not possible until two conditions had been met: 1) the development of a viable rasping machine that could process henequén leaves quickly and 2) a method of financing to meet the tremendous initial outlay of capital the crop demands. Like the biblical Jacob who provided seven years of brideservice to Laban so he could marry Leah and another seven for Rachel, henequén requires seven years of service before it will bear fruit.

The first condition was met in 1854. For decades the state government had been encouraging foreign inventors to develop an industrial rasper, but it did not become a matter of great urgency until after the Caste War of 1848 began. Faced with the destruction of their sugar plantations and the continuing threat of violence on the southern frontier, the peninsular elite had been forced to relocate in the arid northwest quadrant of the state. The commercialization of henequén became a viable option for the first time, and in 1852 the state government offered a 2,000 peso reward to anyone who developed an efficient, economically feasible rasper. Not one but two Yucatecans came up with viable prototypes; they then spent the next decade in court fighting over the reward (Joseph 1982, 24).

The second objective was achieved in 1856 when the export house of Eusebio Escalante organized a line of credit for Yucatecan planters through Thebaud Brothers, a New York brokerage firm (Villaneuva 1984, 71). Having overcome a major technological constraint, and a no less pressing financial one, Yucatecan planters were now in a position to meet the escalating demand for cordage. Between 1855 and 1865, land dedicated to henequén production increased more than sixfold to cover an area of more than 400,000 **mecates** (Cline 1948, 71).[6] With the introduction of the McCormick reaper, which used binder twine in place of bailing wire, henequén production expanded even more dramatically. In just one year, land allocated to henequén cultivation jumped by almost 50 per cent, marking the end of the largely self-sufficient mixed hacienda (which produced corn and cattle as well as fiber) and the triumph of modern labor-intensive industrial plantations.

The most famous properties in the area bordering Maxcanú were Siho' and Acu, a pair of haciendas acquired by José García Morales in 1857. As noted in *Memorias de un ex-hacendado henequenero,* an apologetic treatise written by García Morales's grandson, Alberto García Cantón, the haciendas were acquired for only 15,000 pesos ($7,500 US), although the two properties enclosed 64 square kilometers of land, an area roughly the size of Mérida (García Cantón 1965, 22). At the time of the transaction Siho' contained a mere 600 mecates of henequén; however, by 1916, when the haciendas were passed on to Don Alberto and his brothers, the properties were appraised at 1,100,000 pesos each ($550,000 US), contained a total of 3,000 cattle, and had over 90,000 hectares planted in henequén, placing them among the largest plantations in the state.[7]

Despite their vast land holdings and a lucrative henequén business, the García family may have made more money from speculative land deals than from fiber production, especially during the second generation. In fact, García Cantón proudly mentions that his father, García Fajardo, was a member of a consortium of wealthy planters—including henequén magnates such as Olegario Molina and Avelino Montes—that bought up henequén plantations when fiber prices were low and sold them when the market rebounded.

> In some instances they simply sold the hacienda back to its original owner at a handsome profit: One of the operations [my father] discussed with us that brought fond memories was the purchase made by a group of five or six people, including Don Avelino Montes. They purchased a brilliant hacienda for one million pesos from a wealthy planter who was also a successful businessman. This distinguished gentleman stopped sleeping and eating and became sick for giving up a plantation he felt very attached to. Two months after the transaction the seller began sending offers [to the new owners] in order to reacquire his inheritance, and after a month of struggle paid two million pesos for a property he had sold for a million pesos. (García Cantón 1965, 22)

The second paradox, not unrelated to the first, was the co-existence of a modern capitalist export enclave and a plantation system based on virtual slave labor. Descriptions of Yucatán's turn-of-the-century plantations invariably depict the latter as clean, efficient, and technologically sophisticated enterprises. Friedrich Katz, for example, cites the report of a German engineer who claimed that "on each large plantation are found all the benefits of progress: electric light, the best steam engines, locomotives, etc." (1962, 107). Similarly, Harry Kessler, who visited the plantation of Don Eulogio D. in 1896, remarked that it "was 192 kilometers square [and] equipped with the most modern machinery" (quoted in Katz 1962, 126).[8]

Henequén production also wrought major improvements in state infrastructure. In fact, Yucatán, one of the poorest states in Mexico in 1850, had developed the most extensive rail system in the country by 1890. As Gilbert Joseph writes (1982, 34) in *Revolution from Without:*

> Over 800 kilometers of standard-gauge track constituted Yucatán's main lines and these were augmented by another 600 kilometers of privately owned, intermediate-gauge track that connected the major railheads with the planters *desfibradoras* (mechanical raspers). .... Complementing this remarkable rail hookup was a systematic network of telegraph and telephone lines, that like the railways, connected Yucatán's henequén plantations with their principal market and port.

During the same period, however, the largely Maya work force that planted, cared for, and cut the henequén stalks became the subject of a repressive system of debt peonage that Maxcanú residents now refer to as *la época de esclavitud* (the epoch of slavery).[9] The earliest and perhaps the most influential description of labor conditions in twentieth-century Yucatán is provided by the American journalist John Kenneth Turner, who wrote several articles for *American Magazine* in 1909. In order to gain access to the henequén plantations, Turner posed as a prospective investor and was able to witness the ceremonial punishment of plantation workers by the *capataz* or foreman:

> One of the first sights we saw on a henequén plantation was the beating of a slave—a formal beating before the assembled toilers of the ranch early in the morning just after roll call. The slave was taken on the back of a huge Chinaman and given fifteen lashes across the bare back with a heavy, wet rope, lashes so lustily delivered that the blood ran down the victim's body. The method of beating is an ancient one in Yucatán and is the customary one on all the plantations for boys.... Women are expected to kneel to be beaten, as sometimes are men of great weight. (1969 [1911], 24)

While Turner's account is considered sensational by some, several historians have confirmed the general tenor of his description (Katz 1962; Joseph 1982; Farriss 1984).

In attempting to account for the existence of a brutal compulsory labor system, Katz (1962) and Joseph (1982) have argued that plantation owners were faced with perennial labor shortages during the late nineteenth and early twentieth centuries. As a result of violence stemming from the Caste War, the population had decreased by more than 10 percent, and many more sought refuge in the jungles of Quintana Roo. In fact, the vast expropriation of village lands during the last decades of the nineteenth century was motivated as much by the need to control labor as to control land. With an open frontier to the southeast, such conquests were difficult to maintain without imposing restrictions on movement as well.

After the Mexican Revolution (1915–24) debt peonage was abolished, a minimum wage was established for agricultural workers, and many villages regained lands that had been expropriated during the previous century. However, it was not until the Cárdenas administration took office (1934–40) that Yucatán's henequén plantations became the object of agrarian reform. In 1935, henequén was declared a public utility by the governor of Yucatán, and in the years that followed, henequén lands in excess of 150 hectares were subject to expropriation. As a series of topographic plans in the state archives demonstrates, at least one Maxcanú property owner (Víctor Cicero Cervera) attempted to circumvent the law by dividing his hacienda into eight or nine parcels of 150 to 200 hectares and registering them under the names of different family members. Ultimately, however, his efforts proved futile. On September 13, 1937, residents of Maxcanú and the surrounding communities were given legal title to 37,089 hectares of land, including cultivated and uncultivated parcels.[10] In Maxcanú and throughout the peninsula the size of the *ejidal* (community) grant was calculated on the basis of four hectares per eligible adult, an allotment considered sufficient to support the ejido's population.

The objective of the Cárdenas reform went far beyond land distribution. For Cárdenas, as for other Mexican revolutionaries, education and agrarian reform were organically related. Not only was agrarian reform accompanied by a prodigious expansion of rural education, which provided literate peasants with an entry point into bourgeois society, but in conformity with the new "socialist" pedagogy, the educated peasant/teacher was charged with carrying out the government's reform agenda by petitioning the Department of Agriculture for ejido lands on behalf of the community and aiding in the diffusion of **Cárdenist** political culture. In Yucatán this tendency is, perhaps, best exemplified by the political satires of Santiago Pacheco Cruz, who poked fun at wealthy landowners and portrayed hacienda peons as a group easily moved to action. In addition to Spanish-language dramas such as *El cepo* (The Stocks) and *Justicia proletaria* (Proletarian Justice)—the second of which was performed in Maxcanú on July 4, 1936 by a Cárdenist cultural mission—the theatrical repertoire included a number of Mayan-language dramas such as *In Kat Cambal* (I Want to Study), which were performed on outlying haciendas and aimed at promoting literacy in Spanish.

The promotion of socialist education, however, was not intended to impede capitalist development but simply to bring it in line with the goals of national reconstruction. At the highest level this objective was pursued by the formation of the Instituto Politécnico Nacional in January 1937, which trained technicians and engineers to operate basic industries, thus reducing the nation's dependency on foreign managers and facilitating the expropriation of foreign oil companies.

At the lowest level—the rural primary school—socialist education attempted to create national unity and a more dynamic internal market through the cultural and economic incorporation of the indigenous population. In 1934, the famous labor leader Lombardo Toledano, along with much of the Mexican left, favored an ethnic policy similar to that of the Communist Party of the Soviet Union, which would guarantee greater autonomy to indigenous groups; however, the Cárdenas administration, following in the footsteps of Gamio, Molina Enríquez, José Vasconcelos, and others, continued to emphasize assimilation and a corporatist solution to Mexico's social ills:

> The Revolution has proclaimed as lawful right the incorporation of the Indian within the universal culture; this means the plain development of all the potential and natural abilities of the race, the betterment of its living conditions, adding to its subsistence and work resources all the advantages of technology, science, and art.... As I expressed on a recent occasion our indigenous problem is not to conserve the Indian as an Indian, or in making Mexico indigenous, but in Mexicanizing the Indian. By respecting his blood, capturing his emotion, his love of the land, and his unbreakable spirit, his sense of nationhood will become more rooted and enriched with moral virtues that will fortify his patriotic spirit. . . . (Medin 1972, 175–76)

One way to Mexicanize the Maya, as Salvador Alvarado and other revolutionaries demonstrated, was to preach the gospel of nationalism, a practice that continued undiminished through the 1930s. Another strategy was to promote the national language in spoken and written form. However, for some Cárdenas supporters, such as Humberto Peniche Vallado, a prominent Yucatecan educator, both of these efforts were too intellectual and too indirect. In Peniche Vallado's view, presented in an open letter to President Cárdenas on the eve of the agrarian reform, the socialist school would first have to transform the Indian into a subject of irrepressible desires. The problem was not simply that the Indian had grown averse to physical or mental labor but that he lacked the sentiments and "bodily needs" that linked other subjects to the world of *comodidades* (both commodities and comforts). Moreover, to release the elemental passion of the Maya, repressed by centuries of oppression, Peniche Vallado proposed a curriculum that emphasized competitive sports. Although baseball and tennis, diversions popular among the Mérida upper class, were not considered appropriate because they required too much thought, weightlifting, jumping, and wrestling were considered ideal and would enable the Indian to overcome his "inferiority complex" (Peninche Vallado 1987 [1937], 95). Peniche Vallado's letter, in fact, is peppered with references to Freudian complexes and other psychological ills.

In any case, the redistribution of henequén provided only a temporary solution to the agrarian problem. While the population of Maxcanú has grown steadily since 1940, the ejido has never been amplified, notwithstanding numerous requests. In fact, an unpublished report written by the municipal government in 1983 states that the shortage of ejidal lands is one of the factors responsible for the town's deteriorating economic situation.[11]

Another factor was the gradual disappearance of henequén itself. While Maxcanú produces only a fraction of the henequén it sent to market at the turn of the century, the local population was still largely dependent on the thorny cactus throughout the 1980s. According to the Banco de Crédito Rural Peninsular, 59 per cent of all agricultural workers in Maxcanú still worked in the henequén industry in 1985. At this time, however, there was a concerted effort by the national and state governments to develop new agricultural assets, including cattle ranches, poultry and pig farms, and citrus orchards.

During my first summer in Yucatán (as described in the Preface), I lived in an ejidal community named Calcehtok about five kilometers from Maxcanú and spent most of the time working in an orange grove. It was far from an enjoyable activity; it lacked the romance I associated with fieldwork from reading the ethnographies of Redfield and Villa Rojas, and it helped me understand why many children and teenagers did not want to follow in their fathers' footsteps. In addition to being sweaty, arduous labor, agricultural work is highly stigmatizing. Nonetheless, at that time the government appeared fully committed to supporting and encouraging villagers to work the land. One of the highlights of the summer was the arrival of the governor, Víctor Cervero Pacheco, to inaugurate a pump and irrigation system (*sistema de riego*), a demonstration of his support for agricultural development and diversification. Money flowed freely. This, I would later learn, was the golden age of government involvement in agriculture, although there was also, reportedly, much corruption, an essential element in all narratives involving both local and national governments.

In cooperation with the state government, the National Indigenous Institute (INI)—now the Center for Indigenous Development (CDI)–also invested heavily in experimental plots in order to identify new cultigens and modernize agricultural production. The most successful experiment was Vicente Guerrero, a government farm about seven miles outside of Maxcanú, where agronomists worked alongside *ejidatarios* to develop cultigens that had not been successfully grown in the rocky soils of western Yucatán; these included chiles, pineapples, grapefruit, and other crops.[12] While many residents, even at this time, traveled to Cancún or Mérida in search of work, a large number returned to invest their earnings in private plots, a phenomenon referred to as *re-campesinización* (re-peasantization) by Mexican sociologists.

Another occasional source of income is tourism. During my first stint of fieldwork in the mid-1980s I heard numerous stories about residents who survived the collapse of the henequén market by selling artifacts they collected from Maya ruins or facsimiles they produced on their own. The most popular story involved a clever Maxcanú artisan who purchased a number of plain ceramic vessels from a Mexico City vendor and "Mayanized" them by painting a faint yet identifiably Maya design on the outside. He then gave them an aged, weathered appearance by chipping the edges and boiling them in a concoction of honey, *achiote* (a red spice used extensively in Mexican cuisine), and mud. The facsimiles looked so authentic the artisan was able to sell them to prominent Mérida residents for a hefty price. Not surprisingly, the **federales** (federal police) eventually took notice of his handiwork, and one day as the unsuspecting artisan opened his shed, which was filled from top to bottom with forged artifacts, they arrested him. It is illegal to sell *real* artifacts, not facsimiles, so the wily entrepreneur was able to secure his release by showing the police the tools of his trade. While this story has all the features of a modern trickster tale—outsmarting or evading the federales is a common theme throughout Mexico—an archaeologist from the National Institute of History and Anthropology (INAH) who catalogues Maya artifacts, including the "new" ones, indicated that there were, in fact, some very good forgeries from the western part of the state in the late 1970s (personal communication, 1988).

It was not only wily potters, however, who understood the value of things past. In the late 1980s, the state government in collaboration with private developers began to formulate plans in order to capture more of the tourist traffic between Cancún and Chichén Itzá to the east and the famous walled city of Campeche to the west. In tourism, as in every other discussion of development in this former monocrop economy, the key term was "diversification." How could western Yucatán distinguish itself from other parts of the state and the nation to create a tourist experience that would be interesting and profitable? The answer was to focus on the region's colonial and post-colonial period by creating an artful vision of hacienda life stretching from the eighteenth-century corn and cattle haciendas to the henequén plantations of the early twentieth century. Therefore, in addition to opening the pre-classic Maya site at Oxkintok for public consumption, private investors discussed the idea of remodeling haciendas in Santa Rosa and San Bernardo (discussed in Chapter 4) into museums and five-star hotels. Thanks to a collection of dusty antiques on the second floor, some well-maintained horse-drawn carriages on the first, and interesting Maya artifacts embedded in the hacienda's interior walls, the latter had, in fact, served as a minor tourist attraction for many years.

By the summer of 2007, the date of my last visit, the political and economic landscape had changed dramatically, thanks in large measure to

FIGURE 1.2 The central plaza in Maxcanú in the summer of 2007

neoliberal reforms carried out in the past 20 years; however, much remains the same. Because of its size and proximity to the famous Camino Real—the road leading to Mérida—Maxcanú continues to serve as a commercial, administrative, and religious center for the towns, villages, and populated haciendas in its municipal district. Merchants in the cabecera who purchase goods wholesale in Mérida or hold franchises with major bottling companies supply smaller merchants and bar owners in the surrounding villages with goods for retail. Similarly, schoolteachers from Maxcanú who commute to these villages may supplement their income by selling clothing on credit at greatly inflated prices.

The most significant change has been the decline in agricultural production. With the reform of Article 27 of the Mexican Constitution under President Salinas de Gortari (1992) and the establishment of PROCEDE—a program to map, measure, and title ejidal lands—the infrastructure was put in place to partition and privatize these lands, thereby reversing 70 years of agricultural policy. As a result of this, many individuals who were registered as ejidatarios but who had been absent for many years, came back to claim their parcels. Few, however, stayed to work the land. There was no credit available and little in the way of incentives.

In fact by this time the area where Vicente Guerrero was located was so overgrown with weeds that we had difficulty locating it. After driving about 10 kilometers down a rocky road we were about to turn around when we noticed an old rusted tank on which, with great difficulty, we could make out the name. About 75 yards back through dense weeds we uncovered a

FIGURE 1.3 Vicente Guerrero

burnt-out storage facility but nothing more. Everything of value had long since been removed.

So what do residents of Maxcanú do for a living today? Hundreds travel to Mérida to search for work. Many of the youth who two decades ago would have been working in the fields now work in Mérida or Cancún as masons' or carpenters' assistants. In 1988, one had to run across the plaza early in the morning and push onto a *combi* (bus) to get to Mérida since there were very few around and one could not be sure when the next would come. Nowadays, things are more British: people cue up for combis, which are now more plentiful, but on Mondays and sometimes on other days the lines contain 150 or more individuals. What had been a trickle of out-migration has turned into a torrent.

Getting a job as a teacher is now all but impossible. It used to be that once you completed three years of secondary school and the three-year *bachillerato* (roughly equivalent to high school) you were sure to get a job as a teacher. Now it's like playing the lottery. Each year there are approximately 60 new jobs for public school teachers—and approximately 3,000 applicants. If you place within the top 60, you get a job; otherwise, you take the test again. Consequently, there are now many well-educated residents who make their living by driving tourists and townspeople around on motorized or pedal-powered tricycles. This exemplifies the shift from agricultural work and industry to service, a trend that the economic data for Mexico and Latin America increasingly demonstrate (Gwynne 1999, 89).

FIGURE 1.4 Monty, a textile factory that set up shop in 2002; it currently employs 1,100 workers

By far the largest employer in Maxcanú is now Monty, a large textile factory that relocated from Honduras about five years ago and employs close to 1,100 workers, most of whom come from Maxcanú and the surrounding ejidos. From the outside, the new factory offers a favorable presentation. There is a large well-groomed lawn with a soccer field for employees. The parking lot that faces the street is full of shiny new motorcycles that employees can purchase over time through payroll deductions. The inside—which is very difficult to access due to concerns about terrorism or industrial espionage, a fieldwork dilemma I had not previously encountered—is also clean, well-kept, and well-ventilated. In this sense it is clearly more pleasant than working on the ejido; however, the ten-hour workday at Monty is longer than the average workday of a farm worker or an ejidatario, and the pay scale in this non-union shop is markedly lower than the average daily wage of a farm worker. While the exact wage of a Monty employee, according to the firm's Director of Human Resources, is based on a complex formula that factors in seniority, the complexity of the task, and the employee's speed, it is safe to conclude, based on numerous conversations I had with employees outside the plant, that workers earn slightly above the national minimum wage, which at the time was 71 pesos per day (approximately $7 US). In contrast, Manuel, a friend and informant I have known for 20 years, who works approximately six hours a day planting and clearing weeds for a private landowner, earns 100 pesos or $10 dollars a day and is in his hammock by noon. Workers at Monty also complain that they are docked if they take time off for national or religious holidays; however, the

FIGURE 1.5 Remodeled hacienda hotel in Santa Rosa just a few kilometers from Maxcanú

big losers in the transition are members of the *tercera edad* (the third age), a phrase referring to people over 40 that is used with greater frequency than when I conducted my initial fieldwork. Although representatives of Monty do not publicly acknowledge it, it was clear from my observations inside the plant and from discussions with workers and their families outside that very few people over 35 are hired to work there. Consequently, adults who did not work in the ejido long enough to receive a pension are caught in a no-man's land where they are too old to work and too young, or financially unable, to retire.

Tourism in western Yucatán also has contributed little or nothing to the public good. By the summer of 2007, the new luxury hotel in Santa Rosa was in full operation. As an ad on the Internet notes:

> A small hacienda located near the western coast of the Yucatan peninsula, Hacienda Santa Rosa is a former nobleman's private estate. Hacienda Santa Rosa features uniquely carved columns, ornately furnished gardens, and mysterious evening campfires. Come discover the beauty of 17th century Mayan sites with the service of a world-class luxury resort.
>
> Spend an afternoon discovering the life of the Mayans—historical and contemporary. Stroll through local villages and hear stories of yesteryear and explore unique boutiques of talented craftsmen.[13]

While one reviewer noted that "one of the really cool things about the hotel is their commitment to social responsibility" and praised the hotel for building an "art school" in town where local women can learn and bring crafts to sell, the sense of social responsibility, apparently, did not extend to the small work force. Although the 11-room hotel was charging over $350.00 per room when I visited, the waiter I spoke to was earning about $4 US a day and serving mostly European visitors who do not customarily tip.

By this time, the archaeological site at Oxkintok had also been open to tourists for several years. However, during the summer of 2007 when hundreds of thousands of tourists were swarming to Chichén Itzá to see one of the Seven Wonders of the World, Oxkintok was a well-kept secret. Because of the absence of signage and the long unpaved road leading from the highway to the reconstructed ruins, only a dozen visitors came by in the four hours that I spent there. I had had no intention of staying so long at the site, where it was impossible to purchase a soda, but because there were no tour buses or private taxis and very few visitors heading back to Maxcanú, my son and I spent two hours talking to two former ejidatarios, now employed as part-time guards, until we were able to hitch a ride with a local visitor.

In summary, there is no golden age of Maxcanú to which I can refer. The recent past, which was rank with corruption and sweaty, hard, outdoor labor is not to be envied. I heartily agree with Pierre Beaucage's description of peasants in the upper sierra in Puebla: "After twenty-five years of intense exposure to modernity, nobody wants to return to the old days, where you worked from dawn to dusk, and were happy to have enough corn to eat and a few pesos to spend at a fiesta" (1998, 23). The allure of new consumer goods and non-agricultural work is strong among the youth. Unfortunately, the present, which offers low-paid service jobs, low-paid factory work, and an early retirement that nobody can really afford, doesn't appear to be any better.

CHAPTER TWO

THE GREMIO SYSTEM
The Social Organization of Religious Life

Since the mid-1960s, the study of religious confraternities in southern Mexico and Guatemala, known variously as **cargo systems**, civil-religious hierarchies, or cofradías (brotherhoods), has been a veritable growth industry (see, for example, Annis 1996; Bartolomé and Barabas 1982; Brandes 1988; Cancian 1965; Carlson 1996; Cook 2000; DeWalt 1975; Fernández Repetto and Negroe Sierra 1997; Nash 1970; Nutini 1968; Reina 1966; Slade 1973; Tedlock 1982; Watanabe 1992). A 1990 article by John Chance, which makes no pretense of being exhaustive, contains data from no less than 23 ethnographies of Mesoamerican cargo systems published between 1965 and 1986. If one were to add to Chance's list all the journal articles or unsold inventory in the form of doctoral dissertations, the number would surely ascend into the hundreds. The cargo system is also the central theme of at least one ethnographic novel, Carter Wilson's *Crazy February* (1974), a pious, slow-moving work of fiction that dramatizes the personal sacrifices that cargo holders endure.

Echoing Manning Nash (1958), James Greenberg notes that "[i]n part this emphasis stems from the recognition that these hierarchies, which organize age-grades, do for indigenous communities 'what kinship does for African societies and social class does for Ladino society'" (1990, 95). In other words, the cargo system is the social skeleton or scaffolding upon which prestige, political authority, and power ultimately rest. The other part, presumably, has to do with the nature of anthropological production itself, particularly the intense concentration of research in what Aguirre Beltrán (1975) refers to as Mexico's *regiones de refugio* (refuge zones).

The "anthropological fascination with cargos" (Haviland 1977, 116) has also been nourished by a steady stream of debates about the origin and **ontology** of the institution. Are civil-religious hierarchies a product of Spanish colonialism (Tax 1937; Reina 1966), or are they basically a nineteenth-century invention (Chance and Taylor 1985; Chance 1990)? Do they flourish in communities that are isolated from regional markets (Smith 1977) or those that are closely tied to the market (Favre 1973)? Are they a mechanism for extracting surplus from Indian communities (Harris 1964; Wasserstrom 1983) or a system of exchange that protects community wealth (Dow 1977; Greenberg 1981)? Do they serve to prevent the formation of class differences (Tax 1937; Annis 1996), or do they simply legitimate those differences (Cancian 1965; Farriss 1984)? Are they a symbol of subordination (Warren 1978) or a vehicle for organizing resistance (Bricker 1981; Earle 1990)?

Noticeably absent from Chance's list, however, is any study of Yucatán. While studies of colonial Yucatán by Nancy Farriss (1984) and Philip Thompson (1978) demonstrate the existence of complex administrative systems similar to those in highland Chiapas, Oaxaca, and Puebla, a combination of forces has consigned these associations to the proverbial dustbin of history.[1] Weakened initially by the Bourbon reforms of the late eighteenth century that resulted in the confiscation of many cofradía estates, the cargo system, as well as other "indigenous" institutions, were swept away in the nineteenth century by the liberal policies of independent Mexico and the extraordinary expansion of plantation agriculture. Only in the X-Cacal villages of Quintana Roo, Yucatán's own refuge zone (following the Caste War of 1848), did anything resembling the religious hierarchies in other parts of Mexico and Guatemala survive into the twentieth century. Nor has much been written about cofradías in mestizo towns. The little writing about religious confraternities in the region that does exist is based on ethnographic work in small Maya villages.

Following the Mexican Revolution (1910–20), however, a different type of confraternity began to appear in towns and villages throughout the peninsula. Better known as gremios (guilds), these associations have more in common with cofradías in Mérida and other urban centers than with those found in highland Chiapas or Guatemala. Not only are they less complex than indigenous cofradías, which often include both civil and religious offices, but differences in status or rank are expressed thorough inter-gremial as well as intra-gremial relations. Consequently, ethnographic studies focusing on communities that contain only one or two gremios have failed to see any connection between gremio life and political organization. Indeed, what little has been written about gremios in Yucatán has tended to focus on ritual performance.[2]

In contrast, I argue here that the resurrection of the gremio system (ca. 1925) was not simply a popular attempt to reintroduce religious celebration in public but was central to the reproduction of inequality in Maxcanú and other peninsular towns. Maxcanú's renascent gremio system not only served to dramatize ethnic and status differences but endowed the latter with the sanctity of religious tradition. Moreover, like the social clubs (sociedades) found in Maxcanú, the more prestigious gremios serve as vehicles through which upwardly mobile residents shed their parvenu status and fashion a more respectable past or lineage (*abolengo*). In turn, recruitment of these newly prosperous individuals has helped revitalize lay religious associations of long standing.

An examination of the gremio system also provides much needed insight into the evolving relationship between civil society and the state. While the post-revolutionary Mexican state is often depicted as a modern Leviathan, how it came to be—and how it maintains support in local venues—remains something of a mystery. In the words of the historian Gilbert Joseph, it is a "black box conceptually . . . hovering above (but eerily removed from) the mundane workings of Mexican society" (1994, 137–38). An analysis of the Mexican gremio, and its transformation over time, helps ground this discussion and provides important clues about the nature of power and stratification on the periphery. While colonial-era gremios (discussed below) were compulsory organizations that regulated access to particular crafts and compelled their members to participate in both civil and religious commemorations, the gremios of the post-Independence era were, and are, voluntary organizations that rely on consent rather than coercion. As Victor Turner notes in his description of the gremios of Tizimin, Yucatán, "we were assured by several citizens . . . that 'originally' . . . the gremio in Tizimin was a 'corporation' of workers in a particular trade or craft, and that it was obligatory to join it. Today the gremios are exclusively religious in function and organize the religious aspect of the great fiesta. Affiliation to gremios is voluntary, and many of their members come from outside Tizimin . . ." (1974, 119).[3] While both the number and practice of these associations are outwardly determined by the ritual requirements of the Catholic novena—a nine-day celebration held in honor of the town's patron saint—gremios operate independently and sometimes in defiance of the local clergy.[4]

In short, then, it can be said that the gremio serves two very different masters. As an institution with a long and venerable tradition, it not only structured the spiritual activities and sentiments of its members, it reaffirmed their identity as religious subjects subordinate to distinguished community residents as well as to the saints. In this way, the gremio—like the ejido (Nugent and Alonso 1994), the public school (Rockwell 1994), and even the image of the Virgin (Becker 1994)—contributed to the formation of a new hegemonic order in the 1920s, notwithstanding notable confrontations between the government and the religious faithful.[5] However, as an element of Mexican popular culture, the gremio could—and on occasion did—call into question the authority figures it normally exalted. As Nugent and Alonso (following Gramsci) argue, popular culture is inherently contradictory since it "embodies and elaborates dominant symbols and meanings, but also contests, challenges, rejects, revalues, re-accents, and presents alternatives to them" (1994, 211).

Guild and Devotional Society in Colonial History

While individuals from all social classes belonged to cofradías and participated in the religious life of the Spanish colonies, they generally did not
belong to the same associations and did not participate as equals. The cofradía of St. Peter in New Granada excluded all but the wealthiest citizens
from its membership. Applicants were expected to contribute 200 silver
pesos and a pound of wax in order to gain entry (Graff 1973, 117). Similarly,
in *Las cofradías de Españoles en la ciudad de México,* Bazarte Martínez argues
that Spanish and Creole cofradías were exclusive social clubs where, among
other things, powerful families arranged propitious marriages and negotiated
important business deals:

> In effect, the Spanish cofradía was a select association in which powerful
> Spanish and Creole families weaved matrimonial alliances from biological
> and political kin [and] established political accords, employing diverse
> strategies in order to maintain family wealth, especially between Creole
> oligarchs who held landed estates and mines and Spanish businessman who
> owned capital. (Bazarte Martínez 1989, 16; translated by author)

The order of cofradías in the annual procession was also an important index
of social standing:

> Behind the parish church's crucifix marched the Brotherhood of St. Peter,
> representing the distinguished Spanish and Creole laymen and eminent
> churchmen. Then came the Cofradía of the True Cross, an organization
> dominated by the community's Creole elite, but which also included mes-
> tizos and other non-whites. The Cofradía of the Immaculate Conception,
> another socially and racially mixed sodality, followed. The predominantly
> mestizo and Indian membership of the Cofradía of St. Lucia came next.
> The last of the fraternities was the black Cofradía of St. Peter. (Graff
> 1973, 177)

Cofradías were also popular among the intermediate classes of New
Spain, especially those that functioned as guilds. In the New World, as in
the Old, cofradías were divided into several different types. Associations
dedicated solely to religious or ritual observance were generally referred to
as sacramental cofradías, *hermandades* or *montepíos* (Foster 1953). Those that
combined economic pursuits with religious ones, or that were organized
according to craft, are generally referred to as *cofradías gremiales* or simply as gremios. Unlike many of the sacramental cofradías, the gremios not
only regulated membership and training within their craft but functioned
as mutual aid associations.[6] Most also had their own patron saint and, in

some cases, more than one. The candlemakers and confectioners venerated San Felipe de Jesus; the tailors honored San Homobono; the weavers
and cotton workers made requests of the Virgin of Anguish; and surgeons,
pharmacists, and phlebotomists paid homage either to San Cosme or San
Damian (Carrera Estampa 1954, 89–90). Moreover, while some of Mexico's
less prestigious guilds, such as the *Gremio de los Zurradores* (Tanner's Guild),
admitted Indians, mestizos, and mulattos as apprentices and journeymen, the
more eminent guilds like the *Gremio de los Plateros* (Silverworker's Guild),
excluded these groups altogether. In either case, applicants were expected to
demonstrate that they were financially solvent, in good physical condition,
and Christians of long standing.

In cases where a cofradía functioned as the devotional society for a guild,
a similar ranking system obtained in both. The highest offices were held
either by the guild's master craftsmen or its overseers. Moreover, as Foster
notes in the case of one Spanish gremio, grace was distributed in accordance
with age, gender, and rank. In the carpenter's cofradía, officers would receive
15 masses upon their death whereas others could expect only ten. In turn,
"eight masses were said for wives of *cofrades* [members of the cofradía] and
four for children less than fourteen years of age and for apprentices" (Foster
1953, 13).

The introduction of cofradías among the indigenous population was
primarily intended to facilitate their conversion to Christianity. Cofradías not
only enabled the clergy to indoctrinate and sometimes to conduct surveillance activities among new Christians but provided a means for supporting
these activities. In addition to spiritual guidance, new priests were instructed
to supervise cofradías "so they would prosper and adequately provide funds
and materials for the churches' masses and festivals" (Graff 1973, 101). Indeed,
the contractual arrangement between the cofradía and the clergy was analogous to that between the cofradía and the saints (discussed below).[7] Whereas
the saints provided protection or alleviated suffering in exchange for prayers
and acts of penance, cofradías received specific spiritual benefits and indul-
gences in exchange for the support they gave clergy.

In some cases, Indian cofradías were themselves organized according to
rank. Describing the Maya cofradías of colonial Yucatán, Farriss comments,
that "[i]f the line between civil and religious functions ... was blurred, the
distance between the ranks was not. Only the elite were the servants of the
saints ... channeling gifts in both directions" (1984, 338–39). Indeed, from
Farriss's standpoint, it was the cofradía more than any other institution that
enabled Maya nobility to maintain their elite status during the colonial
period.

While Foster (1953) contends that the *compadrazgo* (spiritual kinship)
was the more successful of Spanish America's two great social institutions,
the cofradía nevertheless played an important role in the economic life of

the colony. In addition to the income accumulated from alms and member-ship dues, many cofradías ran successful businesses. According to Bazarte Martínez (1989, 119), *Nuestra Señora del Rosario* owned a sugar mill in San Lucas Matlala that provided an annual revenue of 373 pesos, and the *Cofradía del Santísimo Sacramento* owned more cattle than the powerful Marquis de Panuco. In general, however, the urban-based Spanish or Creole cofradías derived their wealth from rents, mortgages, or loans. Indeed, cofradías and other ecclesiastical corporations were the credit institutions of first resort in Spanish America (Graff 1973, 248), underwriting major construction projects as well as personal loans.[8]

Even many Indian cofradías ran profitable cattle ranches. In 1782, Luis de Pina, the Archbishop of Yucatán, reported the existence of 159 cofradía ranches in the province. One was the hacienda Loca, which was left to the parish priest of Tixkokob in 1727 by Nicolas Uitz, an Indian noble. If not large by colonial standards, the ranch was well-run and grew steadily over four decades. At its founding, according to Patch (1981, 57), Loca had only 35 cattle; however, by 1764 the herd had increased more than sixfold to 232. Only during the economic downturn of the early 1770s was there a serious decline, and this apparently resulted from the cofradía's attempt to prevent mass starvation.

Under the New Laws (*Leyes nuevas de las Indias*) published in 1542, the Crown encouraged the formation of cofradías in New Spain in the hope that they would establish orphanages and hospitals and carry out charitable works. However, by the end of the century the monarchy had decided it was necessary to regulate their affairs more closely. In 1600 Philip III issued a decree requiring all cofradías to obtain approval from the Council of the Indies as well as local ecclesiastical authorities, and in 1602, based on concerns that black and Indian cofradías were engaging in pagan activities, he decreed that a priest or an appointed representative attend all cofradía gatherings in order to insure that they maintained "decency and good order which is necessary for their education and good living habits" (Bazarte Martínez 1989, 53). In 1604 Pope Clement VIII followed suit, issuing a papal bull that prohibited the establishment of new cofradías that lacked the authorization of the local bishop.

While most sources agree that these regulations were generally ignored, or had little effect on the day-to-day operations of the cofradías, civil and religious authorities did, on occasion, intervene in their affairs. In addi-tion to licensing craftsmen and overseeing the quality of goods produced, the *ayuntamiento* (municipal authority) required cofradías to participate in important vice-regal celebrations as well as major religious events like the fiesta of Corpus Christi and Easter. On such occasions:

The municipal authority convoked the overseer and majordomo of each cofradía gremial in order to give them instructions pertaining to the festival's plan, their order of appearance, the clothing they should wear, and the obligations which, according to custom and the cabido's own long-standing resolutions, correspond to each gremio or cofradía . . . all gremio members were expected to attend the processions accompanied by their titular saints . . . . If they didn't, they were assessed a fine: 30, 20, or 10 pesos plus 30 days in jail for the overseers. (Carrera Estampa 1954, 94–96; translated by author)

In most cases, though, coercion was unnecessary. Gremios participated willingly, and in some cases, fought bitterly for a position closer to the sacramental images.[9]

The Suppression and Reformation of the Cofradía

Historical accounts of the suppression of cofradías in the New World generally begin with a discussion of political economy in the Old World, particularly the emergence of a new brand of economic liberalism in the court of King Carlos III (1759). As Dagmar Bechtloff notes, liberal economists joined with fiscal advisors to the Crown, such as Rodríguez de Campomanes, to condemn the waste and intemperance of Spain's lay religious associations and to promote a new work ethic based on "success and individual merit" (1996, 161). In the words of Campomanes, the endless reunions sponsored by the cofradías gremiales not only diverted skilled artisans from more productive endeavors but ultimately led to their ruin:

Whether for vanity or competitive spirit, the majordomos and other officials of the cofradía gremiales spend more than their treasuries contain and in the year of their service impoverish hundreds of families in the kingdom . . . these heads of families leave their workshops unattended during the year in which they perform gremio duties; they consume their capital; they become accustomed to abandoning their work and the supervision of their workers; and, finally, distract themselves in gluttony and other activities that are contrary to the principles of Christian morality, public and family utility, and the sobriety that is required of artisans. (in Rumeu de Armas 1942, 394; translated by author)

With some exceptions, the Spanish bishops shared the sentiments of the monarchy and its fiscal policy advisors. For example, in condemning the excessive drinking and gluttony of the "popular" cofradías, the Archbishop of Burgos complained that if it wasn't for "wine there wouldn't be cofradías" (Rumeu de Armas 1942, 403).

During this period, cofradías in New Spain also came under attack because of "irregularities" (e.g., failure to obtain authorization from civil or ecclesiastical authorities) or because they lacked the resources to adequately support the parish priest. For example, in 1794, during his investigation of cofradías in central Mexico, Archbishop Alonso suppressed 40 cofradías in the capital and 482 in other parts of the province "because they were found to be in bad circumstances," meaning they lacked sufficient funds or didn't have sufficient members (Bazarte Martínez 1989, 129). Similarly, in Yucatán all cofradía estates held by Maya communities were expropriated in 1780, as noted in Chapter 1 (see p. 20). After monitoring cofradía finances for several years, the Bishop of Yucatán benignly declared that cofradía property was being attached in order to "preserve these pious foundations and avoid the losses to which they are otherwise exposed" (Farriss 1984, 362).

The irony, of course, is that within two decades the expropriators were themselves expropriated as the fiscal crisis of the Spanish state began to be felt in New Spain. In order to avoid bankruptcy as a result of its ongoing wars in Europe, Spain imposed a special tax on church holdings in 1798. This was followed by a royal decree in 1804 requiring the alienation and sale of all church holdings, including cofradías, hermitages, and hospitals, with all proceeds going to the monarchy's consolidated account (*Caja Real de Consolidación*).

However, it was the legislative reforms of Mexico's own liberal economists during the Juarez administration (1855) that affected the gremios most dramatically, eliminating once and for all their economic function. Article Four of the 1857 Constitution formally suppressed the guilds, declaring that "all are free to embrace the profession, industry, or trade which suits him being useful and honest" (Carrera Estampa 1954, 278), and the Law of July 13, 1859 authorized the liquidation of church properties resulting in the confiscation of cofradía funds.[10]

Religion and Revolution

As a religious cult, however, the gremios continued to flourish throughout the late nineteenth and early twentieth centuries. Describing Mérida at the beginning of the twentieth century, Hansen and Bastarrachea Manzano note that:

> ... normal activities in Mérida were practically paralyzed at the end of September and the beginning of October. There was a gremio of hacienda owners, a merchant's gremio, and many other less opulent ones. Celebrations continued beyond the traditional nine days to allow more gremios to participate in the masses and processions. ... In strategic points throughout the city fireworks were blown off during the "entrance" and "exit" of the gremios. (1984, 235)

The Mexican Revolution, however, led to new restrictions on religious activity, and gremios, at least in some towns, were driven underground. While Salvador Alvarado, the Sonoran-born general who brought the revolution to Yucatán, was genuinely impressed by the deference Catholic parishioners showed the clergy—and viewed the church as a model for a new socialist political order—he did not hesitate to expel foreign clerics when Venustiano Carranza, the head of the Constitutionalist Army, ordered it. "Early in 1916," writes James Carey, "the government at Mérida exiled seventeen priests for allegedly having engaged in political activities" (1984, 41). The Alvarado administration also tended to look the other way when churches were vandalized by unruly mobs. On September 24, 1915, for example, a mob entered the main cathedral in Mérida, removed the principal icons, and attempted to burn a famous image known as *Cristo de las Ampollas* (The Blistered Christ) as they sang "La cucaracha," a popular revolutionary song. According to legend, the image had survived a tremendous fire in the church of Ichmul in 1767 and was widely thought to be indestructible. When it failed to burn a second time, the crowd became enraged and carried out other acts of vandalism. Although many of the crimes were committed "less than thirty-five yards from the government palace and the central police headquarters, the rioters were not restrained until the peak of their wild revelry had passed" (Carey 1984, 41).

Similarly, several elderly Maxcanú residents recall the fiery destruction of religious icons that had lined the walls of their church before the Revolution. While Alvarado justified the destruction of church property on didactic grounds—for the deliberate purpose of showing the Indians that lightning would not strike when the church was attacked—not everyone drew the same conclusions. Don Roman Ek, an 85-year-old *rezador* (prayer group leader), recalled watching the saints fly up to heaven like puffs of smoke as flames devoured their wooden bodies. Although the church was closed intermittently during this period, and gremial processions were prohibited, the more devout Catholics continued to meet secretly.

Post-Revolutionary Yucatán: The Resurrection of San Miguel

Following the Mexican Revolution (ca. 1925), religious processions passed through the streets of Maxcanú once again and the town's gremio system was re-established. At this time, according to Don Beto Baas, a well-informed elder, Maxcanú had nine gremios:

1. *Commerciantes y Hacendados* (Merchants and Hacienda Owners)
2. *Señoras y Señoritas* (Women and Young Ladies)
3. *Artesanos* (Artisans)
4. *Mestizos Finos* (Fine Mestizos)

5. *Primera Sección* (First Section)
6. *Segunda Sección* (Second Section)
7. *Tercera Sección* (Third Section)
8. *Cuarta Sección* (Fourth Section)
9. *Músicos* (Musicians)

Nine is a symbolic number since the customary celebration to honor a patron saint, visiting dignitary, or deceased cofrade, is the novena (literally nine), a commemoration taking place over a nine-day period. In fact, in 1989, a second set of confraternities, corresponding to a subdivision of Maxcanú into nine wards, was superimposed upon the older gremio system. These brotherhoods, better known as *"centros de familia,"* were established with the help of the parish priest in order to bolster religious participation, stem the tide of evangelical Protestantism, and increase the authority of the clergy in local matters. Number symbolism thus influences not only the duration of religious performance and the number of devotional societies but ultimately the division of religious labor.[11]

However, as a result of factionalism, shifts in occupational structure, and other realignments of the body politic, many parishes now have a dozen or more gremios. In the town of Tizimin, where Robert Redfield counted nine gremios in the 1930s (1941, 299), Victor Turner found 12 confraternities in 1974 when he went to observe a pilgrimage to the Three Kings. Similarly, the parish in Mérida (ca. 1935) described by Asael Hansen (Hansen and Bastarrachea Manzano 1984) was made up of 14 different gremios, making it comparable in scope to the current parish of Maxcanú. While some Maxcanú residents have suggested that 14 is the upper limit, the town of Ticul, according to Richard Thompson (1974), had 18 active gremios in 1968, enough for two novenas.

Gremio nomenclature is even more complicated. While some bear the name of a particular trade or vocation, such as the *Gremio de Artisanos,* others refer to gender, civic status, or the section of town in which its members reside. Gremios can even be named for something as mundane as a piece of fruit. Like Spanish towns, incorporated villages and towns in Mexico are usually divided into four quadrants, formed by the intersection of two imaginary lines at the town's center (making the sign of the Cross). The gremios that correspond to these sections tend to be large and difficult to manage, and when the gremio of the fourth section in Maxcanú divided some years back, one of the two new associations took its name from a yellow fruit (*sarbay*) that grows abundantly in that part of town. Still other gremios are named after famous religious leaders or saints, such as the *Gremio de Leo XIII* in Ticul. Nevertheless, as discussed below, there is a discernable order within the gremio system that parallels and reinforces the ethnic and status distinctions described by many ethnographers of Yucatán (see, for example, Hansen and Bastarrachea Manzano 1984; Goldkind 1965; Löewe 1995; Redfield 1941; Thompson 1974).

Patronage and Consent

Although none of Maxcanú's existing gremios can demonstrate a continuous existence going back before 1920, participation in the associations is considered a valuable and time-honored activity. Assuming the role of president or host (*anfitrión*) is not simply a religious obligation undertaken in fulfillment of a vow, it is also, in many cases, part of a family tradition. In fact, in the process of collecting information on particular gremios, it quickly became clear that certain families, including a few that are no longer active in gremio life, are widely considered to be repositories of gremio history and lore, not to mention unaccounted-for property or cash.[12]

Nevertheless, it would be difficult to appreciate the importance of gremio participation without a more detailed understanding of religious obligation. Throughout Mexico and much of the Catholic Hispanic world, religious activity is structured by the concept of patronage. In accordance with this theological precept, divine protection is granted conditionally in exchange for the fulfillment of a sacred vow. Indeed, in *Local Religion in Sixteenth-Century Spain,* William Christian emphasizes the parallels between the religious concept of patronage and contract law by noting that the saints selected to defend Spanish communities were commonly referred to as *abogados* (1981, 55), a term that translates as advocate or lawyer as well as protector. Carrying

FIGURE 2.1 Awaiting the arrival of San Miguel, the Patron Saint of Maxcanú

the analogy further, Christian describes how the people of Parraces, Spain put grasshoppers on trial after other efforts at pest control had failed. The prosecution witnesses included St. Jerome, St. Francis, St. Lawrence, and St. Michael the Archangel, the patron saints of nearby villages. The prosecutors, aided by a friar, were three different images of St. Gregory, and the judge was Our Lady of St. Mary. After consulting with the saints and citing judicial precedents, including the excommunication of rats in Osma and of swallows who dirtied a shrine in Cordoba, the judge announced that the grasshoppers would be excommunicated if they did not depart (Christian 1981, 30–31). Moreover, just as God repudiates man for his failure to expiate sin, man can repudiate his freely chosen intercessor for a more effective patron or advocate. Christian notes that vows were conditional on acceptance by the saint: "The extent to which the saint responded would govern the enthusiasm and perseverance with which the villagers maintained the vow" (1981, 63).

Therefore, while a vow, once uttered, must be fulfilled lest the supplicant fall into mortal sin, vows (because they are entered into contractually) are actually "voluntary obligations" and the devotee is thought of as a subject with free will. Indeed, as Victor Turner notes, the boundary between obligation and volunteerism, coercion and consent, is rather amorphous in a pilgrimage as well as in other acts of Christian piety:

> Christian pilgrimages tended at first to stress the voluntary aspect and to consider sacred travel to Palestine or Rome acts of supererogatory devotion, a sort of frosting on the cake of piety. But a strong element of obligation came in with the organization of the penitential systems of the church. When this became authoritatively and legally organized, pilgrimages were set down as adequate punishments inflicted for certain crimes.... Thus, when one starts with obligation, voluntariness comes in; when one begins with voluntariness, obligation tends to enter the scene. To my mind this ambiguity is a consequence partly of the liminality of the pilgrimage situation itself.... (1974, 175)

Acts of penance can be either of an individual or a corporate nature, and while circumstances may impel an individual to endure extreme suffering or mortification, it is the act of *imitatio Christi*, the temporary incorporation of the penitent into the drama of the Passion, rather than the severity of his punishment, which defines the practice. Therefore, even participation in local dramas, such as the re-enactment of the *Via Crucis* (the Way of the Cross) on Good Friday or the gremio processions held in honor of San Miguel Arcángel in Maxcanú may be considered acts of contrition.

What assures gremio participation, then, is the centrality of these confraternities in publicly organized acts of penance (i.e., pilgrimages) that accompany the annual celebration of the town's patron saint. By convention, each

FIGURE 2.2 Re-enactment of the Via Crucis on Easter Sunday in Maxcanú

day between September 15 and September 28 is assigned to a particular gremio, which is responsible for sponsoring a mass and a public procession in honor of San Miguel. And while the daily processions leading up to September 29, the saint's name day, hardly conform to the romantic image of a pilgrimage as a long, arduous trek to an inaccessible holy site, the processions and the requisite expenditures—always a topic of public discussion—provide an opportunity for townspeople to demonstrate their identification with the exemplary model of San Miguel and help fulfill the town's corporate contractual obligation. Gremio members, in fact, not only refer to themselves as "pilgrims" but actually traverse a circuit between the gremio president's home and the church, creating a sacred space over a two-day period. Moreover, as noted below, by carrying standards that resemble the Mexican flag or tricolor, gremios also highlight their identification with the nation state.

Fieldnotes: September 18, 1990
At around 6:00 p.m. the church bells began to clang wildly, indicating that one of the gremios was about to enter. The procession, by contrast, was a rather dispassionate affair that started at the house of the outgoing president whose last responsibility was to provide a meal for gremio members and other invitees. From there the gremio made its way down one of the town's main arteries, circled the main square, and proceeded to the front entrance of the church. At the head of the procession was a group of teenagers igniting fireworks and small percussion bombs as they walked. Following a short distance behind were two single-file lines composed of gremio members and their supporters. First in line were the children, waving pink, green, and white crepe paper flags (emulating the Mexican flag). Behind them were several dozen young women dressed in *huipils* or

nylon dresses and holding fresh bouquets of pink and white gladiolas. In third position was the gremio's color guard bearing aloft the church ensign and the Mexican tricolor minus the national seal. In fourth place came the gremio's standard-bearers carrying elaborately embroidered velvet standards with the gremio's name, the date of the relic's construction, and an artistic rendering of San Miguel vanquishing the devil. Marching last, and in no apparent order, were the rest of the gremio's male members and a three-piece brass band, which played "Viva Cristo Rey" (Long Live Christ the King) for the duration of the procession. At the church door the gremio was met by Padre Justo who recited a benediction, sprinkled holy water on the assembly, and then led them into the church for mass. The following day at noon, following a rosary and a mass, the gremio made its "exit." After lining up in the same fashion, it passed through the center of town once more and headed off to the house of the new president.

The aura of pilgrimage was enhanced by the arrival of outsiders on September 29, including gremios from nearby towns who had made vows to San Miguel. In addition to Maxcanú's 14 gremios, religious confraternities from the nearby town of Cuch Holoch were present at the annual celebration.

The Gremio Hierarchy in Maxcanú

At the summit of the religious hierarchy resurrected in the mid-1920s stands the *Gremio de Comerciantes y Hacendados,* a consortium of wealthy landowners and businessmen that organized impressive processions for many years. With the exception of a handful of Lebanese merchants who owned fabric shops or dry goods stores in the center of town, this gremio was, reportedly, exclusively Hispanic in composition, based on surname, dress, residence (in the town's center), and ethnic ancestry.[13] According to several elderly residents, the town's butchers—a well-remunerated occupation—also marched with this gremio; however, it is not clear whether they were actually full-fledged members. As noted below, hacienda workers marched with this gremio as well—presumably to enhance the grandeur of its procession—but were clearly not considered members. In fact, the phrase "marched with" seems to signal a status distinction between different participants of a gremial procession. Of all the gremios this one alone is described in the Archives of the Archbishop of Mérida since in 1927 it requested permission to hold its annual procession on a Sunday rather than the previously scheduled weekday, so that it could pay tribute to San Miguel without interrupting the hacienda's normal work schedule. Whether the **hacendados** were more interested in maintaining production quotas or sponsoring a

FIGURE 2.3 Procession of San Miguel, Patron Saint of Maxcanú

spectacular procession that included their work force is not clear since they appear to have been interested in both.

In the early 1960s, this prestigious gremio entered the church for the last time. If its demise remains something of a mystery, it is not because residents are reluctant to talk about it. Quite the contrary. As in Garcia Márquez's popular novel, *Chronicle of a Death Foretold* (1984), many people claiming first-hand knowledge of the gremio and its history were eager to tell their story. Indeed, there are more conflicting accounts than cats in a litter.

The most popular version concerns the unpardonable heresy of the gremio's last president, Don Julio, a leading merchant who later served a term as municipal president of Maxcanú. In the early 1960s, according to this account, Don Uyé designed an authentic-looking priestly frock for Maxcanú's pre-Lenten carnival celebration and proceeded to march through town with a male transvestite on each arm. Although carnival is generally considered an appropriate occasion for sacrilegious parody, the parish priest was so infuriated by this performance that he refused to let the *Comerciantes y Hacendados* enter the church that year.

Others maintain that while Don Julio's carnival antics poisoned relations between the gremio and the church, it was not the decisive breach. That occurred when the former president deliberately burned the gremio's standards in a fit of rage. Still others claim that the standards were never willfully destroyed but were simply left in the rain, an all-too-common form of religious neglect. In any event, Maxcanú residents continue to debate Don Julio's fate to this day, some contending that he was formally excommunicated by the Vatican, others maintaining that he was merely humiliated by the parish priest. Don Julio himself has remained silent on the matter.[14]

According to a third account, the demise of the once venerable gremio had more to do with financial malfeasance than sacrilegious display. On several occasions, according to a merchant and erstwhile member, the gremio's treasurer invested the association's assets in his personal business. This, not surprisingly, undermined confidence in the association, and members eventually stopped donating money.[15] Finally, other informants insist that the gremio was undercut by a special sinod held in Mérida in the early 1960s that decreed that gremio members, or at least the leadership, be limited to "perfect Christians," that is, individuals married in the church. While this regulation certainly would have affected the membership of *Comerciantes y Hacendados,* it also would have undercut other gremios that are still in existence today.

Two of the other gremios resurrected in the 1920s—the *Gremio de Mestizos Finos* and the *Gremio de Artisanos*—were clearly **fino** organizations, associations of intermediate standing within the town. Although there is some disagreement concerning the name of the former,[16] it is generally acknowledged that the association was started by the foremen of the hacienda Chencoh, one of several henequén plantations located on the outskirts of Maxcanú. As some historians have noted (Joseph 1982; Katz 1962), the owners of Yucatán's lucrative henequén plantations were seldom involved in the day-to-day operations of their enterprises. These functions were handled by a trusted manager (**encargado**) and several foremen (mayokoles) who were responsible for assigning jobs, enforcing production quotas, preventing theft, and meting out punishment when necessary. In short, the mayokol was an intermediary or broker whose knowledge of Mayan and Spanish, and his ability to perform basic accounting tasks, put him in a class by himself.[17]

FIGURE 2.4 Mestizos finos. Courtesy of the University of Yucatán

As a mestizo fino, or fine mestizo, the mayokol was entitled to wear a more elegant version of the folk costume than other mestizos or Mayas. According to informant accounts and photos taken a half-century ago, finos distinguished themselves from other mestizos on festive occasions by wearing a distinctive white sandal known as an **alpargata,** which featured a metal buckle, an elevated heel, and a thick sole made of several layers of leather (*tiras*). Finos wore white pants; however, unlike the crude cotton pants worn by Indians or mestizos, their pants were made of *dril,* a tightly woven fabric. Finos might also sport a white, panama-style hat made from *jipi,* a soft flexible fiber that is easily distinguished from the rough-hewn straw hats of the agricultural worker. In fact, the mayokol's costume is very close to that of the jarana dancer described in Chapter 3 (see p. 73).

The *Gremio de Artesanos,* Maxcanú's other fino association, was dominated by tailors during its early years. In the 1920s, there were many workshops for the manufacture of apparel in Maxcanú, and several residents who recall this period described the gremio's original membership as "*puros sastres*" (all tailors), although sandal makers and a variety of other artisans were also included. Following the demise of the *Gremio de Comerciantes y Hacendados,* the town's butchers joined as well. Although Maxcanú was also home to a considerable number of potters at this time, the latter were generally considered peasants and, apparently, were not included in this gremio.[18]

Unlike other towns its size, Maxcanú has only one confraternity of artisans rather than several organized according to craft; nevertheless, the *Gremio de Artisanos* has fared well in inter-gremio competition and maintains a reputation for hosting spectacular celebrations in honor of San Miguel. The gremio's principal figures were also instrumental in establishing the *Club Montessori,* a lineal descendent of the fino social clubs begun in 1953. While members of Maxcanú's upper crust, the *Comerciantes y Hacendados,* belonged to Maxcanú Social, an exclusive club that was formed and disbanded many times over the years, the *Club Montessori* was the secular social organization of Maxcanú's intermediate social class.

With the exception of the *Gremio de Señoras y Señoritas,* discussed below, the remainder of Maxcanú's gremios correspond to the Spanish cuartel system and are numbered from one to four in clockwise fashion beginning in the town's northwest quadrant.[19] Because the imaginary lines that divide the town into four sections bisect one another in the main plaza, the four gremios share the "center" equally and, thus, are of equal stature. It would be more accurate to say that they are of equally low stature since the sectional gremios are made up primarily of peasants, ejidatarios, and others who are unable to participate in any of the previously named gremios.

The sectional gremios are also well known for their factionalism. Because they tend to be large and unwieldy—too large for the communal meal that the gremio president hosts in his yard—they are subdivided internally into a number of smaller units known as *particulares.* Each *particular* organizes its own festive meal and takes responsibility for supplying the gremio with some item (e.g., flowers) used in the religious procession organized for San Miguel or for the "profane" celebration that follows. In most cases, the relations between *particulares* are cordial, and the leaders of the various subgroups take turns filling the role of gremio president. Nevertheless, the *particulares* mark the fracture planes where gremios divide when egotism, caprice, or allegations of fraud rise to the surface.

Women's Gremios

The religious hierarchy or triarchy noted above emerges with even greater clarity when one begins to trace the fault lines that traverse the women's gremios. The oldest and most prestigious of these sodalities is the *Gremio de Señoras y Señoritas*. Often referred to as the *crema y nata* (cream of the crop) of Maxcanú, this gremio is best remembered for its elite membership and their elegant white gowns, a trait that distinguishes them from other gremio women who don brightly colored *huipils* or **ternos**.[20] In describing its founding members, emphasis is always placed on the proximity of their homes to the town center, or to 20th Street, a paved street that runs alongside the church and slopes gently up toward the foothills of the Pu'uk Mountains at the southern edge of town. In the 1920s this street served as a part-time residence for wealthy plantation owners who divided their time between Mérida, Maxcanú, and the gambling houses in Havana. According to property records found in the town hall, the value of these houses greatly exceeded any other residential constructions, even those in adjacent blocks.

The social composition of this gremio, however, was more complex than first appears. During the early years, according to older, well-informed members, it was composed of two distinct social groups: 1) wealthy mestizas (mestizas finas),[21] an intermediate strata that included the wives and daughters of the artisans and mestizos finos described above; and 2) women purportedly free of Indian blood, most notably the wives and daughters of hacienda owners. While both groups participated in the same procession honoring San Miguel, the mestizas finas were obligated to march at a respectable distance behind the leading ladies, and at gremio socials the mestizas were served lemonade while their wealthy counterparts sipped champagne.

The unique configuration of this gremio was no accident but the by-product of an unresolved tension between the elite's desire to reaffirm old social boundaries and their obligation to organize a celebration worthy of San Miguel. Although the *crema y nata* lived in impressive cement houses in the center of Maxcanú, they formed only a small minority of the town's population and, therefore, lacked the numbers, if not the resources, to host an impressive public feast.[22]

Contradictions such as these reveal the ambiguity inherent in local social relations. Notwithstanding changes wrought by the Mexican Revolution, the social order continued to rest on a complex chain of analogies—similarities and invidious distinctions—extending from the top of the social spectrum to the bottom. For example, the terms "señora" and "señorita" can be thought of as the Spanish equivalents of Mrs. and Miss, generic titles that index age and marital status and apply to women of all social classes. In this sense, the mestizas finas were clearly señoras and señoritas. In other instances, though, the terms are used in a more restrictive manner to refer to women who are chaste, of high social standing, or (in some cases) incarnations of the Virgin Mary (e.g., *Nuestra Señora de las Lágrimas*).[23] Indeed, the virginal white gowns worn by this gremio's top tier is best understood as a mimetic device, a way of proclaiming their purity and their difference from the mestizas finas who always donned the traditional folk costume. In others words, if the mestizas finas were "señoras" in one sense of the term, or more nearly "señoras" than Maxcanú's less refined mestizas, it did not mean they were señoras in every sense, and the gremio's wealthier members went to great lengths to remind them of this.

In the early 1930s the *Gremio de Señoras y Señoritas* divided at its weakest link, and a second women's gremio known by the name *Unión Católica Popular* (Popular Catholic Union) came into being. Although there are several contrasting accounts of this epochal event, most residents contend that it was actually the mestizas finas who, weary of being treated as second class citizens, fomented the split. The formation of *Unión Católica* did not, however, eliminate social boundary disputes; it simply displaced them to a lower level. If the terms "señora" and "señorita" are ambiguous, the terms "mestiza" or "mestizo" are even more equivocal. On the one hand, "mestizo" is frequently used as a euphemism for farm laborer or Indian since the Spanish term "indio" is no longer acceptable in public discourse. At the same time, however, individuals of considerable wealth often refer to themselves as "mestizos" (mixed) simply by virtue of the fact that they dance the jarana or participate in other forms of the regional mestizo culture discussed in the next chapter. Indeed, the notion of Yucatecan society as a confluence of two great traditions, Maya and Hispanic, is such an intrinsic element of regional statecraft that local and state politicians seldom miss the opportunity to self-identify as mestizos. Finally, as noted above, the term "mestizo" also at times refers to an intermediate social segment previously known as "mestizos finos," who distinguished themselves through occupation, residence, and dress from their less-affluent neighbors.

It is not surprising, then, that a new "mestiza" gremio would attract a wide range of members. Indeed, the new organization had only been in existence a few years when the original members decided that gremio activities were attracting too many poor mestizas. The situation finally became so intolerable that Doña Socorro, one of the founding members, stood up and announced that the association was for finas only, prompting a second split. Although both entities continued to use the name *Unión Católica,* the two resulting gremios are respectively known as "mestizas finas" (fine mestizas)[24] and "mestizas devotas" (devout mestizas), and each now holds separate processions in honor of San Miguel. As Don Mario, Maxcanú's most unabashed atheist once remarked, "one has a little more money, the other has a little more religion."

The formation of three separate sodalities distinguished according to class can, of course, be viewed as an historical event, a fortuitous set of incidents unfolding over time (in this case two decades); however, it would be more appropriate to view it as a dramatization of social structure. Indeed, the formation of a religious triarchy—señoras and señoritas, mestizas finas, and mestizas devotas—can be viewed as the religious analogue of the tripartite ethnic system that has existed in Yucatán since the colonial period. In the *Folk Culture of Yucatán* (1941), for example, Redfield not only notes that Indians were denied certain civil rights that vecinos held but that vecino was a more or less legal term that included *two* groups distinguished socially: whites and mixed bloods who wore the same garb as Indians. Although the relationship between whites and mestizos was clearly asymmetrical, both groups fit within the broader category of vecino, which denoted their identity as fully vested citizens, equivalent in some ways to the title of "burgher" in medieval Europe. Similarly, reflecting on his childhood in Temax, Yucatán, William Brito Sansores distinguished between the two *non*-Indian social groups that vied for political power in the early 1920s:

FIGURE 2.5 *Gremio de Unión Católica*, otherwise known as the *Gremio de Mestizas Devotas*

After some time I began to realize that the town contained two major groups who were enemies; in a hushed, silent manner they grappled for power that was vested in the municipal presidency of Temax. There was a group led by Pastor Castellano Acevedo, which included the owners of the nearby henequén haciendas, the proprietors of cattle ranches in the region, and the principal businessmen of the town. The second group was led by Señor Pedro Crespo, an elegant mestizo, a short, brown-skinned man with a large mustache and revolutionary ideas as he was a follower of Felipe Carrillo Puerto. This group included several merchants, a number of public employees, and the majority of peasants. . . . (Brito Sansores; translated by author)

In short, then, while the fate of Doña Socorro and other members of *Unión Católica* were not recorded in the prophecies of the Chilam Balam, the intrigues played out in public and in private, and the segmentation of the women's gremio, might have been predicted on structural grounds.

A Truncated Hierarchy

Since the 1960s Maxcanú's status hierarchy has undergone change as new occupational groups have entered the religious arena hoping to convert recently acquired wealth into symbolic capital. For example, the *Asociación de Ferrocarileros* (Railroad Workers Association), begun in the 1970s, is currently one of the wealthiest and most vigorous confraternities in Maxcanú. As members of one of Mexico's most powerful trade unions, the *Ferrocarileros* not only earn several times as much as agricultural workers or teachers but are the beneficiaries of an excellent pension plan. As wage laborers they are also unaffected by the declining market for handmade goods, something that has plagued Maxcanú's artisans in recent years. At the annual fiesta in 1990 the relative prosperity of this gremio was demonstrated in several ways. Most notably, the *Ferrocarileros* entertained the town by sponsoring a popular dance with a well-known and very expensive band. This much-discussed event was underwritten by the gremio's younger members, each of whom contributed 40,000 pesos, a sum equivalent to the wages an ejidatario earns in two weeks. In addition, elaborating on tradition, the gremio women donned elegant ternos (along with a blue canvas engineer's cap) in place of the simple huipils and nylon dresses worn previously.

During the same period, several of Maxcanú's more prominent confraternities entered a period of decline or disappeared altogether. As noted above, the *Gremio de Comerciantes y Hacendados* entered the church for the last time in the early 1960s. While several competing accounts are given to explain its disappearance (see above), the important fact is that there have never been any serious attempts to revive it.

Similarly, the distinction that once existed between the fino gremios and the other mestizo gremios (e.g., *Unión Católica*) is no longer in force. Indeed, a curious semantic detail provides evidence that the *Gremio de Mestizas Finas*—long abandoned by Doña Socorro—is no longer what it used to be. As noted above, the poorer of the two mestiza gremios is popularly known as the mestizas devotas (devout mestizas). Yet, as one informant noted with a touch of irony, many townspeople now think of them as the *mestizas de botas* or the "mestizas with shoes." Unlike Castilian Spanish where the /v/ and /b/ represent distinct phonemes, in Mexican Spanish the two are virtually homophonous, so a "mistake" of this nature is clearly understandable on phonological grounds. Nevertheless, the fact that so many people consider the mestizas devotas to be the well-shod gremio—in a setting where footwear correlates closely with social standing—indicates that status differences between the two gremios have all but disappeared.

Even the prestigious *Gremio de Señoras y Señoritas* has lost much of its previous luster. Not only does it now include an ample number of poor women, but, as it made its way to the church in 1990, one onlooker, a peasant in his fifties, described the pilgrims as *chen ichcallilobo*, a Mayan-Spanish neologism meaning, "just street people."[25] While all members of this gremio are still drawn from residential blocks located near the center of town, a spatial index of prestige, the center has begun to expand outward as Maxcanú's wealthier residents move to Mérida or simply stop participating in gremio activities. As one gremio officer admitted, "every time we recruit new members we include a new block a little further away from the town square."

The gremio system has also been greatly affected by the rapid growth of evangelical Protestantism in the last 20 years. While charismatic churches, such as the Church of God and the Jehovah's Witnesses, appear to attract mostly poor people, Maxcanú's Presbyterian church has recruited many upwardly mobile shop owners, individuals who in former times would have belonged to one of the town's more prestigious gremios.

Even the Catholic Church has contributed to the leveling tendencies in religious life. In an attempt to stem the growth of evangelical Protestantism, a second set of confraternities was superimposed upon the older gremio system in 1988. These associations, better known as centros de familia, were established to bolster religious participation in the community and receive regular visits from the parish priest; however, unlike the older gremios, they are organized geographically—based on a subdivision of Maxcanú into nine wards—not on the basis of occupational affiliation or status.

Finally, the gradual erosion of Maxcanú's religious hierarchy can be linked to a global shift in the relationship between secular and religious authority since the Mexican Revolution. Since the 1920s the Catholic Church has been officially off limits for schoolteachers and other public officials, a circumstance that makes it difficult, if not impossible, for the gremios to recruit educated, upwardly mobile residents. During certain presidencies this prohibition was greatly relaxed. Don Manuel Coello, a retired teacher whose name now appears on one of Maxcanú's primary schools, recalls how he started attending church in the 1940s after President Ávila Camacho proclaimed himself a believer in the Roman Catholic faith; nevertheless, then as now, the idea of a schoolteachers' gremio was unthinkable.

Notwithstanding these changes, the gremio system not only continues to function as a mechanism for ranking local residents but helps facilitate the transformation of pecuniary success into symbolic capital. If *Señoras y Señoritas* is not what it used to be in the eyes of some onlookers, its emphasis on abolengo—ancestry, lineage, and tradition—serves as a vehicle for cloaking or concealing the parvenu status of its new, economically active members. While both the incoming and outgoing presidents in 1990 were married to men with working-class jobs rather than businessmen or landowners, they were accumulating wealth at a rapid pace. The latter, the daughter of a well-to-do mestiza fina, not only operates the town's only telephone concession but recently purchased the rights to a new cable television franchise, which she plans to run out of her clothing store. Moreover, because of her role in the gremio, her mother is now welcome to participate in *Señoras y Señoritas*. Similarly, Doña Socorro, the 80 year-old mother-in-law of Maxcanú's wealthiest man (a large beer distributor), is now described as a founding member of *Señoras y Señoritas* even though she belonged to the second tier of the gremio and left on bad terms 50 years ago. Therefore, if the gremio is no longer an exclusive sodality of the rich (and perhaps it never was), it is the only gremio in which wealthy residents still participate.

Conclusion: Between Exclusivity and Grandeur

Yucatán's renascent gremio system helped re-establish order and privilege at a time in Mexican history when such principles had been called into question by the dissolution of the Porfiriato. Religious confraternities in the peninsula, however, function quite differently than the civil-religious hierarchies in Chiapas and other regions of Mexico where, according to Chance, "offices are usually ranked hierarchically in a more or less clear-cut order" (1990, 30). In fact, the operative principle in Yucatán appears to be ambiguity. Gremio life is governed by a notion of grandeur that encourages wealthy residents to invite Maya and poor mestizos into their confraternities in order to orchestrate a religious demonstration worthy of San Miguel. Broad and ambiguous ethnic/gender categories like "mestizo" or "señora" not only reflect this process of accommodation but point to the need for a different notion of hierarchy (see Sahlins 1985; Dumont 1970), one in which salient social distinctions are enveloped, at least temporarily, within a broader social unity. Eventually, however, envy, pretension, and exclusivity rise to the surface, resulting in the fragmentation of these fragile social units. While in some instances these social dramas or social intrigues are played out over long stretches of time, the structural impediment to unity is generally present from the very beginning.

The dialectic between exclusivity and grandeur is not played out solely at the organizational level (i.e., within individual gremios) however. It exists at the level of the community as well. While intra-gremial disputes become inter-gremial competition, and inter-gremial competition is ubiquitous, these rivalries continually unfold within a field of custom, community obligation, and festivity that evokes unity out of difference or, as Victor Turner notes in his account of the annual fiesta of Tizimin, helps participants disengage "from participation in structural role playing and status incumbency" (1974, 221). In addition to the normal sequence of bullfights, jaranas, and popular dances leading up to the annual fiesta, the evening mass gives way to nightly revelries in which individual gremios entertain the whole town by mounting large mythical beasts onto wooden carts and racing them through town as they burn or by sponsoring dramatic fireworks displays designed to incite mass hysteria. At other points, such as the final procession held in honor of San Miguel on September 29, the gremios march together in silence and join in solemn fellowship as the patron of Maxcanú is restored to his throne.

In the following chapter, we move from the always messy business of understanding the relationship between actual social groups to a somewhat more refined model of ethnic and status relationships based on an analysis of named social categories, labels, and other aspects of identity.

CHAPTER THREE

MAKING MAYA INTO MESTIZO
Identity, Difference, and Cultura Regional Mestiza

Ethnicity Above and Below the Belt

If not a topic of perennial concern, discussion of ethnic relations in Mesoamerica is certainly never far from the surface of intellectual life. Like debates over exchange in the western Pacific, cannibalism in the Amazon, and hierarchy in the Indian subcontinent, discussion of ethnic relations in Mesoamerica seems to follow a natural rhythm, re-emerging every 17 to 20 years and eating everything in sight before vanishing as quickly and mysteriously as it appeared. In the 1940s and 1950s ethnographers (Tax 1942; de la Fuente 1951) not only attempted to draw a clear conceptual distinction between ethnicity and race but to demonstrate that the relationship between Indians and **Ladinos** in Guatemala was fundamentally different—more fluid or more changeable—than the relationship between blacks and whites in the United States. When the topic re-emerged in the mid-1960s, attention, not surprisingly, turned to the relationship between ethnicity and class (Stavenhagen 1975). Should ethnicity be conceptually distinct from social class, or should the former be thought of simply as a distorted image of the latter? The social implications of the question were clear. If an ethnic group was simply a class with certain cultural trappings (e.g., a folk costume and a certain way of speaking) then reaffirming one's ethnic identity would do little more than "fix," so to speak, one's lowly place in the world.

More recently discussion of ethnic relations has focused on the origin and nature of key terms like "Maya" and the question of self-ascription (Castañeda 2004; Cocom 2004; Eiss 2004; Fallow 2004; Gabbert 2004a; Restall 2004; Sullivan 2000). Why does the term "Maya" appear so infrequently in colonial documents? Was resistance to public education in rural Yucatán around 1930 really rooted in concerns about preserving Mayan language and culture, or were locals more opposed to co-education? Do the Maya really think of themselves as Maya, or is "Maya-ness" a colonial—or even a post-colonial—construct imposed on Mesoamerica from without? In *Becoming Maya* (2004a), for example, Wolfgang Gabbert argues that the Maya have rarely been a cohesive self-conscious group. Maya ethnicity, to the extent that it exists, is an ephemeral, highly localized phenomenon, limited to certain periods and places. While I am reluctant to delve into a discussion based on historical documents covering a time period that ends precisely where my expertise begins (i.e., 1935), the questions that historians like Restall (2004) and Gabbert (2004b) raise may well serve as an historical predicate to the present discussion. Indeed, the promulgation of a regional culture that emphasizes the "mestizo" or "Yucateco" over the Maya—the topic of this chapter—may help to explain why Maya identity (i.e., the tendency toward self-ascription) remains weak in Yucatán, especially when compared to Guatemala or highland Chiapas.

At the same time, however, I hope to shift the emphasis from the problem of **essentialism** and Maya identity writ small to an analysis of the broader semantic and political fields in which group and category operate in contemporary Yucatán. As Ueli Hostettler notes in his rejoinder to Restall (2004), Gabbert (2004b), and others, the task is not complete once "we detect ethnicity" or isolate the tendency to essentialize identity: "We need to document the social processes that draw culturally defined groups into hierarchically structured fields of power, status, and wealth . . . to document how such processes operate in everyday practice . . . and under what circumstances ethnic identifications are perpetuated, modified or discarded" (2004, 195). In my view this requires examining not only past and ongoing forms of prejudice, insult, and innuendo but also the habitual pairing of the lovely mestiza, the pride of Yucatán, with images of vulgar or unsightly Indians.

Reluctance to identify oneself as Maya—the central paradox of regional ethnography—must also be understood as a result of a long history of defamation and **semantic derogation**; repeated attempts to depict **indigenas** as cannibals, wild animals, or rebellious savages (*rebeldes*); and a social system in which social mobility was and is achieved through assimilation or cultural **hispanicization**. Nevertheless, the latest round of discussion (see Castañeda 2004) has, in my view, served to rekindle important questions about ethnogenesis, the relationship between ethnicity and statecraft, and the nature of ethnic labels.

What are ethnic labels? Are they like the taxa or nomenclature that zoologists created to classify the natural world? Such a comparison is not as absurd as it first appears; after all, the mission of colonial Spain was to introduce order in the New World by domesticating nature, including its pre-Columbian inhabitants, *los naturales*.[1] How better to accomplish this task then by cataloging residents of New Spain according to phenotypic characteristics? This, indeed, can be seen in the painting "Las Castas," which adorns the cover of this book and depicts the physical appearance of the New

Spain original Castes. However, as Gonzalo Aguirre Beltrán notes in his *Obra polémica* (1992, 130), Spanish authorities soon came to grief trying to create legal or scientific-sounding categories, if this was, in fact, their intention. After applying the familiar *Español, indio, negro, mestizo,* and *mulatto* to the appropriate populations, the authorities drew on an incongruous collection of mathematical terms, animal names, and insults—e.g., *cuarterón* (¾ Spanish, ¼ African) from the Spanish *cuarto* (quarter), *lobo* (wolf), *zambo* (knock-kneed), *jarocho* (rude, brusque), *chamiso* (half-burnt log), *albarazado* (black streaked with red, having leprosy), *gíbaro* (Caribbean Indians known for shrinking heads), *cuatralbo* (animal with four white legs)—illustrating both their interest in biological precision and the supposed continuity between phenotype and moral character (Montalvo and Codina 2001). And in a "final act of desperation," to borrow Aguirre Beltrán's words, the authorities resorted to derogatory phrases such as *torna atrás* (throw back), *ahí te estás* (there you are), and *no te entiendo* (I don't understand you), a belated recognition of the enormity or the absurdity of the whole enterprise.[2] Therefore, if ethnic labels are one part science or taxonomy, they are certainly also one part insult or innuendo.[3]

Starting with this insight, I argue that ethnic categories of the Maya region, particularly Yucatán, are best understood as figures within a broader discourse, a regional rhetoric in which the mestizo or Yucateco is the master trope. The "mestizo," like Marx's commodity, at first sight appears to be a trivial and easily understood object. As the subject of anthropological discourse, it is sometimes thought of as a unitary being, the inexorable product of biological miscegenation or cultural assimilation; however, this abstract, essentially mechanical view of ethnic group formation not only obscures the deliberate syncretism of religious revitalization movements—the rhetorical genius that has led to so many brown virgins and Indian kings in Mesoamerica (Bricker 1981; Lafaye 1976)—but the nature of Mexican nationalism more generally.[4]

What I propose, in contrast, is a close analysis of mestizaje (political syncretism) in a regional setting that not only highlights the polysemy, or multiple meanings, of key terms (e.g., mestizo) but demonstrates how ethnic groups relate to one another structurally as well as symbolically. Yucatecan towns like Maxcanú are composed of several named groups—*mayero, catrín, ts'ul, blanco*—but the members of these groups are always also "mestizos" in some form or fashion. In this sense, named groups are analogous to names given to religious images like the Virgin of Guadalupe or the Virgin of Remedies. While the latter retain a unique history and hagiography, they are ultimately incarnations of the Virgin Mary and share in her importance. And while I confess to a latent structuralist impulse, an artifact of my interest in hierarchy, my goal is to understand ethnicity as it is manifest in performance and other cultural practices. After all, it is only by participating in specific folk performances (e.g., regional theatre, dance, etc.) that many Yucatecans become "mestizos" at all.

Here special attention is given to the jarana or vaquería (cattle dance), a dance originating on the eighteenth-century corn and cattle hacienda. Now thought to epitomize the unity of Maya and Hispanic culture, the dance has become a familiar feature at political events and tourist venues as well as village fiestas. While, in theory, the jarana is open to all residents, in practice it has become a spectacle in which well-to-do Yucatecans don an elegant version of the traditional folk costume and publicly represent themselves as *mestizos legítimos* (cultivated or legitimate mestizos), the first among equals. In this way, this chapter demonstrates how invidious distinctions between groups persist within a regionalist ideology or rhetoric that emphasizes common heritage and equality.

The Many Meanings of Mestizo: Modeling Ethnic Relations from the Ground Up

MESTIZOS AND THE WORLD OF WORK

In ethnographic accounts of the Yucatán (Redfield 1941; Hansen and Bastarrachea Manzano 1984; Villa Rojas 1987; Thompson 1974; Press 1975), the term "mestizo/a" is most commonly employed in its most restrictive sense, that is, as a way of denoting individuals who wear the traditional folk costume or what little remains of it. In this instance, however, dress is less an indication of one's fealty to regional tradition than a way of signifying work or occupational differences: farming :: manufacture, outdoor :: indoor, etc.[5] Indeed, as Irwin Press notes in *Tradition and Adaptation* (1975), mestizos often point to the impossibility of using catrín attire (city clothes) for work in the fields. Such clothes—and presumably the people who wear them—are simply too delicate. Similarly, farm workers in Maxcanú say that they dress as mestizos because they work in the *campo* (fields), although it might be more accurate to say that they work in the campo because they wear mestizo clothing, given the tendency of parents to dress and socialize a certain number of their children as mestizos in order to tie them to the homestead.[6]

Moreover, because agricultural work is generally considered the defining feature of Indian-ness, mestizo, in this sense of the term, is really a euphemism for the forbidden *indio* or a synonym for *mayero,* a name that points to the close association of ethnicity and work. By affixing the Spanish "-ero" to the nominative *Maya,* an ethnic label is effectively transformed into an occupational category similar in form to the Spanish *carpintero* (carpenter) or *mesero* (waiter). And while the term "indio," according to Fischer and Hendrickson (2003, 26), is sometimes used by Guatemalan intellectuals as a way of defusing "the destructive power of the term just as some African-Americans use 'nigger' in English," I have not noted this usage in Yucatán.[7]

TABLE 3.1 Multiple Meanings of Mestizo in Yucatán

Mexican National	**Mestizo/a$_3$** Includes all Yucatecans who dance the jarana regardless of class or racial background. Anyone who participates in *cultura regional mestiza*. Excludes residents of central Mexico.		
	Dzul Yucatecans of putative Spanish ancestry. Effeminate mestizos.	**Mestizo/a$_2$** Includes individuals of mixed ancestry regardless of dress.	
		Catrin Individual who wears western dress and does not work in the fields. Effeminate mestizo.	**Mestizo/a$_1$** Agricultural worker or individual (generally female) who wears the folk costume. Euphemism for the prohibited *indio*.

Mestizos and Race

The term "mestizo" is also understood in a more inclusive sense in which the opposition noted above (mestizo::catrín) is resolved. This necessarily brings us to the issue of race, since it is bodily images, that is, notions of inherited traits or shared substance, that both unify this dichotomy and distinguish this broader concept of mestizo from **ts'ul** or *blanco* (white) at a higher level of the social order.

While ethnographers since the early 1940s have attempted to minimize the importance of race[8] and, more specifically, the tendency to reduce culture or ethnicity to human biology, Yucatecans do pay attention to physical or anatomical differences when it comes to questions of health and illness, sexual prowess or sexual orientation, or simply when they are trying to come up with an appropriate nickname. Thus, residents of Maxcanú referred to a wealthy shop owner in the center of town as *mulix* (literally, mound) because of his kinky hair and affectionately applied the name *chino* (Chinese) to the commissar of the ejido because of his straight, flaxen hair. Similarly, they addressed the municipal president's personal chauffeur as *box pato* (black duck) due to his dark complexion. And, while the standard binomial invective is composed of the Mayan term *box* (black) and a reference to one or another orifice (e.g., *box it,* black anus; *box pel,* black vagina), *boxita,* formed by adding the Spanish diminutive "-ita," is generally used as a term of endearment, if in a rather paternalistic way:

Boxita, tu tia y tu madre	Little black one, your aunt and mother
me ponen tremenda cara;	gave me terrible looks;
no le hace, las meto en varas	don't worry, I caged them
y que otro perro me ladre	as any other barking dog.
Por ti perdería la vida	For you I would kill myself
si me niegas tu querer	if you deny me your love
y entonces negra querida	and then my precious negress
no me volveras a ver	you shall not see me again.
Por eso cuando tu cantas	Therefore when you sing
mi dulce y bella morena	my pretty, sweet brown woman
el anima me levantas	my spirit rises
y se me olvidan mis penas	and I forget all my troubles.

(Menéndez Díaz 1986, 80; translated by author)

One of the more interesting examples of race consciousness is the belief surrounding the *wah* (literally, tortilla) or *makal* (literally, tuber), a birthmark that appears on certain infants and is considered proof of their Maya ancestry. Indeed, as noted by Amparo Gamboa, the author of a popular encyclopedia of peninsular slang, the arrival of a newborn produces an irrepressible desire in certain "aging hypocrites" to check for the infamous spot:

> It is a . . . custom among old gossips . . . to visit women who have recently given birth, and with the pretext of admiring their infant's beauty, they . . . discretely observe the lumbar region . . . in search of the Mongolian spot . . . which is present among newborns of Indian ancestry; this spot . . . if it is indeed present, produces a triumphal joy among the *comadres* and if absent they announce it in front of the contented mother who, if not a cretin, will understand why the intrusive visitors have come. (1985, 267; translated by author)

And while the wah reportedly fades away by the time the bearer reaches adulthood, youth who have it often go to great lengths to conceal it.

The wah is also thought to be the outward sign of the Indian's/mestizo's inner essence (*naturaleza*) as well as a logical explanation for his "unseemly" comportment. Indeed, expressions like "Eduardo has retained his wah" or "Josúe must have a tremendous makal" are used to embarrass individuals who display their anger in public. In other words, bodily features taken as a set of symbols—a set deceptively close to nature itself—can be seen as a foundation upon which other cognitive or affective features rest. Just as nature, conceived as *el monte* (the untamed forest), is thought to determine the kinds of clothes men must wear, the Maya mark points to an underlying conception of nature (in this case biological substance) that accounts for the difference between angry, brutish mestizos and genteel, effeminate ts'ules, a category I discuss below.

In fact, the use of the term "makal" might be seen as an attempt to relate racial differences or human taxa to differences occurring elsewhere in nature. As Amparo Gamboa notes (1984, 267), the makal is actually a type of tuber that grows abundantly in Yucatán and is found in two varieties: a small, light-skinned variety (*Xanthosoma Violaceum*) and a larger dark-skinned type (*Colocasia Antiquorum*), which is commonly referred to in Mayan as *makal box* (black makal).

Similar to the wah is the *sinik* (literally, ant), a Yucatec Mayan term referring to red spots that are said to appear on the necks of Indians or mestizos when they get angry, thus revealing their true identity. Indeed, both the sinik and the wah point to the prevalent belief that the fine clothing worn by the catrín simply serves to disguise a more enduring, biologically rooted identity. As a popular Mexican expression, quoted in the Introduction, states: "*La mona aunque se vista de seda, mona se queda*" (a monkey dressed in silk is still a monkey). Or as Víctor Suárez plainly comments, the catrín is simply "a mestizo who abandons the traditional folk costume in order to wear European dress" (1979, 167). In other words, the catrín is not simply the mestizo's counterpart but also a species of a more inclusive mestizo genus (also see Hervik 1999).

Taking this analysis further, it can be argued that the catrín is also a feminine or feminized mestizo. Here, it is important to note that Yucatecans draw a distinction between an individual who adopts western dress as a young child—which is less problematic—from one who embraces the style as an adult by referring to the latter as a *catrín forzado,* a phrase translated as "forced" or even "raped" catrín. In other words, by westernizing his attire and demeanor, a Yucatecan moves along a gender continuum towards ts'ul; a sophisticated individual who is prone to hair loss is considered effeminate or gay and seems to lack stamina.[9] As Redfield commented, "The Indian can work, work, work, eat only a little atole and some dried tortillas, and endure the heat . . . but 'the blood of the *dzul* is weak'" (1964, 157).

Politics, Parody, and El Catrín

While ethnographers have tended to emphasize the opposition between mestizo and catrín, they frequently overlook or fail to comment on the important distinction between the *catrín simple* (poor catrín) and the ts'ul (the gentleman or foreigner). In part, this can be attributed to the fact that Yucatecans with money and a little common sense are seldom found in the places anthropologists perennially inhabit; however, the oversight also reflects a lack of curiosity about the origin and meaning of key terms, a failure, in short, to do the necessary historical spadework.

The term "catrín," as noted above, is applied to individuals who compare favorably with others mestizos in terms of education, occupation, and dress; however, the term has other, more negative connotations that reflect a bitter history of class struggle.

As several authors have noted (Joseph 1982; Loewe 1995), education and agrarian reform were co-equal aspects of the Cárdenas reform in Yucatán. By recruiting the sons and daughters of Maya agriculturalists to serve as rural educators, the Cárdenas administration not only began to break down occupational and class barriers but developed an effective cadre organization to carry out the political objectives of the administration. Rural educators were expected to petition the Department of Agriculture for ejido lands on behalf of their communities and aid in the diffusion of Cárdenist political culture through drama and art.[10]

Rural teachers were also encouraged to wear contemporary garb (e.g., leather shoes, colored slacks) as part of a deliberate attempt to subvert established ethnic/class codes. Consequently, poor mestizos dressed in city clothes began to appear in towns and villages where even some of the wealthiest merchants still spoke Mayan and wore the traditional folk costume, a situation that all but insured biting insults—dandy, fop, catrín—from more conservative Yucatecans.

In fact, while Redfield (1941, 64) notes that this unusual moniker (that is, catrín) was just beginning to grace the lips of Dzitas residents during his stay in the peninsula,[11] he either failed to mention, or was unaware, that the term actually comes from a satirical novel entitled *Don Catrín de la Fachenda* (The Pretentious Don Catrín) by José Joaquin Fernández de Lizardi, a humorist and pamphleteer who lived in Mexico City in the early 1800s. In Lizardi's novel the protagonist, Don Catrín, comes from a family of very modest means. His father assumes that his son will be groomed for an honest trade such as carpentry or tailoring; however, his mother, who claims to have the "blood of the Ponces, Tagles, Pintas and Velascos" in her veins (Spell 1931, 74), will hear nothing of it. She insists that her son be sent to a good preparatory school. Don Catrín follows the course his mother sets for him but only succeeds in acquiring an unhealthy disdain for honest labor. Unable to complete the work required for a professional degree, and unwilling to serve anyone "unless it was the king himself" (Spell 1931, 75), he moves from one ill-reputed occupation to another. Beginning as an attendant in a bordello, he briefly becomes an actor and, finally, ends up as a gambler's assistant. Although Don Catrín eventually goes broke, he continues to try to impress others by wearing stylish apparel that he purchases at a Chinese market in Mexico City:

> I was simply floating in the air, without education in military matters, business, farming, the arts or anything worthwhile, just a clean and simple citizen [*paisano mondo y lirondo*], when my old comrades "the officials" turned their back on me. None of them showed me the least respect; they even refused to greet me. Perhaps it was because I was broke, since in those days my clothing was not indecent, because with the money I earned from selling my uniform, I purchased a blue shirt with tails [*fraquecillo*] at the Chinese market [Parián], a top hat, a pair of nice boots, a watch for twenty *reales,* a stylish chain for six pesos, a little cane and a handkerchief.
> (Fernández de Lizardi 1944, 45; translated by author and Rosa Vozzo)

In short, the use of the term "catrín" to denigrate rural educators and other "pretentious" Yucatecans was not simply a rhetorical strike against the Cárdenas administration but an ardent attempt to reinforce distinctions within the upper tier of Yucatecan society, a boundary marked by the distinction between *gente de vestido* (individuals who wore European dress) and mestizos who didn't.[12]

A similar attempt to defend ethnic and class boundaries can be seen in contemporary jokes about undiscerning Mayas or mestizos who attempt to raise their stature by translating Mayan surnames such as *Ek* (star) into the Spanish equivalent, *Estrella.* Because the Spanish equivalent is often a common noun, rather than a recognizable Spanish surname, nobody is fooled. The effort, as the jokester notes, simply draws attention to the ignorance and vanity of the individual in question. The jokester also invariably adds that nobody named *Pech,* a common Mayan surname, ever assumes the equivalent Spanish name *Garrapata* (tick or bug) since that would just compound their shame.

And then there is the tale of Juan Mierda (Juan Excrement), which I heard several times but never actually recorded. Juan Mierda, as the story goes, decides to change his unusual name and goes to the civil registry or to court:

> Juan: I've come here to change my name.
> Judge: So you have. And what's your name?
> Juan: Juan Mierda, your honor.
> Judge: Oh I see. Well, have you thought about a new name?
> Juan: Yes, I'd like to change my name to José.

Ts'ul: A Gentleman and a Devil

Continuing up the social ladder, we arrive at ts'ul, alternately defined as "gentleman," "foreigner," "white person," and "Satan." While ts'ul stands at the height of the social order, it is by no means clear who, aside from anthropologists or visiting government functionaries, merits this designation in rural communities. It is a social category that currently has few if any members in Maxcanú. In fact, one way to generate an interesting bar room debate is to ask a group of drunken schoolteachers whether the son of a former hacienda owner is a ts'ul.

During my initial stay in Yucatán I was privy to two such debates, and in both instances the arguments centered on the status of Don Felipe Josúe Téllez y García (a pseudonym). Don Felipe was a friendly man in his early sixties who spent a good part of the day reading the newspaper and sipping whiskey in his matrimonial-sized hammock; however, he also found time to tutor high school students in French and Latin, teach ballet and folk dance (the jarana), handle government correspondence for illiterate farm workers, and talk with anthropologists sent his way. He was quite proud of his ability to speak Mayan, something the children of hacienda owners commonly know and, thus, a mark of distinction, although a rather ironic one given the prejudice toward indigenous Mayan speakers. In short, it is one thing to be an indigenous Mayan speaker and quite another to be a wealthy, non-indigenous Mayan speaker.

Felipe had no children of his own but was the *padrino* (baptismal godfather) of more than 80 children, so many, in fact, that he finally lost count. The feat was especially impressive because he had, reportedly, never set foot

FIGURE 3.1 "Say No to Drugs": poster next to an advertisement for beer near the Capilla Sistina

in church. Felipe was not only a die-hard empiricist who believed only what he saw with his own two eyes, but he considered the parish priest a hypocrite for railing against sin in the pulpit and fathering illegitimate children on the side. Indeed, Felipe often bragged that the only church he attended was the *Capilla Seistina* (6th Street Church), his way of referring to a cantina on Sixth Street, and a play on the Spanish name for the Sistine Chapel (*Capilla Sistina*).

Felipe was comfortably retired in the home his parents had owned, a heavy cement structure that sat across from the church about 100 yards off the main square. At one time, according to Felipe, the building covered almost an entire city block; however, as time passed and his siblings settled in Mérida, the house was partitioned into several separate apartments. In addition to his own, one unit was occupied by his sister, Elda, and her husband, Pablo, Maxcanú's leading loan shark. Several other rooms had been rented to a young doctor from Mérida who transformed the space into a small examining room and pharmacy. The remaining apartment was entrusted to Felipe's nephew who briefly operated a cantina and, when this failed, began renting the space to transients, this author included.

The interior of Felipe's apartment was simply yet tastefully decorated with curios from different parts of the world and a few antiques that had been in the family for years. The most important item in his house, however, was an old album that sat open on a wooden coffee table and contained photos of actors, dancers, and filmmakers he had met in Mexico City. Although Felipe originally went there to study medicine, he dropped out after one year and began to dance with the *Ballet Folklórico,* a vocation that took him to Europe and the US. As a result of his travels, Felipe learned a little Italian and a touch of English; he even managed to get a minor role in a film.

Upon his return to Maxcanú, following an injury that ended his dancing career, Felipe continued to be something of a showman, displaying articles and affectations he picked up in Mexico City. To convey the image of a cultivated man, or simply to ruffle the feathers of his compatriots a bit, Felipe would appear in public with a stylish top hat and a cane or would address people in Italian. And while most people accepted Felipe as a walking anachronism, a "fossil" as one teacher blithely put it, others were clearly bothered by what they considered an attempt to put on airs. For them, even his good posture, the telltale sign of a former ballet dancer, appeared exaggerated and arrogant.

Felipe was an ebullient, talkative person who had an opinion on practically everything, but when it came to discussing his family he was more selective. He was quite comfortable talking about his mother, the daughter of a refined Oaxaca family. On several occasions, in fact, he pulled out pictures of her posing in an elegant gown and recalled her stern, forceful manner.

Because of her insistence on proper etiquette, especially around the dinner table, Felipe and his siblings learned the meaning of manners at an early age. Felipe, however, was reluctant to talk about his father. Although Don Sebastián had, apparently, made a small fortune by purchasing henequén plantations and putting them to productive use in the 1930s, he was not a cultivated person. Felipe's mother had, by all accounts, married below her station, and it was this that raised questions about his place in society.

The fact that Don Felipe still resided in Maxcanú also mitigated against his inclusion in the ts'ul category. Place, ethnicity, and class are intimately related in Yucatán, and ts'ul has always been defined more by his absence than by his presence. As an absentee landlord, he belonged to a social class that owned splendid stone houses in the center of rural towns yet chose to spend most of the year in Mérida. As Alberto García Cantón (1965, 10) notes in his nostalgic *Memorias de un ex-hacendado henequenero* (Memories of a former henequén hacienda owner), only during the summer months, when family reunions were held, did the hacendado and his family spend much time on their rural estate.

In short, then, if Felipe was considered by some to be Maxcanú's last ts'ul, it was not based on his ability to speak proper Spanish or his use of a particular garment, things that define the ordinary catrín. Nor was it a question of wealth. Though wealthy enough to live off the interest from his savings account and a rental property or two, he had been surpassed long ago by the town's mestizo merchants, men who in Felipe's view had sullied their reputations by bootlegging whiskey. Rather, it was a question of lineage or abolengo, and his ability, for better or worse, to maintain the image of a knowledgeable, well-bred gentleman. In other words, while all ts'ules are by definition catríns insofar as they wear western attire, speak good Spanish, and purchase prestige items in the market, not all catríns are ts'ules.

The Legitimate Mestizo

At the highest level of society, even the intractable opposition between catrín and ts'ul is reconciled, this time by a conception of mestizo that emphasizes the cultural unity of all Yucatecans regardless of ethnicity, status, or class. Taken in this final sense, the mestizo is the central figure in the highly celebrated *cultura regional mestiza*.

When Yucatecans speak of regional culture, they refer to two separate but related practices. On the one hand, regional culture is thought to be a body of custom, gesture, and disposition that not only unifies the peninsula but sets Yucatecans apart from residents of central Mexico (better known as *waches*).[13] Notwithstanding the criticism of Don Felipe's exaggerated posture, Maxcanú residents insist that there is a distinctly Yucatecan gait, which is infinitely more graceful than the central Mexican stride. When asked to account for this difference, one primary schoolteacher explained that Yucatecans, including a good number of ts'ules, practice the *hetsmek,*' a Maya "baptismal" ritual in which a newborn child is placed on the hip of a godparent of the same sex and is carried nine times around a table arrayed with gender appropriate objects. Straddling the godparent's broad hip, I was assured, opens the newborn's young legs so that he or she can walk properly.

Similarly, despite the middle-class penchant for ridiculing the Spanish syntax of poor peasants (that is, individuals who speak Yucatec Mayan as a first language), educated Yucatecans proudly note the distinctiveness of peninsular Spanish that results from neologism, semantic transposition, and the hybridization of Spanish and Mayan forms.[14] One oft-cited example, drawn from popular books by Alfredo Barrera Vásquez (1957) and Víctor Suárez (1979, 176), is the verb *apesgar,* meaning to "hold down" or "put pressure on an object." While *apesgar* has all the morphological features of a regular Spanish verb, it is unique to Yucatán and is thought to derive from a homophony between the root of the Spanish verb *pesar* (to weigh) and the Yucatec Mayan *pets'ah,* meaning to hold down with one's hand (Barrera Vásquez 1980a, 649; future references to this work will be cited as DMC and page number). In short, Yucatecans tend to view the regional vernacular as both more expressive and more melodic than the Spanish spoken in central Mexico.

Regional culture, however, also refers to a set of standardized performances that both symbolize and articulate the unity of many Yucatecans. They are performances, moreover, that frequently receive government sponsorship or support and are rapidly becoming **folkloric**. These include such things as *teatro costumbrista* (popular theatre),[15] certain types of handicraft production, and poetic verses that artfully combine Yucatec Mayan and Spanish.

By including well-known Mayan phrases in lyrical Spanish sonnets, Yucatecan writers illustrate the mestizo character of peninsular speech as they transform a widely disseminated poetic genre into a more popular, regional form of expression. The poetic fragment reprinted below—with Mayan phrases enclosed in quotation marks—is but one of several pieces published in *Novedades,* a regional newspaper. Needless to say, the sonnet also depicts Mayan speakers as vulgar individuals, an example of how the valorization of mestizaje in form is paired with an insulting view of indigenous people in content.

El Bracero	The Migrant
Me llamo Tiburcio Euan	My name is Tiburcio Euan
Pero me dicen "El Xix"	but they call me "residue"
porque de catorce hermanos	because of fourteen siblings
yo viné a ser "el dziriz."	I was the last one through.
Crecí como un "Xlucuncan"	I grew like a "Xlucuncan"
flaco, feo, un "malix"	skinny, ugly, a mutt
tomando "choco zacan"	drinking hot corn gruel
y comiendo "pac," "kut bi"	and eating ground chiles.
Pronto aprendí a trabajar	Quickly I learned to work
y desde entonces yo fuí:	and from then I was:
ejidatario en Texán	a farm worker in Texán
un vaquero en Tizimin	a cowboy in Tizimin
camionero en Tepakan	a truck driver in Tepakan
y torero en Yobain	and a bullfighter in Yobain.

(From "El Bracero," Vasquez López 1987; translated by author)[16]

The Jarana

The crown jewel of regional culture, however, is the jarana, a dance that has been popular among Yucatán's Creole population since late colonial times. Originally part of the vaquería, the jarana has become an emblem of regional identity and is currently part of the annual fiesta held to honor the patron saint of a town or village.

In Yucatán, the jarana has two common variants: a slow waltz choreographed in ¾ time similar to the **Jota Argonesa**, a Spanish dance, and a livelier dance in ⅝ time, which derives from the fandango of Andalucía (Pérez Sabido 1983). However, despite the many similarities between the Spanish and American forms,[17] Yucatecan writers are quick to point out that the jarana contains several aboriginal traits that distinguish it from the Spanish jota. The rigid vertical position of the torso, the relative absence of arm movements, and the marked hieratism of the dance are all said to distinguish the former from the latter. The musical accompaniments, appropriately known as *sones mestizos* (mestizo sonnets), often involve indigenous instruments like the *güiro* (an instrument made from a perforated gourd or wood in the shape of a fish) that give the jarana a more percussive flavor. In fact, according to Pérez Sabido (1983), none of the instruments that originally accompanied the fandango—guitar, violin, castanets, and cymbals—is still used by jara-nero musicians. Nowadays, a typical ensemble contains two trombones, two clarinets, two trumpets, a tenor saxophone, a bass, and a güiro. Other native percussion instruments such as the *rascabuche* and *zacatán* are also sometimes used. Similarly, Maya influence, particularly the indigenous love of wildlife, is revealed in the names and lyrics of the more popular jaranas, such as *El Ch'om* (The Vulture), *El Xulab* (The Ant), and *La Tsutsuy* (The Wild Dove)—names, incidentally, that combine Spanish articles with Yucatec Mayan nouns (*Enciclopedia yucatanense* 1977, 779).

Other characteristics of the jarana that make it a symbol of regional pride are the novelties or *suertes,* neither Mayan nor Spanish, that have grown up alongside it, embellishments such as waltzing with objects balanced precariously on one's head or dancing atop a narrow, wooden box used to measure maize (*almud*). These tricks not only distinguish the jarana from the jota, while highlighting the abilities of more talented dancers, but are the subject of numerous anecdotes that emphasize the color and creativity, not to mention the drinking prowess, of famous Yucatecan performers (Pérez Sabido 1983).

Standard female attire for the jarana is an elegant version of the mestizo folk costume. Female dancers dress in a resplendent terno (literally, three), a dress that, thanks to a cloth overlay extending from the waist to the knee, has three rows of brightly colored embroidery. To make the costume even more elegant, the dancer wears a decorative slip (*fustán*) with a lace border that hangs at ankle length just below the hem. The third element of the outfit is a *rebozo* (silk scarf) called the Santa María, which came into vogue in the late nineteenth century and has since served to distinguish wealthy mestizas from poor ones. The dancer's status is also displayed by the medallions and gold chains she wears conspicuously around her neck. Customarily these include a rosary made of red coral beads, gold filigree, one or more gold coins, and a gold medallion embossed with the image of the Virgin of Guadalupe.

Male attire is equally elegant but less complicated and less colorful. Typically male dancers will appear in a *filipina,* a long-sleeved white cotton shirt with a round collar, which may have gold buttons connected to one another by a thin gold chain that runs down the inside of the garment. In keeping with tradition, the dancer's pants are white, lack a crease, and are made of a tightly woven fabric. Similarly, the dancer wears the distinctive white sandal with a decorative leather band that crosses the toes, an elevated heel, and a thick sole made up of several layers of leather (*tiras*). In the past, "social standing" could be measured quite literally by counting the number of tiras a dancer could legitimately wear; however, nowadays elevated sandals connote femininity or homosexuality and have been abandoned for the most part, a change, quick frankly, that has done little to break the association between jarana troupes and homosexuality. The last element in the outfit is a narrow-brimmed white panama hat.

It is this refined, meticulously dressed individual that Maxcanú residents have in mind when they speak of the *mestizo legítimo* (legitimate mestizo). Since the term "legítimo" is generally understood as "pure" or "unadulterated"—as in *legítimo Maya,* a phrase referring to the supposedly uncontaminated spoken Mayan of times past[18]—the idea of a "mestizo legítimo" at first appears to be a contradiction in terms, namely, an "unmixed mixture."

Contradictory propositions, however, have a way of revealing interesting secrets, and the unspoken truth in this case is that the jarana dancer *par excellence* is not a mestizo at all—at least not according to any of the previous definitions—but ts'ul. Ts'ul, who in every other instance stands apart from and above the society of mestizos, is ritually reintegrated through the jarana. Situated in the hallowed space of an open-air dance floor, he is no longer a secluded individual but the primus inter pares, first among "half breeds." In short, once the jarana is understood as a forum in which ts'ul and a few well-heeled catríns gain legitimacy by becoming mestizos, the concept of a "mestizo legítimo" begins to make more sense.

Indeed, from John L. Stephens's account of the "Dance of the Mestizas," a jarana he observed in Ticul in 1842, it is clear that this colorful pageant has served as a Yucatecan saturnalia for more than 150 years:

> El báyle [sic] de las Mestizas was what might be called a fancy ball, in which the señoritas of the village appeared as las Mestizas or in the costume of Mestiza women: loose white frock with red worked border round the neck and skirt, a man's black hat, a blue scarf around the shoulder, gold necklace and bracelets . . .
>
> To sustain the fancy character, the only dance was that of the *toros* [toritos]. . . . This over, all dispersed to prepare for the báyle de dia, or ball by daylight. . . . At length a group was seen crossing the plaza: a vaquero escorting a Mestiza to the ball, holding over her head a red silk umbrella to protect her from the scorching rays of the sun; then an old lady and gentleman, children, servants, a complete family group, the females all in white with bright-colored scarves and shawls. *The place was open to all who chose to enter, and the floor was covered with Indian women and children, and real Mestizos, looking on good-humouredly at this personification of themselves and their ways.* (1963 [1843], Vol. 2, 63–65; emphasis added)

Noting that the dance was intended to provide a vivid picture of hacienda life, Stephens goes on to describe the behavior of two *fiscales* (hacienda foremen) dressed in filthy white shirts, crude cotton drawers, ridiculously oversized sombreros, and "long locks of horse hair hanging behind their ears" (1963, 65). They were the masters of the dance and demonstrated their authority by forcibly seating vaqueros on the floor and threatening to whip the "mestizas." At the least provocation, they would expel male dancers from the hall and steal their partners or make idle males sing a song in "alternate lines of Mayan and Castilian" (1963, 69). To Stephens's surprise, the person chosen for this role was not one of Ticul's refined young gentleman but a common pig butcher known for his sense of humor.

At noon the "Dance of the Mestizas" ended with a hearty meal of tortillas, beans, eggs, and meat, but much to Stephens's chagrin there were neither forks nor knives. And just to make sure the meaning of the event did not escape their distinguished guests, one of the fiscales pulled Stephens's hat down over his eyes when he attempted to thank a "mestiza" for serving him and informed him that there was no need for compliments since "we [are] all Indians together" (Stephens 1963, 69).

If Stephens had missed something of importance, it is probably the numerous gender inversions that occur in the vaquería, since he mentions that the mestiza's "black hat was repulsive" (Stephens 1963, 69) but avoids further comment about this typically male piece of apparel being worn by a woman. In contemporary jaranas, women are thought to have greater stamina than their male counterparts and will accept new partners as the vaqueros wax weary and retire to the sidelines. In fact, these gala performances are often extravagant dance contests whose competitive character increases as the night progresses. Since there is no conventional endpoint, couples vacate the dance floor only when bored or exhausted, and, as long as there are dancers present, custom dictates that the band must continue playing. When only two couples remain, the male onlookers will line up behind their favorite female contender and will place their sombreros on her head, offering encouragement in the form of a symbolic coronation. When the dance is finished, the victor will be honored with a silk sash and small gifts and will be referred to as "*t'ok xich*," a Mayan phrase that translates as "exploding tendons" *(Enciclopedia yucantanense* 1977, 789).

A similar inversion occurs in "Toritos" (Little Bulls), which, according to Stephens's account, was the only piece performed in Ticul in 1842. In this dance, performed in 6/8 time, the vaquero removes a large red handkerchief from his hip pocket and attempts to parry the charge of his female "bull" as he dances. The "bull," however, makes no pretense at dancing; her only objective is to knock the toreador down and penetrate him, yet another example of the transformation of ts'ul into a feminine or feminized mestizo.

Ultimately, though, the importance of the jarana as a token of regional unity or regional statecraft is revealed not by what happened 160 years ago but through the actions of the state government over the last two decades. At present, the jarana still opens the traditional four-day fiesta; however, there is an ever-present fear that the next fiesta organizer will replace it with a more popular dance (e.g., rock, salsa, or tropical music) in order to ensure a healthy return on his investment. Suspicions of this sort are, apparently, not unwarranted given the recent tendency of fiesta organizers to economize on the jarana by hiring little known bands or to charge steep admission fees. Therefore, while the jarana is a ubiquitous feature of regional politics and can be found at campaign speeches, public dedications, official commemorations, gubernatorial addresses, and dozens of tourist venues, the dance is threatened with extinction in the one place it counts most, the rural town or village. This, not surprisingly, has led to several attempts by the state government to preserve or revitalize the event, a process referred to as *rescate cultural* (cultural rescue).

One of the more notable attempts at revitalizing the jarana was the *Vaquería de Rescate Cultural* held in Maxcanú on April 16, 1983, a carefully scripted and highly publicized event organized by a prominent resident and then minister of cultural affairs for the State of Yucatán. Unlike most pre-dance advertisements, which typically sport the logo of the beer company that underwrites expenses, posters announcing this event promised "good clean fun in remembrance of times past," and specifically prohibited the sale or consumption of alcoholic beverages. The publicity also contained a series of rules that participants should follow. Women were expected to wear the regional costume, a terno or huipil. Men were to wear the filipina described above or a *guayabera* (a short-sleeved white shirt with ribbing), and all participants were strongly encouraged to be punctual.

Further, in a break with custom, not to mention the normal rhythm of rural life, the promotional literature for Maxcanú's first state-sponsored jarana

FIGURE 3.2 Governess of Yucatán in an elegant terno as Maxcanú celebrates its 150th anniversary as a town

listed the order and precise starting time of each event in the "traditional" opening ceremony. Residents of the town's four principal barrios would be summoned by the explosion of fireworks at 8:00 p.m. They were to arrive at the center of town by 8:20 with ribbons, canes, and a decorated pig's head to request permission to enter the municipal building. At 8:25 the band was to play "*La Angaripola*," the musical piece typically used to signal dancers that they can enter the dance floor. Finally, the dance was to commence at 8:30 p.m. with "Aires Yucatecos" (Yucatecan Airs) and end promptly at 12:00 a.m. with "Toritos" (Little Bulls).

The pre-dance publicity was also much more didactic than usual. Unlike other advertisements, which generally contain only the date, the name of the band, and a few adjectives describing the festive atmosphere one can expect, promoters of the *Vaquería de Rescate Cultural* produced a 30-inch flyer, which contained a detailed description of pre-Columbian dance as well as an account of the unique character of the *Jarana Yucateca:* "what is certain . . . is that it is executed in a unique way, with artistry, with its own unique style that varies according to region, [and] in which every individual places his own unique, ancestral experience . . . in front of others . . . a condition that must not be lost or confused with modern rhythms or styles that are not characteristic of this performance" [translated by author].

Finally, underscoring the political character of the event, special invitations were sent to Alpuche Pinzón, the Constitutional Governor of Yucatán, the First Lady, a dozen prominent state politicians, and the municipal presidents of 15 cities and towns.

Conclusion

At this point it is worth repeating that the objective of this chapter is not to develop a model of ethnic relations that stands apart from other aspects of social life, a neutral, colorless representation whose "only job is to represent something else, to become the vehicle of a meaning conceived quite independently of itself" (Eagleton 1983, 136). On the contrary, the aim is to highlight the interconnectedness of ethnicity, culture, and statecraft in one remote corner of the republic, to analyze, as it were, an "ethnic rhetoric" or ideology that relies heavily on euphemism, parody, insult, and innuendo.

Despite many excellent studies, the ethnography of Yucatán sorely lacks a sense of irony. Fernández de Lizardi's fictional Don Catrín de la Fachenda—used to great effect by Yucatán's upper class—has been hypostatized by Redfield, quantified by Thompson, and used as a taxonomic category by many other anthropologists who show no awareness of the conservative parody embedded in this term. Equally conservative in its effect is the jarana, a public spectacle that links the nostalgia residents feel for the Yucatán of their youth, and their interest in conserving cultural traditions, to the preservation of a political order rooted in ethnic and racial difference. Above all, the jarana is an attempt to measure the present in terms of the past. Amidst all the discussion of mixed codes, histrionic social inversions, and elegant costumes, it is important to remember that Maxcanú residents feel that by preserving the jarana and vaquería they are preserving a way of life, a moral order that is threatened not only by economic and political transformations but by aggressive, well-financed evangelical groups, foreign companies, and new and unusual forms of music. Within this milieu, the mestizo legítimo is a symbol of virtue, an incorruptible figure whose elegance and simplicity recall a more honorable past. He is a romantic figure who treats women with respect and has the decency and preparation to place a handkerchief between his sweaty palm and the shoulder of his female consort during the dance.[19]

Nor is the model outlined above intended to be the final word on ethnic relations in Yucatán. While I believe that it helps to illustrate the dominant (i.e., nationalist) conception of ethnic relations, it is neither a unique or uncontested view of things ethnic. However effective the rhetoric of mestizaje is in creating unity out of difference, it is an ethnic discourse that has begun to fray around the edges as indigenous community leaders reassert their identity as Mayan speakers. Not only do many young teachers from rural areas bristle at the suggestion that they are mestizos or catrines, but the rough outline of an alternative political current rooted in Maya identity can be seen in campaigns to promote Mayan literacy and to make Mayan an official language of government.[20] And while it is true that many Mayan speakers do not readily identify themselves as Mayas, the situation in Yucatán is, perhaps, not unlike Guatemala a generation ago: "Twenty years ago the only Maya in Guatemala were on thousand-year-old glyphs and in tourism literature. Until about the mid-1980s the word *Maya* was primarily used in archaeological discourses to refer to the builders of Tikal.... Maya was not used popularly, or by those self-identifying, to refer to existing indigenous people" (Nelson 1999, 6). However, in the wake of the quincentennial of the Conquest and the protests against it, there has been a dramatic increase in identity politics in Guatemala and the willingness of people to think of themselves as Maya rather than simply as residents of a particular town or as speakers of a particular linguistic group. Could something similar be brewing in Yucatán?

PART II

Critical Perspectives From Below

CHAPTER FOUR

YUCATÁN'S DANCING PIG'S HEAD (*CUCH*)
Parody as a Weapon

One of the standard features of Mesoamerican ethnography is a chapter describing the annual fiesta held to honor the patron saint of a town or village (Friedlander 1975; Hansen and Bastarrachea Manzano 1984; Smith 1977; Vogt 1969; Watanabe 1992). Thanks to the formative influence of anthropologists like Robert Redfield and Alfonso Villa Rojas in Yucatán, and the Harvard Chiapas Project of the 1960s, one can find dozens of descriptions of village fiestas spanning the last half-century. As noted in Chapter Two, anthropologists have also expended a great deal of energy and ink describing and analyzing the religious organizations—cafadías, gremios, or civil-religious hierarchies—which play a central role in organizing the fiesta.

A third focus of ethnographic inquiry—and the subject of the present chapter—is the Maya **cuch** ceremony (Loewe 1995; Pacheco Cruz 1960; Pérez Sabido 1983; Pohl 1981; Redfield 1962; Villa Rojas 1987). Literally "burden," the cuch is a type of investiture ceremony in which responsibility for organizing the fiesta is passed from one cofradía to another. At its most basic, it involves the parading of a cooked and decorated pig's head around the town, accompanied by music and various performances. It is also considered by some to be the fiesta's central performance (c.f., Redfield 1962).

However, notwithstanding this ethnographic bounty, the anthropology of performance remains fragmented. Performances of the cuch and its transformations are presented as spatio-temporal isolates, reflecting a view of indigenous or community life prevalent in Mesoamerican ethnographies of the 1940s and 1950s (c.f., Tax 1937, 1942; Wolf 1957). Indeed, the multiplicity of labels in Spanish and Mayan used to describe the cuch and its transformations—*cuch, k'ub pol, ok'ostah pol, baile del cochino*, etc.—leaves the impression that different enactments of this ceremony have little relationship to one another.

In revisiting this staple of Yucatecan ethnography, my first goal is to highlight the intimate relationship between the cuch and its various transformations. Like the ideal or "prototypic" performance outlined by Bauman and Briggs in their review of performance studies, the cuch indexes a broad range of speech events, religious rituals, stories, negotiations, and prior performances and, thus, challenges the "reified, object-centered notions of performativity ... that presuppose the encompassment of each performance by a single, bounded social interaction" (Bauman and Briggs 1990, 61). Indeed, following Bakhtin (1984), I argue that the rich parody that permeates the *k'ub pol* (literally, head delivery), a transformation of the cuch performed in San Bernardo and other former haciendas, is invariably lost or reduced to innocent burlesque if one fails to recognize the references to more sober interpretations of the ceremony. Similarly, while middle-class Yucatecans have developed a more aesthetically pleasing interpretation of the cuch for tourist consumption, referred to as el *baile del cochino* (the dance of the pig), I argue that the *value* of the performance depends less on its intrinsic merits (i.e., its artistic quality) than on its assumed connection with the vulgar "folk" performances of the rural hacienda. In short, **ludic** performances of the vaunted cuch not only gain meaning and sustenance from more orthodox enactments but lend authenticity and value to a new genre of performance dedicated to the tourist. Furthermore, participation in the k'ub pol can also be seen as an indicator of one's attitude toward Catholic orthodoxy.

Secondly, in line with José Limón's call for a more politically conscious approach to performance studies (1989), I have attempted to delineate the contending structures and agents that shape the fiesta and its key performances. For example, while the clergy insist on strict adherence to the Christian calendar and aim to make solemn religious observance the centerpiece of the fiesta in obeisance to Catholic tradition, the state and the tourist industry exalt artistically refined secular performances of the k'ub pol, which illustrate the convergence of Spanish and indigenous cultural forms and, thereby, lend support to a multi-ethnic state. However, as I demonstrate, fiesta organizers and performers may subvert either or both of these agendas in the name of Maya tradition or simply to ensure a return on their investment. As Susan Gal (1989) and others (Briggs 1988; Levine 1977; Limón 1983; Paredes 1966; Weigle 1978) have noted, performances by subaltern groups at the periphery of the capitalist system are often explicitly aimed at deconstructing dominant ideologies and artistic forms.

In particular, I take issue with Peter Hervik's recent study of the k'ub pol in Oxkutzcab (1999). While Hervik provides an interesting and very personal account of the competition and ill feelings that exist between journalists, anthropologists, and folklorists (i.e., second-line interpreters) who observed this performance, the actual performers are given short shrift and are considered to lack both artistic temperament and desire. Describing the Campeche residents who help with the performance, Hervik, following Boyer (1990, 11), argues that they "know how to make the ritual, but they do not rationalize it.... In this case, ritual competence is passed on automatically 'i.e., through a process that is quite independent of people's desire.'" Elsewhere Hervik comments that "They enact the celebration . . . through what has been called a form of unreflective common-sense and habit'" (1999, 145–46). In contrast, following Geoffrey Bent (1991)—who thoughtfully compares Richard Burton's rendition of Hamlet with that of Laurence Olivier and John Gielgud—I consider the performers to be first-line interpreters.[1] What, after all, is performance if not an act of interpretation? Similarly, desire, in my admittedly partial view, is virtually unbounded, ranging from the monetary to the libidinous!

My final objective is to draw attention to the politics of ethnography by demonstrating how second-line interpreters privilege or essentialize certain interpretations of the cuch in their accounts and implicitly align themselves with local agents or institutions. For example, while Redfield clearly favored the more sober "Catholic" interpretation of the cuch in Chan Kom (1950) and ignored Villa Rojas's description of a more raucous performance in Tusik (1987), leading Yucatecan folklorists like Pérez Sabido (1983) maintain that vulgar performances of the cuch (e.g., the k'ub pol) are among Yucatán's most traditional performances. Only in this way is it possible to understand the fragmentary nature of ethnographic description as it relates to performance.

The Cuch as Icon

In many accounts of the village fiesta, traditionalists allow for no creative genius. Activities that make up the annual fiesta are prefaced by adjectives like "customary" or "typical," suggesting the existence of well-established norms. Conceived in this way, the ethnographer's task is simply to describe the time-honored division of labor, the rules of reciprocity, the norms governing the selection of officers, etc.

This conception of the annual fiesta as a labor of mindless conformity is, perhaps, most pronounced in *Cultura popular y religión en el Anahuac,* in which Gilberto Giménez reduces the "traditional peasant fiesta" to seven cardinal rules, a kind of catechism for students of anthropology and religion. According to Giménez, all fiestas have the following characteristics:

1. a rupture in the normal flow of time;
2. a collective expression of the local community in which no class is excluded;
3. a global celebration that includes the most heterogenous elements (games, dances, etc.);
4. a celebration that requires wide open space and "free air" (the plaza, the atrium of a church);
5. a celebration that is strongly institutionalized, ritualized, and sacred (i.e., the traditional fiesta is inseparable from religion);

6. a celebration that is impregnated by the logic of use-value (in which fiesta equals participation); and

7. a strong dependence on the agricultural calendar. (1978, xx)

Similarly, in *The Folk Culture of Yucatán*, Redfield, following Durkheim, highlights the consensual aspects of the fiesta as well as its division into discrete categories of religious and profane activity,[2] with only a passing reference to the authority of the Catholic Church:

> The activities which make up these fiestas are much the same in all communities of Yucatan. They form a regional style, a special type, within the more general outlines of Middle American, or of Catholic American, folk festivals of patron saints. . . . Whatever else the festival is, it is both worship and play. The presence of these two elements is recognized in the program of the festivals and in such accounts of them as appear in the newspapers: those which are *religiosas are set off against those which are profanas*. (1941, 270; emphasis added)

Having witnessed the severity of Protestant evangelicals in Chan Kom, it is not surprising that Redfield saw the Catholic Church as a benign presence. For the villagers, as Redfield notes, words such as "religion" or "Catholic" were rarely spoken prior to 1930 when the first Protestant missionaries arrived (1950, 88). The Maya-Catholic syncretism of rural Yucatán was *doxa* (Bourdieu 1977, 168). Still, Redfield's treatment of religion is somewhat ironic, given the fact that Catholic authority, far more than Protestantism, is beholden to ritual schemes that purposely distinguish between sacred and secular, faith and frivolity. Whereas evangelical Protestantism is totalizing and seeks to reform the sinful nature of man, the Catholic Church operates by establishing boundaries between different spheres of human activity and deliberately setting off the sacred and profane activities that Redfield refers to in passive voice. The debaucheries associated with carnival pose no threat to the moral order and the Church so long as the perpetrators conclude their activities on time and show up for mass on Ash Wednesday.

Through his writings, however, Redfield did more than simply reify the administrative practice of the church, transforming its agency and authority into "custom"; he simultaneously bolstered the clergy's emphasis on solemn ritual, whether Catholic or Maya, as the core feature of the fiesta. As the following description of the fiesta of X-Kalakdzonot reveals, the cuch, in Redfield's view, was not only an extremely solemn occasion, but the very essence of the fiesta:

> At noon the present **cargador** [majordomo], together with his wife and his associate organizers, the *nakulob*, go to the house of the future *cargador*,

whom he thereupon invites to his house, that he may deliver the *carga* or *cuch*. *This is the essential part of the fiesta and gives its name (cuch) to the whole.* On a table the *kulelob* (assistant) places a cross, a clay vessel containing the cooked head of a pig, a pile of tortillas, several bottles of rum, and on a little plate, some cigarettes. The present *cargador* carries the *cuch:* a decorated pole from which hang many colored paper streamers, packages of cigarettes, cloth dolls and loaves of bread made in the form of an eagle. He addresses the *cargador* of the fiesta to be celebrated next year, saying: "In the name of the Father, the Son and the Holy Ghost, I deliver to you this charge (*cuch*), and that which is upon this table, so that next year you may make your fiesta to the holy cross." . . . Then he tells the three *nakulob* . . . to take what is on the table. Lifting up the various objects, these men move around the table, turning about as they go, and dancing a slow dance, with little leaps, while the musicians play the air of an old Spanish song—"La Carbonerita." (Redfield and Villa Rojas 1990[1934], 155; emphasis added)

In *The Folk Culture of Yucatán,* Redfield reiterates his views on the cuch, describing it as a sacred vow "by which the community is perpetually bound to its supernatural guardian" (1941, 277) and noting that in X-Cacal, one of the two remote villages studied by Villa Rojas, the "ceremony is attended with much religious significance" (1941, 286). However, by omitting any reference to the investiture ceremony in Tusik, Villa Rojas's other field site, Redfield carries out what might be described as an ethnographic *auto-da-fe* or defense of the faith. Indeed, in *Los elegidos de Dios* (1987), Villa Rojas's seminal monograph on the Maya of East Central Quintana Roo, one finds two radically different descriptions of the investiture ritual or **ok'ostah pol** as Villa Rojas refers to it. While the performance in X-Cacal was, as Redfield noted, characterized by its sobriety, the dance in Tusik was most notable for its irreverent humor.

As in X-Cacal and San Bernardo (described below), the Tusik offering was adorned with polychrome paper, sweet breads (*arepas*), corn husk cigarettes, male and female Castillian rag dolls (*dzulitos*),[3] and a sweet bread (*chuchuc-uah*) placed between the jaws of the newly anointed swine. The only apparent difference was the presence of a bamboo crown, suggesting the head's function as a mock Jesus, and a thick tortilla with four sticks arranged in a quadralinear fashion, representing the spatial coordinates of the Maya cosmos. The performance, however, was quite frivolous:

> The activities of the following day began in the early morning hours with a dance called *okostah pol.* For this dance, which represented the sale of a pig, nine women . . . were selected. The dancers were organized as follows: in the first place was an individual who played a rattle made by placing corn

kernels in a gourd shell and wrapping it in a handkerchief; this individual, who represented the owner of the pig, pretended to lead the animal with a cord that hung down from the head/offering. [The offering] was carried by a man who followed the owner; immediately following were the women with their gourds. The musical accompaniment recalled an old Spanish melody known as "La Carbonerita." The individual who opened the march was proposing the sale of the pig with these words: "Who will buy the pig that I bring tied up, who will buy it from me?" Two other individuals assumed the role of buyers and responded by offering a very low price. This led to bargaining between the two parties, and comic exaggeration of the defects and fine qualities of the animal that produce laughter from those present. The joyous event reached its climax when the bearer of the pig's head takes on the role of the pig, "cuts" the cord with his teeth, and escapes from the room, bringing the negotiations to an abrupt halt. The owner and the musicians chase after the "pig," capture him, and return him to the hall, whereupon the dance is resumed and the 18 turns are completed. It was at this point that the host of the fiesta, using the musicians as witnesses, "purchased" the "pig" saying: "I place on this table 100 cigarettes in payment of this 'pig' which I have bought today." (Villa Rojas 1987, 358; translated by author)

Redfield's reluctance to mention the more satirical Tusik performance is, no doubt, bound up with his conception of the village as the sacred pole of a sacred/secular continuum stretching across Yucatán. X-Cacal, nestled deep in the jungles of Quintana Roo, was considered the *sanctum sanctorum* of the peninsula, a place of utmost privacy and reverence, and Tusik was one of nine "homogenous" folk villages that supported it.

By pointing out the sober, serious-minded tone of Redfield's work, my intention is not to argue *contra* Redfield that the cuch is really ludic but simply to note the unmistakable convergence between Redfieldian ethnography and the orthopraxis of the Catholic Church with regard to tradition and festive activities. After all, to be effective, parody requires a set of rules that are recognized and generally respected. As Umberto Eco notes in *Carnival!*, "the law must be so pervasively and profoundly introjected as to be overwhelmingly present at the moment of its violation" (1984, 6).

This process can be seen even more clearly in the Mexican *coloquios* (traditional nativity plays) described by Bauman (1996, 318). In these plays satire is effected by enabling the audience to hear both the narrator or prompter's rendition of a written religious text (the straight verse) and the actor's parodic counterstatement, a type of word play in which syntactic and phonological parallelism foregrounds humorous semantic differences. For example, while the prompter states, "It appears that I am getting out without losing a step" (*Parece que voy saliendo sin perder una pisada*), the Hermitaño, the parodic figure of the drama, remarks, "Now I am getting used to it without missing even a single fuck" (*Ya me estoy poniendo sin perder ni una pisada.*). In the **ok'ostah pol** the religious referents may be more hidden than those of the *coloquio,* but the "audience" is presumably conversant with religious norms and knows what's being satirized.

The Fiesta of San Bernardo: The Cuch as Carnival

THE SETTING

It is, perhaps, ironic that the fiesta of San Bernardo is now considered one of the state's most traditional fiestas. Located in the state's northwestern quadrant, the *zona henequenera* (sisal zone), San Bernardo is not only far removed from the *zona Maya* (Quintana Roo), but has never led an independent existence. Like many communities in this part of the state, San Bernardo was for many years little more than an appendage to the great sisal plantation of Las Palmas, supplying workers to plant, harvest, and process sisal in semi-feudal conditions (Katz 1962; Joseph 1982; Turner 1969). Even today, it retains the juridical status of a hacienda rather than a *pueblo* (village), a grim reminder of its former dependent status (Loewe, 1995).[4]

San Bernardo is also an auspicious site since it figures prominently in the regional development of western Yucatán. Over the last two decades the state government, in collaboration with private investors, has begun to lay the foundation for an expansion of tourism in this part of the state. In addition to preparing the archaeological site at nearby Oxkintok for public consumption, Las Palmas is one of several former haciendas that investors hope to turn into a luxury hotel and henequén-era museum, thus offering tourists an array of images of Maya life from pre-Conquest to post-colonial times, a strategy that reflects the new, almost obsessive concern for diversity in this former monocrop economy. (See Chapter One for a description of the hacienda hotel in Santa[?] Rosa.)

Although access to San Bernardo is presently limited to a rocky dirt road, the partially restored plantation has served as a minor tourist attraction for many years. Visitors who pass through the wrought iron gates find themselves in a nicely manicured yard punctuated only by an occasional ceiba tree. Inside are several partially finished exhibits: a dining room whose former elegance can still be detected amid the aging furniture; an office with dusty, early-model typewriters and adding machines; and, finally, an exhibition room with a horse-drawn carriage and a series of lithographs depicting the evolution of ground transport in Yucatán.

The main attraction, however, is the plantation's decorticating equipment, which rests above the north wing like the *chacmool* (sacrificial altar) found atop Mayan pyramids. Indeed, the development of a viable rasping

machine is one of the major leitmo-
tifs of contemporary Yucatecan folklore. As the historian Gilbert Joseph
notes (1982), it is a matter of great
pride that a native Yucatecan rather
than a foreign national developed
the first prototype in the early 1850s,
thus bringing progress and prosperity to the peninsula.

However, notwithstanding its
early integration into the global
economy through sisal production,

FIGURE 4.1 Machinery formerly used to process henequén fiber at the Las Palmas hacienda

San Bernardo is considered a Maya preserve of sorts, and, according to Pérez
Sabido, the k'ub pol performed by its former work force is described as one
of only five dances that have "resisted the passage of time and can still be
seen in . . . the interior of Yucatán" (1983, 129). Not surprisingly, perhaps,
such comments—echoed in newspapers, magazines, and even a few television
documentaries—have served to transform the fiesta into a popular regional
celebration, which draws hundreds of visitors from nearby towns and villages
as well as the state capital.

THE PERFORMANCE

Fieldnotes: San Bernardo, June 4, 1989[5]
Arrived in San Bernardo around 8:00 a.m. to observe preparations for the
k'ub pol. By this time a group of men had gathered around a long wooden
table on the dirt road leading into the plantation and were beginning to
minister to a 400-pound pig that had been slaughtered and disemboweled
the night before. While one *campesino* (farm laborer) was busy shaving the
upper portion of the body to remove unsightly hairs, a second was brushing
the pig's teeth, and a third was scrubbing its body, removing soot and grime.

One resident asked me if I thought the pig was beautiful. When I
said "yes," he asked if I would like to have sex with her. I declined, saying
that my wife was likely to show up at any minute. Also present were three
students from Mérida dressed in leisure clothes and sharing a camera among
them. They admitted to understanding Mayan but responded to questions
in Spanish and watched the preparations from a distance.

After the pig had been cleaned and groomed, she was turned on her
back and bamboo rings were inserted in the body cavity in order to restore
her figure, since without her entrails the body had a rather collapsed appearance. As the pig was being sewn up, one of the attendants pulled out a bottle
of rum, took a swig, and commented that it was rum that had led to the

poor pig's demise. The last step before transferring the animal to the dance hall was to pry open her jaws and insert a wood block.

Once inside the dance hall, the pig was set in front of an image of San Bernardo, the town's patron saint, and his two companions, San Antonio de Padua and the Virgin del Carmen. At this point the women took over and began to decorate the animal. The first step was to construct the *ramillete,* a makeshift cage made by arching a series of branches over the table supporting the pig. From the *ramillete* were hung bottles of rum, coca cola, and mineral water; gingerbread cookies shaped in the form of men and animals; flowers; and a number of mestiza cloth dolls. The finishing touch was provided by placing two elegantly dressed plastic dolls (*ts'ulitos*), one male and one female, at the front of the ramillete. While the ramillete was being prepared, other decorations were attached to the pig directly. Perforations were made in its sides and tinsel flowers mounted on sticks were inserted into the openings. Silver coins wrapped in pink cloth were affixed as earrings, and another coin, rolled up in a bright bandanna, was tied around its forehead. Finally, the offering was completed by placing cigarettes, bowls of rice, candied papaya and *ciruelas* (plums) on the table next to the beast and inserting a large square cake in her mouth.

Around 5:00 p.m. the procession began. A group of 20 or so residents assembled around the table, took hold of the two beams extending out from either end, and with a collective groan hoisted the beast onto their shoulders. In front of the group stood the **chik** or clown, a lanky mestizo about 35 years of age who was dressed in tattered clothing. Stationed next to him was his *maestro,* a much older man who had taught him several verses

FIGURE 4.2 The altar of St. Pig is almost complete; some festal offerings are yet to make their appearance

for the occasion. Also present were two mayacoles, or assistants, who had handkerchiefs tied over their heads. The first was a man from Maxcanú nicknamed *Tierra Linda* (beautiful land), a poor mestizo who spoke little Spanish. In one hand Don Tierra held a rattle made from dry corn kernels and a hollowed-out gourd (*jícara*). This was used to "summon" the pig. In the other hand he held an empty jícara, which he used to bathe the animal. Meanwhile the second mayacol stood ready with a bottle of rum. Posted next to the two mayacoles was a small group of musicians, a drummer wearing dark sun glasses and two men with brass wind instruments.

As the band struck up "La Angaripola," a popular dance tune, the chik and his assistants filed out of the dance hall, followed by the pig bearers. The latter moved like drunken sailors, weaving back and forth as they attempted to throw their companions off balance. As the entourage emerged from the hall, one person shouted "*la capilla*" (the chapel), and the entourage staggered off toward a simple thatch-roofed hut. About 20 yards from the hut, the pedestal was lowered for the first time as the mayacol shouted, "*hap a chi'o,' hap a chi' o*" (open your mouth), insisting that the pig was thirsty. With this he filled his gourd container with rum and threw it over the animal's body. Then, while the others shouted "*ba'ax tawalah*" (What did you say?), the chik stepped forward to recite the first of many humorous **quatrains** or *bombas*.

From the "church" the pig bearers reversed direction and headed off toward the house of the new president, the villager who would take responsibility for organizing next year's k'ub pol. En route the pig was lowered every 20 yards to be watered and to give the chik an opportunity to recite another bomba.

FIGURE 4.3 Emulating the procession of the saints, St. Pig is carried around town on her altar

Several of the quatrains below refer to illicit sexual episodes while others highlight the antagonism between villagers and the state (*la federación*). These original and, in some cases, impromptu verses reinforce the image of the chik as a wanton, carefree individual, a character unbeholden to laws or moral constraints. Other quatrains (not shown below) were clearly stock, ready-made verses heard at jaranas and found in pamphlets sold in Mérida bookstores. All the verses, however, became less intelligible as the procession advanced and the chik became increasingly drunk.

1.

Le tun tech ukichpam ch'up
ka' manen tuhol abel
[inaudible] *yaan ump'e luch*
ka'ten soten wech inpak'tik kep

ka' bin la puch [ka'] bin la tuch

As for you, beautiful young woman,
when I passed the entrance to your street
... there is a bowl [made from a gourd]
two times I inflated the "armadillo," I thrust my member
when the back goes, the navel goes

2.

Federación bin inkahal bin xan

presidente kumanik bin
yeetel inhijo [le tusah] bix u tak'in
kusik bin tinwotoch xan

The federal authorities left, my "mistress" left too,
the president reportedly paid them
and my son [remitted the money?]
he reportedly gave them my house as well

3.

Oxtun federación kutal u k'axten xan

mix un tohol yaan in bo'ot(ik)
tumen tulak(al) inwatan tintsa'h xan

Three federal police are coming to look for me too
not even a "cent" have I to pay them
because all of it I gave to my wife also

4.

[Ts]'ok bin tak'in ti[n] kahal bin xan

Maxcanú bin u taal bin
San Bernardo bin kuchu[I] xan
yeetel ulak' inwatan yak xan

The money ran out, my mistress ran out too
[To] Maxcanú she will come they say
[In] San Bernardo she will arrive also
my wife is with another person too

5.

Oxp'e dia ma' haantken tinwatan
mix inwatan tsenken xan
yaan tun kubo'otik bin up'ax
[inaudible] *ko'olibi bo'otik xan*

For three days my wife doesn't eat me
nor does my wife feed me either
she must, then, pay the debt she owes
... the virgin pays it too

6.

Cinco lequas intak ink'aan	Five leagues I come for my hammock
yeetel uxay unabil chi'	with the woman with the wide mouth
yeetel bin ukaxah wupik inwatan	and go to search for the slip of my wife
chen ubin ukaxah bin upik bin yaan	she reportedly just goes to search for her slip

When the entourage finally arrived at the house of the incoming president, the decorations and festal foods were removed and distributed among the cofradía's members along with an admonition that they donate a similar or larger item the following year. The pig was then handed over to a team of talented butchers who quickly reduced her to one-kilo portions.

Discussion

While the activities that make up the k'ub pol take place within a two day-period, the spectacle can be seen as the culmination of a lengthy, sometimes acrimonious struggle between fiesta organizers and the clergy. The organizers want the local priest (a resident of Maxcanú) to visit San Bernardo and perform mass during the fiesta; however, the year I witnessed the fiesta (1989), Padre Justo repeatedly told them that he would do so only if the celebration was held on the day corresponding to San Bernardo's feast day in the Christian calendar. From his perspective, the sacred character of the event was undermined by festival promoters who scheduled it on a weekend (even when the saint's day fell on a weekday) in order to attract more visitors and increase revenues.

In deference to a tradition of their own, k'ub pol organizers insist that the celebration cannot be held until the pig has reached the appropriate size, a date that rarely coincides with the official saint's day.[6] Along with his quota of pig flesh, the deputy selected to organize the k'ub pol is given a length of rope to measure the beast's enormous paunch. When the circumference of the pig's belly matches the length of the rope, it is time for the sacrifice and celebration. Therefore, while the saint's day is May 28, the actual date of the k'ub pol is indeterminate. In 1974, according to Pérez Sabido, it was held on May 23, and in 1989, as noted above, it was held on June 4.

While this breach of the liturgical order is, perhaps, the most blatant challenge to priestly authority, it is merely the first in a series of acts that seek to nullify the ecclesiastical opposition of sacred and profane activities. The others occur within the spectacle itself.

FRAME 1: THE BURDEN BEARER AND THE DEVIL

Although the San Bernardo k'ub pol refers directly or indirectly to a variety of texts, events, and other performances, and defies any desire for analytic closure, the leading referent or frame is unarguably the cuch (cf. Redfield 1964). At the same time, however, it distinguishes itself from more solemn enactments of the cuch through a series of unconventional substitutions or permutations. Most notable is the substitution of devils and drunkards for the traditional *dramatis personae*. The chik, described above, is everything the cargador (burden bearer) is not. While the latter is considered a model of moral rectitude, an individual who literally carries the obligation of the community on his back, the chik is thought of as a playful animal like the *coatí* (badger) for whom he is named.

A similar effect is achieved by the substitution of mayokol for the *naku-lob* or *noox* (ritual assistants). In describing the cuch ceremony in Chan Kom, Redfield noted that the cargador is assisted by several subordinates who help cover the expenses of the fiesta and perform certain tasks. In referring to these helpers, Redfield used two Mayan terms interchangeably—*nakulob,* which is defined simply as "a subordinate of a *cargador*" (1941, 393) and *noox,* which is described as a person or an object used to support someone or something else.[7]

In the San Bernardo performance, however, neither of these ritual specialists is present. The two assistants who minister to the pig, and repeatedly ply her with rum, are referred to as "mayokoles," a term normally applied to plantation foremen, that is, devils of a different kind. As older villagers recall, the daily operations of a henequén plantation were generally left in the hands of a trusted administrator (encargado), a well-to-do mestizo who spoke Spanish as well as Mayan and who handled the plantation's accounts. The encargado, in turn, supervised the mayokoles, who were responsible for meeting production quotas and who administered corporal punishment to Maya peons who worked too slowly or stole plantation property.

The mayokol's reputation is, perhaps, best revealed by a rather interesting folk etymology. The word is neither Mayan nor Spanish but a Yucatecan neologism formed from the Spanish word *mayor* meaning "elder," "principal," or "main" and the Mayan word *kol,* which translates as "field." It is, therefore, clearly a regional variant of the Spanish *mayoral* (foreman, boss) or **mayor-domo** (majordomo), heard in other parts of Mexico. However, Yucatecans familiar with the mayokol's role in protecting plantation property suggest that the term really derives from two Maya morphemes: *ma,* a negative particle that precedes the verb stem, and *okol,* a verb meaning "to steal." In short, while the mayokol was a native Mayan speaker, he was an anathema in the eyes of the Maya work force because of his loyalty to ts'ul, the plantation owner.[8]

Evidence that the k'ub pol, and the fiesta more generally, is intended as a humorous representation of hacienda life is also found in Villa Rojas's description of the fiesta in X-Cacal. Here, he notes that the event was officially inaugurated at two o'clock one morning with a nominating ceremony in which individuals were selected to play the part of hacienda administrators. In all, 25 individuals were selected to fill different roles, including:

U nohoch dzulil ixtancia (the owner of the hacienda)
U x-nuc xunanil ixtancia (his wife)
U chan dzulil ixtancia (the owner's son)
U chan xunanil ixtancia (the owner's daughter)
U nohoch mayordomoil ixtancia (the first majordomo)
U chan mayordomoil ixtancia (the second majordomo)
U nohoch capularil ixtancia (the first corporal)
U x-nuc capularil ixtancia (the corporal's wife)
(Villa Rojas 1987, 362; translated by author)

To round out the staff, seven cowboys and five cowgirls were selected along with four men and women who were responsible for taking care of the pigsty (cuidadores de chiqueros). Predictably, those selected to play the part of the hacienda owners did little but issue orders, while the majordomos and corporals were obliged to carry out the numerous tasks associated with a village fiesta (Villa Rojas 1987, 363). Similarly, in reflecting upon the k'ub pol he observed as a young boy, Santiago Pacheco Cruz, another well-known folklorist, remarked that it was a feature of hacienda life, not something found in the city or the town.[9]

In short, then, by historicizing and politicizing the omnipresent cuch, the San Bernardo performance not only continues a satiric tradition going back half a century or longer but challenges the romantic conception of plantation life proffered by the Las Palmas museum.

Finally, the subversive character of the k'ub pol is manifest through an implicit comparison between the moral economy of a religious offering and the mercantile ethos of the market place. In the cuch ceremonies described by Redfield, it was understood that the pig's head, and the delicacies that accompany it, are offerings made on behalf of the community, or cofradía, and constitute the fulfillment of a sacred vow to the patron saint. Those who accept the offering are expected to make an equal or greater contribution the following year. However in the performance described by Villa Rojas (the ok'ostah pol), two "buyers" haggle with the owner of the pig in order to purchase the animal at the lowest possible price, inverting the traditional relationship between donor and recipient, and transforming an august exchange (i.e., a gift) into a vulgar economic transaction. Indeed, after the pig's escape, as described in the quote above (p. 86), the host of the X-Cacal fiesta purchased her back for a mere 100 cigarettes!

FRAME 2: THE PARADE OF SAINTS

The other principal object of k'ub pol parody is the *santa procesión* (saints' procession), a solemn activity that occurs on the last day of the annual fiesta. On this occasion the patron saint is lowered from his pedestal and carried through the streets on a portable altar.

For example, following the mass said in honor of San Miguel, the patron saint of Maxcanú, the congregants pour into the street behind the church and reassemble in their respective cofradías or gremios. The image of San Miguel is lowered from his pedestal and set on an altar at the front of the procession. An altar boy leads the procession, swinging a ball of incense. Close behind are the priest and four litter bearers who agonize in silence under the tremendous weight of the altar and image. From the church the procession enters the main square, silently circles the plaza in a slow deliberate manner, and returns to the starting point. After a rosary is recited, the patron saint is returned to his pedestal (see Figure 2.3).

The similarity between this procession and the San Bernardo k'ub pol is revealed through a series of indexical relationships: the raiment of the pig with jewelry (e.g., earrings) and ornaments in emulation of Catholic images, which must be properly attired before they go out in public; the position of the finely manicured beast on a portable altar similar to that used to carry religious images; its association with the images of St. Anthony of Padua, the Virgin of the Conception, and St. Bernard in the corner of the hacienda's outdoor shelter; and, finally, its incorporation into the procession that enters the church. Indeed, the procession that Pérez Sabido witnessed in San Bernardo in 1974 included the three Catholic saints named above as well as a 400-pound pig. After several stops, during which the chik recited "strophes in Maya" (1983, 140), the holy trinity were returned to their modest temple. Only then was the pig delivered to the incoming president and divided among the villagers.

At the same time, the satirical nature of the k'ub pol is revealed through a series of paradigmatic shifts: the insertion of a raucous shoving contest in place of the silent pilgrimage described above and, of course, the substitution of a raw, corpulent beast for the saint or the nicely adorned and well roasted pig's head that accompanies the cuch. In other performances, such as the k'ub pol Pacheco Cruz observed in Santa Cruz de Bravo, the chik irreverently combines iconic representations of the devil and the priest into one role: "The joker had a painted face; the same was true of his naked body in which nothing but 'the parts' were covered; a diadem of turkey feathers and a pair of horns in imitation of the devil replaced his sombrero, he even had a long tail ..." (1936, 30). Dressed in this fashion, the chik goes about his priestly duties. Following the delivery of the pig's head to the incoming deputies and an "epistle" by the outgoing president, "the *chik* lightly sprayed everyone with **balche** (holy water), which according to them, is the benediction which authorizes the new deputies" (1936, 130).

Including the clergy in a satire of hacienda life is only fitting, given the fact that throughout the nineteenth and early twentieth centuries the cleric and the hacienda owner were frequently one and the same. For example, Robert Patch notes that priests were quite often estate owners: "Two priests ... Miguel and Pedro Antonio de la Paz ... owned ten haciendas. Miguel had two in Mérida, one in Uman, one in Motul and one in Mococha, while Pedro Antonio's five estates were in Mérida, Conkal, Acanceh, Mochocha and Motul" (1993, 191). Similarly, Rugeley disputes the notion that clergy had a difficult time adjusting to the world of commerce by noting that the priest of Sotuta, José Manuel Pardio, owned multiple estates, including haciendas as far south as Tekax: "The padre's economic success, together with his warm ties with the town's leading citizens, provides a classic example of clergy adapting themselves into the local bourgeoisie ... through their shared interest of estate ownership" (2001b, 133–34).[10]

The most seditious act, however, is the recitation of the vulgar Mayan/ Spanish quatrains during the procession. These are doubly subversive since they not only evoke the festive image of the jarana in what would normally be an extremely solemn affair, but they debase the refined character of the Spanish verse itself. The bomba's predictable rhyme scheme, consistent meter, and long association with genteel courtship rituals have, in recent years, become so attractive to the Yucatecan middle class that its poetic form is now frequently used in advertising jingles on television. Urban consumers are entreated to purchase anise liquor and other goods through clever bombas. However, in the k'ub pol, the quatrain is irreparably damaged. Its gentle sexual allusions are rendered overt, and its poetic form is distorted almost beyond recognition as the drunken chik stumbles through each verse.

Indeed, while several aspects of the k'ub pol may be evocative of indigenous rites and practices, it is less the content of the performance than its ribald style that leads observers like Pérez Sabido to view the ritual as part of an unbroken Yucatecan tradition. What makes it truly "authentic" are the grotesque movements of the performers and their slurred, piquant speech— in short, a code of conduct that conforms to popular stereotypes of rural mestizos or Indians. In regional parlance such individuals are referred to as *che' che winik,* a Mayan phrase translated as "raw or unseasoned people,"[11] or *werek,* a term of unknown origin, used to designate grotesque or unsightly persons. Similarly, the rural mestizo is ridiculed for his irregular Spanish syntax. He is said to jabber (*chapurrear*) rather than speak properly. In short, the grotesque beast in San Bernardo's k'ub pol is a perfect homology of the "grotesque" men who carry it on their shoulders.

Here it is worth noting that the "*Danza de las Cintas*" (The Ribbon Dance), a Yucatecan version of the Maypole Dance, also appears on Pérez Sabido's list of most traditional performances. In this case, he makes no attempt to trace the event's origin but simply notes that the dance is performed in a rural location (Ticul and Santa Elena) by "**autochthonous** groups" who lack sophistication (1983, 146). To emphasize this, he mentions that in the performance he witnessed a strange person suddenly appeared and attempted to join the dancers. The dance group stopped, and the pole man asked the intruder in Mayan to explain what he wanted. "I want to dance with you," remarked the intruder. "No you don't," countered the pole man, "you're a dog and you want to urinate on the pole, get lost!" (1983, 146).

By equating authenticity with profanity and crude irreverent acts, Pérez Sabido's account of the k'ub pol and other traditional dances can be seen as the antithesis of Redfieldian ethnography. While the latter highlights the sacred, the former exalts the primitive and the profane. However, like Redfield, Pérez Sabido ultimately fails to recognize the dialogical relationship among performances, the political and performative context in which the k'ub pol is enacted. Consequently, the meaning of its countless tropes is lost or reduced to signs of mere "primitiveness." Like Roland Barthes' mythical signifier (form)—a signifier that is already a sign (1972)—these interpretations rob the k'ub pol of its original set of meanings and place it at the disposal of a new signifying consciousness. They reduce parody and satire, the *raison d'être* of the k'ub pol, to an innocent burlesque that offends no powerful institution or individual—an image of the "folk" that will henceforth serve as the foundation, alibi, or "raw material" upon which an aesthetically pleasing, nationalist folklore is constructed.

The Cuch as Commodity and Symbol of the Nation

Since the early 1960s the phenomenal growth of tourism has not only led to the development of new forms of handicraft production in the peninsula but has refocused attention on the value of things past. In fact, following the disappearance of henequén in northwest Yucatán, a process essentially complete by 1980, some Maxcanú residents make their living by selling artifacts they scavenge from nearby archaeological sites or from facsimiles produced in their homes.

The growth of tourism and tourist consumption has also enhanced the appeal of folk goods, such as huipils, among middle-class Yucatecans. In the late 1960s, upwardly mobile women from Ticul and other towns would not be caught dead in huipils or other vestments associated with indigenous women (Nathanial Raymond, personal communication, 1989); however, by the late 1970s, thanks to the buying habits of North American tourists, the mini-huipil—a dress that resembles the original but which is tapered along the sides and considerably shorter—had become popular among middle-class Yucatecans. This new style, worn without the typical insignias of Indian identity (e.g., long lace slip, scarf) not only allowed middle-class women to show off their figures but enabled them to demonstrate regional pride, or simply a more folksy appearance, in a non-stigmatizing manner. In short, as a result of a few alterations, a sign of subordinate status was transformed into a symbol of regional identity.

The re-valuation of regional custom has also been stimulated by a shift in the attitude of federal agencies such as the National Indigenist Institute (INI)—recently renamed the Center of Indigenous Development (CDI)—and the Secretary of Public Education (SEP) toward indigenous communities. Although the overriding concern of such agencies is still to foster economic growth and promote assimilation, vigorous debates within Mexican anthropology in the early 1970s and charges of ethnocide[12] have modified their ideology and practice. Indeed, the preservation of indigenous culture (rescate cultural) is now seen as one of their most important functions.[13]

It is hardly surprising, then, that the k'ub pol and the jarana have gained the attention of cultural workers interested in celebrating and preserving local custom. While one can still see raucous performances of the k'ub pol in San Bernardo, San Fernando, and other former plantations, this colorful performance has, for the most part, been appropriated by Yucatán's increasingly nostalgic middle class.

FIGURE 4.4 Close-up of the pig used in San Fernando's k'ub pol, a less well attended celebration

In Maxcanú the task of preserving regional culture in the late 1980s had fallen to Don Ponso, a merchant who owned a small café in the center of town and who was one of Maxcanú's leading folk dancers (*jaraneros*). Don Ponso is also a proud descendant of a mestizo fino family, an intermediate social group composed primarily of craftsmen and small merchants who wore elegant versions of the traditional folk costume until the 1960s. At closing time each night Don Ponso would remove the tables from his café, pull out a tape player, and provide dance lessons—interspersed with stories of the unusual places he had performed the "Dance of the Pig's Head"—to anyone who cared to learn.

Learning from Don Ponso was no easy task since he was a perfectionist. He was, however, a very well respected teacher, and when word got out that he was going to open the fiesta of Guadalupe with a choreographed version of the baile del cochino, the town turned out.

Fieldnotes: Maxcanú, December 1989

Around 9:30 p.m. Víctor Soberanis's orchestra, one of the most popular and most expensive jarana orchestras in Yucatán, gave the musical prompt and Don Ponso's entourage entered the dance floor. In the first position was Don Ponso, elegantly dressed in thick-soled white alpargatas; a brilliant, long-sleeved filipina with gold buttons; freshly creased, white linen pants with a large, red-and-white handkerchief hanging carefully from his right front pocket; and a new, white, derby-style hat made from *jipi* (a soft flexible fiber). Standing on either side of Don Ponso was an attractive young woman, dressed in a finely embroidered terno, a long silk scarf, white high-heel shoes, and liberal quantities of facial makeup. Behind each of the women was a column of six dancers in which men, dressed exactly like Don Ponso, alternated with females dressed in brightly colored ternos. Finally, in the center, several paces behind Don Ponso, was a young man balancing a large platter on his head. The platter contained a roasted pig's head decorated with large tomatoes, several loaves of white bread, a number of brightly colored streamers, and a half-dozen green, white, and red pennants. As the dancers moved through the hall, each of them held one of the colored streamers connected to the pig's head. At the end of the hall the dance troupe stopped; the performers danced in place for several moments, executing graceful pirouettes and demonstrating stylistic variations on the basic jarana dance step. Next, the dancers circled the pig bearer, moving first in a clockwise and then a counterclockwise direction. After completing several circuits, they stopped, exchanged places with their partners, and began to circle the pig bearer in opposite directions, weaving their streamers into a tight braid and transforming the man in the center into a human Maypole. Finally, with equal grace and solemnity, the dancers reversed positions and unwound the braid. The performance was considered a smashing success and was rewarded by enthusiastic applause from the crowd.

The irony of this event—at least at first glance—was that Don Ponso did everything to minimize his own creative genius. Despite his carefully choreographed entrance and the intensive labor he and his assistants had put into their costumes, the baile del cochino was, in his view, more an act of cultural *preservation* than an act of artistic *interpretation*, a point he underscored repeatedly by noting his dependence on the cruder, less refined performances of the hacienda. In retrospect, however, Don Ponso's attitude appears to be less an example of false modesty than an acknowledgment that the authenticity and value of his performance depended on its acceptance as a faithful representation of performances found in more remote, autochthonous Maya villages.

However, despite the emphasis on preservation, the baile del cochino transforms the k'ub pol in several obvious and profound ways. For one thing, it transforms ritual (irreverent as it may be) into a form of theatre. While the audience was clearly incidental in the latter case, consisting as it were of an anthropologist and some adventurous tourists, the baile del cochino was created specifically for an audience. Chairs were set up around the perimeter of the open air pavillion where Don Ponso performed, and printed programs were distributed to the guests. By charging admission, the baile also transformed the cuch (and k'ub pol) into a commodity. Unlike tropical or salsa dances, fiesta organizers have traditionally covered the cost of the jarana through the sale of alcohol, the fees they charge concessionaires, or the profits they make on other dances. However, much to the chagrin of Maxcanú residents, fiesta organizers had begun charging admission to the Friday night jarana by the late 1980s.[14]

The baile also surreptitiously transformed the cuch (and k'ub pol) into a symbol of Mexican nationalism by substituting one set of decorations for another. As noted above, the pig used in the k'ub pol contained several icons of hacienda life—effigies of the hacienda owner and his wife—as well as numerous luxury goods found in the cuch (e.g., cigarettes). While most of these artifacts are missing in the baile del cochino, one new element appears, that is, green, white, and red pennants in emulation of the Mexican tricolor. Like the cuch that Redfield described, the baile del cochino was a solemn event, quietly and respectfully observed by the audience; however, it was by no means a religious event. It was a secular ritual honoring Mexico's national **patrimony** and the state that seeks to preserve it.[15]

Most importantly, the genteel baile transforms the k'ub pol into a performance acceptable to the middle-class aesthete and the foreign tourist by removing the course language, grotesque movements, and overt sexual humor found in the latter. It is a transformation in no way different than the aesthetic transformation of carnival described by Bakhtin in *Rabelais and His World*, a bourgeois reinterpretation in which the coarse humor of the French peasantry was first reduced to bare mockery by Voltaire and eventually was sanitized by pious French abbots.

> The influence of carnival forms, themes, and symbols on eighteenth-century literature is considerable. But this influence is formalized; carnival is merely an artistic means made to serve aesthetic aims. . . . Voltaire uses carnival forms for satire which still preserves its universality and its philosophy, laughter is reduced to bare mockery. Such is precisely the famous "laughter of Voltaire": its force is almost entirely deprived of the regenerating and renewing element. . . . In his *Modernized Rabelais* the Abbé Marsy not only stripped the novel's language of its dialect and archaic forms, but also mitigated the book's indecencies. The Abbé Perraud went even further when he published in 1752 . . . the *Ouevres Choisies*. All that was . . . indecent was removed from this selection. (Bakhtin 1984, 118–19)

Indeed, current attempts to cleanse the k'ub pol can be seen as a continuation of a more general effort to tame religious celebrations throughout the peninsula. Summarizing the work of Oliver de Cásares, Rugeley notes that in the early part of the nineteenth century religious festivals still contained a great deal of trenchant political humor. Processions included "*gigantones* . . . giant two-man costumes associated with the Carnival of Vera Cruz," which were sometimes used to poke fun at hypocrites within the Church.[16] However, as Rugeley adds, the "real stars . . . were the *diabletes* (devils), the virtually naked men who painted themselves from head to toe in black and yellow paint, wore horns, and carried large whips. These pranced their way through the parade gyrating, leering, leaping, and pouncing, and dealing out whiplashes to anyone who appeared insufficiently reverent" (2001b, 90). Within a few decades, however, most of these figures had disappeared. The gigantones reportedly disappeared in 1812, the diabletes were not seen after 1827, and the Maya dancers departed a couple of years later.

Thus, in the final analysis, whatever else the baile is—an act of preservation, a form of artistic expression, a boon to local commerce—through the performer's attempts to cleanse the k'ub pol, it also becomes the most recent attempt, conscious or unconscious, to bolster the colonial-era distinction between a primitive untamed Maya hinterland (San Bernardo) and a civilized semi-urban mestizo community (Maxcanú).

Conclusion

Interpreting the cuch and its transformations is a complex task but one that provides several lessons in ethnographic interpretation as well as a better understanding of the annual fiesta and its place in regional politics. The first lesson, obvious to some, but one that bears repeating, is that the performance itself is an act of interpretation, an interpretation that receives close public scrutiny and, thus, provides an opportunity for demonstrating conformity or making provocative statements, not to mention making money. The annual fiesta is the mass media of the poor.

The second lesson concerns the complications introduced by the second-line interpreter, the ethnographer or folklorist, especially when he or she essentializes a particular performance or aligns himself or herself with a particular group of performers. While Redfield clearly favored the more sober "Catholic" interpretation of the cuch in Chan Kom, others like Pérez Sabido maintain that bawdy heterodox performances of the k'ub pol are among Yucatán's most "traditional" performances. Neither writer, unfortunately, recognized the potential for political satire, a third option illustrated in accounts left by Alfonso Villa Rojas and Santiago Pacheco Cruz.

Through these latter texts we begin to recognize the dialectical relationship between different performances. Rabelaisian laughter is the overwhelming sentiment at many village fiestas; however, it is by no means universal. Were it not for the more stolid religious performances described by Redfield and others, the rich parody that characterizes the San Bernardo and Tusik performances would be difficult to sustain; it would be reduced to simple burlesque. By the same token, it would be wrong to view the more aesthetically pleasing baile del cochino as a completely distinct form or as the end product of an evolutionary trend toward commercial culture. These enactments (or entextualizations) found in large towns and cities ultimately depend on the crude peasant humor found on rural haciendas like San Bernardo since the authenticity and value of the former is based on the assumption—sometimes stated, sometimes not—that it is a faithful representation of the latter.

In the following chapter we examine another form of popular culture, namely, myth. The similarity, though, ends there. If the k'ub pol is a satirical look at the past, the tale of *Way Kot* (Eagle Witch) is a type of horror story that examines the present (or at least a more recent past) and looks into the future.

CHAPTER FIVE

THE JOURNEY OF *WAY KOT*
Myth as Cultural Critique

Narrative and Economy

As many anthropologists have discovered, strange and wondrous things occur at the margins of the world system where different economies collide. Airport runways suddenly appear in the rain forests of Papua New Guinea (Worsley 1986 [1968]); stories of the devil are heard with increased regularity on coffee plantations in Colombia's Cauca Valley (Taussig 1980); real estate in "Manhattan" can be purchased at rock-bottom prices (Graeber 2001); and tales of buried treasure break like news items in Michoacán, Mexico (Foster 1967). Little wonder, perhaps, that surrealists and ethnographers have time and again found inspiration in each other's work (Clifford 1988).

Two things, however, should be said about these stories. One is that little attention is generally given to the narrative itself. In most cases, readers are lucky to get a summary or a small snippet of the exemplary text since the latter is employed primarily to demonstrate a broader lesson about exchange, the nature of commodities, or the difficulty of economic development. Nor, in many cases, does the ethnographer discuss the status of the narrative. Is it considered a factual account, a true story? Is it an allegory? Or does it, perhaps, belong to a genre that doesn't exist in the ethnographer's vernacular? These questions are, of course, asked and answered quite well in ethnographies of communication (Bauman and Scherzer 1974; Haviland 1977; Hanks 1990; Sherzer 1983) and in studies of oral literature (Boccara 1997; Bricker 1981; Burns 1983; Gossen 1974; Ligorred Perramón 1990). The latter, however, clearly come from a different part of the anthropological animal and generally do not attempt to answer broad questions about economy or exchange.

The second point, not unrelated to the first, is that such narratives are generally intended to demonstrate the mystification or **fetishism** of people living at the periphery of the world system. Such bewilderment may be attributed to the limitations that social organization (Godelier 1977) or the mode of production (Taussig 1980) impose on consciousness[1] or simply to the distance that separates production from distribution or consumption. As Appadurai explains in his oft-cited introduction to *The Social Life of Things,* "such stories acquire especially intense, new, and striking qualities when the spatial, cognitive, or institutional distances between production, distribution, and consumption are great.... [T]he institutionalized divorce (in knowledge, interest, and role) between persons involved in various aspects of the flow of commodities generates specialized mythologies" (1986b, 48). In either case, the ability of indigenous groups to understand the world without the aid of the anthropologist is considered to be gravely in doubt. Economic dependency gives way to anthropological dependency.

In this chapter I shift the normal division of anthropological labor by foregrounding the imaginary—a popular Yucatecan tale—without losing sight of the broader picture, the relationship of narrative to history and political economy, particularly the political economy of early twentieth-century Yucatán. While Way Kot reveals a veritable fantasy world populated by animate objects and inert humans, I reject the idea that these images are simply manifestations of a bewildered, alienated subject. Building on the aesthetic theory of the Frankfurt School—particularly Adorno's "exact fantasy" (1997) and Benjamin's "mimetic transformation" (1977)–I argue that the production of such incongruous figures can be seen as an attempt to reveal the contradictory essence of the commodity form, the first step of a critical interpretation.

If Adorno considered fetishism or reification an inherent aspect of human creativity or art (Jay 1973, 181–82), it was not an Alcatraz of consciousness, a prison house from which no daring individual ever escaped. On the contrary, employing the messianic language of his friend Walter Benjamin, Adorno considered reification or objectification the first act of "revelation." Through "ciphers" or "riddle-figures," music, art, and other forms of expression high-lighted the contradictory nature of social life. Greater truths concerning the contingency or historical construction of the "given"—what Adorno referred to as "second nature"—would then be revealed through critical exegesis, a precursor of sorts to deconstructionism. Moreover, if art or other forms of representation were intimately tied to the world—or imminent within the object—they were neither static nor totally contained within the object. In fact, in articulating the concept of exact fantasy or mimetic transformation—deliberate non-sequiturs—Benjamin and Adorno ran the gauntlet between theories of art as a reflection of the real world, then popular among Marxists in the 1930s, and bourgeois idealism, which saw the artist as a free and unfet-tered creator of beautiful objects. While the artist was hemmed in by the particularities of bourgeois social life (i.e., the concrete particular), he was still free to rearrange the pieces—which Adorno likened to Leibniz's monads or

Marx's fetish objects—in a manner that anticipates Lévi-Strauss's "bricoleur" and his science of the concrete (1969). As Susan Buck-Morss writes:

> Exact fantasy was thus a dialectical concept which acknowledged the mutual mediation of subject and object without allowing either to get the upper hand. It was not imagination in the sense of subjective projection beyond the existing world either into the past or into the future; it remained imminent within the material phenomena, the factuality of which acted as a control to thought. Exact fantasy was scientific in its refusal to step outside the perimeters of the elements. Yet like art, it rearranged the elements of experience, the riddle figures of empirical existence, until they opened up to cognitive understanding. It was this interpretive rearrangement which brought to light what Adorno meant by the logic of matter. The subject yielded to the objects, yet it did not leave them unchanged. (1977, 86–78)

What remains troublesome, at least to me, is the relationship within critical theory between the artist, or front-line interpreter, and the critic, or second-line interpreter. Since there are always at least two interpreters of art, myth, music, or drama (i.e., the creator and the critic), the question becomes: who does the heavy lifting? With the exception of Schonberg, whom he considered a true revolutionary at least in a musical sense, Adorno felt that the weight of interpretative activity fell mostly upon the philosopher-critic and his use of juxtaposition to explore or break apart the essence of concrete phenomena. In other words, while the artist/storyteller was quite capable of forming riddles, he was not, in Adorno's view, very good at solving them.

However, in interpreting the myth of Way Kot, I argue that the story-teller does a good job of solving its own riddles. While the myth's verbal iconography can be compared to the radical juxtaposition of antithetical elements in surrealism, it does not simply replicate the phenomenal forms (appearances) of consumer society—a charge Adorno leveled against surrealism—but provides a novel interpretation of its object through the deft arrangement of its "fetishes" in narrative structure. Indeed, through the subtle play of images, Way Kot not only reveals the mystery of the commodity form (i.e., the relationship of labor, commodities, and money) but provides a critical perspective on consumption itself, a rhetorical counterstroke to the commodity aesthetics of the period. Whereas institutions of modern society attempt to make commodities enchant, Way Kot presents commerce as a form of witchcraft and consumption as a form of cannibalism in which unsuspecting Maya consumed their own relatives. In short, I suggest that the best place to look for "unfetishized consciousness in non-Western societies ... is precisely around objects Westerners would be inclined to refer to as 'fetishes'" (Graeber 2001, 248).

The Oral Literature of Yucatán

Although critical analysis of Mayan folktales is a recent and still relatively rare pursuit, anthropologists and folklorists have been collecting stories, proverbs, and riddles in Yucatán for well over a century. An early sampling is contained in Daniel Brinton's 1883 *Folk-lore of Yucatan,* a publication of the London Folk-lore Society (see Brinton 1976). While his study is by no means systematic and contains no complete texts, Brinton identified several important characters and motifs that appear in later collections and are discussed throughout the peninsula today. One such character is the **x-tabay**, a seductress who captures the attention of hunters by combing her beautiful hair in front of the ceiba tree she inhabits. When a hunter approaches, she runs away, but slowly enough and with an occasional glance over her shoulder, so that he knows to pursue her. The unsuspecting hunter easily catches x-tabay and embraces her, but not before the seductress is transformed into a cactus or thorny bush with huge talons. Heartbroken and bloody, the hunter returns home, develops a fever, and in most versions becomes delirious or dies.

Because Maya villages were despoiled by large henequén (sisal) plantations that supplied the world market with fiber needed for cordage in the late nineteenth and early twentieth centuries—and henequén is a type of cactus (*agave fourcroydes*)—it is possible that the popularity of this story relates to Yucatán's early insertion into the global economy. Brinton, however, was content to compare x-tabay with legendary women of the Old World (e.g., the sirens of Greek mythology) and saw little need to contextualize or historicize the story. Indeed, while one would expect henequén to figure prominently in regional folklore because of its impact on village life, little or nothing has been written about this devilish plant. On the other hand, untold volumes have been written on maize deities and other Ur-Maya constructs.

A more systematic approach to Mayan oral literature can be found in Margaret Park Redfield's "Folk Literature of a Yucatecan Town" (1937), a study conducted in Dzitas, Yucatán in the 1930s. Here, Park Redfield follows the example of earlier mythographers such as Malinowski by dividing oral literature into three broad categories: the *cuento,* a fanciful tale; the **ejemplo**, a more or less true story with a moral; and, finally, the *historia,* a more or less true story without a moral. While the cuento—which includes animal stories as well as tales of European origin—was considered a stable, well-defined form, Redfield politely noted that the historia violated the taxonomies laid down by previous mythographers, veering off in the direction of fantasy or anecdote. Nevertheless, like other ethnographers of her time, Redfield considered herself a functionalist and viewed folk literature as a method of reinforcing community norms, not as a critique of the social order. Ejemplos, in particular, were considered tools for teaching children to avoid saying inappropriate things: "People said that I had twins because the children had two fathers. But God punished them for talking this way. It is not good to talk about other people, and so these same women had twins too" (1937, 26).

A more contemporary approach to oral literature can be found in the work of Allan Burns. In *An Epoch of Miracles* (1983), Burns not only broadens the scope of oral literature by including narratives concerning esoteric phenomenon and dreams but relates his typology to indigenous speech categories rather than the categories employed by Malinowski and others. Burns also places considerable importance on the contextual and performative aspects of Mayan storytelling. In addition to noting that Yucatec Maya like to tell riddles at wakes, he argues that storytelling is best understood as a dialogue or conversation (1983, 19–20). More importantly, at least for the present study, Burns argues that oral literature, especially "counsels of a historical nature" (i.e., historias), be understood as a form of rhetoric or argumentation rather than a recitation of tales frozen in time or space. For example, he notes that one informant rejected his scientific explanation of rainfall and evaporation by performing a counsel (historia) that "included a reference to a time during the Caste War when the water from the sea joined the water from the sky to destroy many enemy troops" (1983, 71).

Another important contribution to Mayan oral literature is Michel Boccara's *Encyclopédie de la mythologie Maya Yucatèque,* a 15-volume work published in French and Yucatec Maya (1997). In the introduction in Volume 1, Boccara lays out a general theory of myth that sharply distinguishes the "myth" from the "account" (or myth text) and emphasizes the affective or unconscious nature of myth (1997, 16–17). In contrast to Lévi-Strauss and the structuralists, Boccara argues that myth is really a special kind of speech (*parole*), a primeval form of communication based on song or chant. This not only helps to explain the recurrent comparison between human beings and birds in mythology but the fact that many myths contain a prologue concerning the origin of language or a reference to mythic ancestors who laugh and sing but do not speak (Boccara 1997, 20).

Notwithstanding the importance of bird-lore in Yucatán, Boccara's general formulations are obviously remote from my way of thinking about myth. Nevertheless, the *Encyclopédie* is an invaluable resource. Unlike many previous collections, which sacrifice depth for breadth and offer little contextual information or analysis, it focuses on a limited number of motifs, including commerce and Way Kot, and provides multiple versions of each tale as well as commentaries, historical and ethnographic notes, and other supporting documents. Boccara, as I note further on, also does a good job of pointing out how myths evolve over time, incorporating new elements or characters as the historical context changes.

Meeting Way Kot

My interpretation of Way Kot is based on five versions of the myth. The first, which appears below, was recorded and transcribed in Maxcanú in the summer of 1989. The narrator, Don Román, was an 80-year-old *rezador* (prayer leader), who said that he first heard the tale as a young man. Don Román lived in a small, thatched-roof hut on the edge of town and was considered a master storyteller as well as an authority on local history. The complete version can be found in Chapter 6 of my dissertation (Loewe 1995); the other four versions, along with English translations, can be found in the Appendix to this book.

Version 2 is from Ligorred Perramón's bilingual (Mayan/Spanish) study of Mayan oral literature (1990). Version 3 was handwritten in Spanish by Manuel Dzib Palominos, a young resident of Maxcanú who helped me with several projects. Manuel, in fact, often referred to himself as a Way Kot because of several trips he took to the US while I was living in Yucatán. Version 4, the Yaxcaba version, refers to a summary of the tale published by Michel Boccara in Spanish (see Boccara 1985). Since then Boccara has published the complete version of the tale in Yucatec Maya and French in Volume 6 of his encyclopedia, so I have been able to consult the full form as well as other versions published in that collection. Version 5 is a literary rendition published by Luis Rosado Vega (1957, 168–75). Although the latter is entitled *El uay pach,* it discusses the collaboration between *way pach'* and Way Kot. A brief description and a picture of a Way Kot can also be found in Redfield and Villa Rojas (1990 [1934], 178–80) and Brinton (1976 [1883]).

My first meeting with Way Kot occurred shortly after my arrival in Yucatán, although at the time I assumed I was simply dealing with the curiosity of a six-year-old child. My wife, Helene, and I had just completed a quick tour of handicraft stores in the town of Ticul and were waiting in 100 degree heat at the local bus depot. As I scanned the area for *boli bolis,* the local version of a popsicle, a young girl approached and, selecting the less threatening of the two gringos, directed a question to Helene. Still in the process of learning Spanish, Helene cast a confused glance in my direction and asked: "What's *agarran* mean?"

"Grab," I said, noticing a broad smile on the face of the woman standing next to her. Something was up. I moved closer and asked the girl to repeat the question. Reluctantly, but more annoyed than frightened, she turned and asked if it's true that gringos grab young children, take them up north, and make ham out of them. Peals of laughter rippled from every corner of the dusty depot. Unsure how to respond, or to whom I was responding, I paused, turned back to Helene, and translated the question. Finally, not wanting to appear too defensive, I smiled and said, "No, actually gringos prefer hamburgers, they make hamburger out of them." Undaunted, but recognizing that caution is the better part of valor, the girl stepped back and buried herself in the folds of her mother's huipil.

Back in Maxcanú (my primary field site) I repeated the story to friends and informants, hoping to elicit similar stories about "los gringos." Few were forthcoming. Although I was privy to endless stories about the archaeological team from Madrid that was allegedly stealing gold artifacts from nearby Oxkintok (a pre-classic Maya site) and shipping them back to Spain, people were hesitant to talk about "los gringos Americanos," at least to me. Eventually, however, Don Román admitted that the episode in Ticul reminded him of an historia—a tale that combines fantasy with historical fact (Sullivan 1989, 186)—he had heard as a young man, and he told me to return the next day to hear the tale of **Way Pop** [Way Kot].

THE STORY OF WAY KOT (THE EAGLE WITCH)

FIGURE 5.1 Way Kot, the eagle witch. Artwork courtesy of Krystal Kittle

Version One

... había un encargado que habitaba en una finca. Entonces a lado de la finca todos
... there was a foreman who lived on a small hacienda. Back then they imprisoned

los que no obedecían a el los encarcelaba, pero dice que cuando amanece ...
those who didn't obey him next to the hacienda, but they say the next morning ...

no esté allí. Y entonces le dice a sus compañeros: "señores, éste no está, se huyó,"
[the prisoner] wasn't there. Then he says to his friends: "Gentlemen, he's not here, he escaped,"

y despúes está cerrado con llave. ¿Quien sabe como se fue? Bueno, cada vez así ...
and then [the prison] was locked. Who knows how he left? Well, each time it was like that.

Como hay uno de ellos también que sabía ese de convirtirse en *way pop* desobedicío al encargado.
Since one of them also knew how to convert himself into *way pop* he disobeyed the foreman.

Entonces lo metieron al bote. Ah, entonces como a media noche oyó que se estaba abriendo
So they threw him in the prison. Ah, then around midnight he heard someone opening

la llave del carcel y lo sacaron. "Bueno, pues pasa a subirte aquí, que voy a llevar en Mérida."
the lock on the prison and they took him out. "Okay, climb up here, I'm taking you to Mérida."

... obedecío y se trepó entonces y vio que abre sus alas entonces y voló y va volando y ve que éste
... he obeyed, climbed up and saw [foreman] open his wings and fly, he was flying and saw the

tenga narices a con que así llevan los demas, pensó el. Pues ... en medio camino habia una
[creature] had a beak with which he carried the rest, he thought. Well ... about half way there was

mata de arbol, pero vio que era un desierto, pero ese mata estaba muy frondoso y muy alto.
a tree, but he saw that it was in a desert, but this tree was very florid and very high.

Allí descansó ... entonces vio que llegó en un pueblo. Y vio que se bajó
There he rested ... then he saw he had arrived in a town. He descended onto

sobre una azotea y que le decía: "bajate." Vio que no tenía alas, nada ...
a long flat roof and was told: "Get down." He saw [way pop] had no wings, nothing ...

Y empujó la puerta y entró. Y agarró la mano del señor y vio que se le entregan a
[Way Pop] pushed the door and entered. He grabbed the hand of the man and delivered him to

otro señor. "Aquí trajé ... otro. Está bueno ... ya tengo para mi mercancia,"
another man. "Here I brought another one. He's good ... now I have [enough] for my

que dice. "Ah, éste es tan poco mas gordo, hay para preparar para vender," que dice.
merchandise," he said. "Ah this one is a little fatter, there's enough to prepare for sale," he says.

Ah, creo que son los que se preparan de jamón para vender. Ah, entonces agarraron su mano
Ah, I think they are the ones they make ham from, for sale. Ah, then they grabbed his hand,

y llevaron y lo metieron ... en una una caseta así, y vio que allí están a sus amigos allí
they carried him away and put him in a little house like this, and he saw his friends were there

y le tienen cortado los pies ... Cerraron con llaves a todos. Entonces el como nada sacó la llave
and their feet had been cut off.... Everyone was locked in. Then he casually pulled out the key....

Bueno, pues abrense. Uno de sus, que es muy conocido de el ... "Pues, hoy te voy a llevar," dice.
Well, it opened. To one of them, who is very close to him ... he says, "I'm taking you today."

Y lo sacó.... entonces al otro cuando lo sacó así entonces ahora así que abre sus alas también.
And he took him.... Then to the one he took out, he [shows] him he has wings too [and says],

"Subate allí en mi espalda, vamos" ... Muy alto empezó a ir y vio hace rato que
"Climb up there on my back, let's go." ... He began to fly very high and he saw after

está yendo hasta que asomó en el desierto, a éste a que pasamos y empezó
awhile he was going to the place they landed in the desert, the one we passed, and he began

a ver donde está el arbol donde descansaron … Entonces cuando llegó allá a la finca …
to see the tree where they rested. … Then, when he arrived there at the hacienda …

Abrió donde están cerrado los demas, vio que no había ni un preso allí.
he opened the place where the rest were and saw there wasn't even one prisoner.

Ya había amanecido entonces. Cuando si antojó al encargado fue a echarse allí en la carcel.
The sun was already up then. When he noticed the foreman he threw himself in the jail.

Y vio que allí estaban los dos personas, personales y achechó. Y vio que es el que llevó.
[The foreman] saw there were two people and stared. He saw it was one he already took.

Y entonces el señor lo vio y no hable ese. Ah, se le quitó allá. … Es que se estaba huyendo. … .
The [foreman] saw him, but he didn't speak. Ah, he just got out of there. … He was really escaping. …

Despúes que salió el encargado salió tambien y fue a la comandancia. Entonces le dijó que
After the foreman left, he left as well and went to the police. He told the police to

agarran a ese encargado: "Ya descubrí donde acaban la gente que a veces," que dice,
grab the foreman: "Now I discovered where the people sometimes end up," he says.

"que lo meten en el calabozo y cuando amanece que no está allá pues el lo lleve. Los lleva a vender.
"They put them in prison and when morning comes they're not there since he takes them. He sells them.

Ah, porque yo ya fui. Yo ví allí están mis compañeros. Hay que ya comieron, hay que
Ah, because I just went. I saw my companions there. Some had already been eaten, some

todavía, ya le tienen cortado sus pies a todos …" Entonces … la comandante fue … a ver el calabozo
still hadn't, they all had their feet cut off. …" Then … the police chief went … to see the prison

y vio que allí esté el señor. Entonces al agarrar entonces ese encargado, no lo agarraron. Se huyó
and saw the [foreman] was there. He then tried grabbing the foreman, but he couldn't. He escaped

… volvió en su casa … lo agarraron y … metieron en el calabozo … entonces lo metieron en los separos allí.
… he returned to his house … they grabbed him and … put him in jail … they put him in solitary confinement.

En los separos no dejan nada. Si tienes faja te lo quitan … Solo te dejan tu pantalon y tu camisa …
In solitary nothing is allowed. They even take your band-aids. … They only leave your pants and your shirt. …

Nada le dieron para comer y cuando amaneció, cuando fueron a ver allí, estaba colgado.
They didn't give him any food and the next day, when they went to see him, he was hanging.

Se ahorcó. … Ya se acabó el *Way Pop*. … Entonces el otro citaron para que se presenta otra vez y se fue.
He hanged himself. … *Way Pop* was finished. … They set a date for the other [*Way Pop*] to appear and he left.

Y dijó como descubrió. "¿Pues … cómo ese oficio lo sabe?" "Tambien lo sé, pero yo no para hacer daño.
And he told what he learned. "Well … how do you know this business?" "I know it too, but not to do harm.

No mas lo aprendí y nunca he hecho ningun maldad. … Solo así a veces voy a buscar mercancia. …
I just learned it and I have never done anything evil. … Only on occasion do I go looking for merchandise. …

Eso es lo que hago, pero ese señor que lo descubrí, tenía un comercio de pura lozanía." [R: ¿De puro que?]
This is what I do, but this man I discovered, he sold pure luxury goods." [R: Pure what?]

De pura lencería. Ah, entonces en ningún lado encuentran esas cosas que tiene el … no se veo.
Pure linen and lingerie. Ah, back then you didn't find the things he had anywhere … they weren't seen.

El va por extranjero, pero asi lo trae cargado. Y nunca se vio que se estaciona un coche en la puerta de
He goes abroad, but brings them back like this. Nobody ever saw him park a vehicle in front of the

la lencería. Cuando se abre la casa está lleno de puras cosas así … Le dieron su libertad … No le
clothing store. When they opened the house it was full of things like this. … They let him go. … They

hicieron nada. Porque el confesó que no era para hacer daño. Que el iba al extranjero a comprar mercancias.
didn't do anything. Because he claimed he didn't cause harm. He went abroad [simply] to buy merchandise.

Discussion

PRIMITIVE ACCUMULATION

In this version, and other versions of Way Kot/Way Pop, the myth begins by posing a solution to a specific problem; however, the problem it purports to solve is not identified until the very end when the narrator notes the mysterious character of the clothing store (*lencería*). Although no one ever sees a delivery being made, the store is always stocked with costly and unusual goods. Where does this merchandise come from? Moreover, how does a merchant who doesn't engage in productive labor, or directly exploit the labor of others, amass such great wealth? The problem, of course, is a familiar one. It is the same problem Peter Worsley identified in his study of cargo cults and the basis for the imitative magic he described in *The Trumpet Shall Sound:* "As far as the natives are concerned the Whites received the goods by steamer from unknown parts; they did not manufacture them, and merely sent pieces of paper back.... Who made these goods, how and where were mysteries—it could hardly be the idle White man" (1986 [1968], 97).

The Mayan solution, however, is a bit more "sociological" than the New Guinea one. In the tale of Way Kot the merchant, in the guise of a large bird, emanates directly from the foreman, an individual well known for his ability to appropriate the labor power of others. Known in Yucatán as the mayokol (see Chapter 4, p. 93 for a discussion of this term), the foreman was hated by the Maya workers. In other versions of the tale, the foreman is replaced by a priest, another well-known usurper,[2] but the outcome is the same.

The tale of Way Kot also resembles the treasure tales told by the peasants of Tzintzuntzan, tales that were used to explain a resident's sudden rise to prominence. Indeed, most of Foster's treasure tales, though purportedly examples of a general worldview (i.e., the idea of limited good), deal specifically with the genesis of mercantile capital.

> 1. Salvador Enríquez was a potter, so poor he lacked animals to carry clays. Like other poor potters, he packed his raw materials on his back, and his tumpline had worn all the hair off his head, he was that poor before he began to live well. His daughter, after cutting her bare foot several times on a stone in the yard, lifted the slab out with a hoe and to her astonishment found a pot containing pure silver. Salvador bought the village's first sewing machine, *opened a store,* built a fine house and began to live on a scale previously unknown in Tzintzuntzan.
>
> 2. Several boys were playing in the *aljibe,* a vault beneath the cloister adjacent to the church. One of them, Jaime Enríquez, struck an old chest and saw something gleaming behind the rotten wood. He ran to tell his father, Gaudencio, the sacristan, who ejected the boys and locked the

room. That night Gaudencio sent his eldest son, Angel, who took his friend Eleno Miranda, and the two removed the treasure which in part consisted of golden sandals left there by Tarascan kings. Shortly thereafter, Eleno opened a *fine store on the plaza with clothing and everything. Angel entered commerce,* bought a truck ... and became Tzintzuntzan's richest man. (Foster 1967, 146–47; emphases added)

The difference is that while the treasure tales of Tzintzuntzan attribute the genesis of mercantile capital to fortuitous circumstances, or in some cases to simple theft, the tale of Way Kot proposes a more sober economic solution by linking commerce to production and highlighting the dependence of the city on the countryside. Once again, however, the fragmentary character of Foster's published narratives makes a more detailed comparison impossible.

EAGLE EXCREMENT AND GOLD SHIT

Having resolved the problem of "primitive accumulation," Way Kot moves on to other matters. At this point, however, the serious reader confronts an interpretive stumbling block. Although in all versions of the tale the role of the kidnapper/usurper is of central importance, his identity remains somewhat in doubt. While in Versions 1 and 2 he is referred to as *Way Pop,* which might be translated as "the witch of the mats" (*Diccionario maya cordemex* 666), in Version 4 he is referred to as *Way Kot,* "the eagle witch" (DMC 338). Moreover, in Version 5, a literary rendition composed by Luis Rosado Vega, *Way Kot* acts in concert with a third evil-doer, *way pach'*, a long, slender creature who can "slip through the smallest fissures" (1957, 168–75).[3]

Prima facie evidence, of course, supports the choice of *Way Kot* since the usurper in each case is a large, winged creature. Moreover, the collaboration between the Way Kot and the serpentine *way pach'* allows for a rather intriguing comparison between the usurping villain and the Mexican peso (i.e., money) since, based on mythic imagery of an earlier era—the Aztec origin myth—the back of a peso features a ferocious eagle perched atop a cactus (*nopal*) with a serpent dangling from its beak. Following this scenario, the florid desert tree where the way kot rests in Version 1 can be interpreted as the nopal upon which the Aztec eagle sits. In fact, the nopal, a cactus found throughout Mexico, is well known for its flower.

Moreover, thanks to a popular jingle preserved by José Bolio López, we know that the eagle and his droppings have served as metonyms of token money since the time of the Mexican Revolution, if not earlier. Referring to the worthless *carrancudos* that General Carranza used to pay his soldiers, one anonymous poet wrote:

El águila nacional	The national eagle
es un animal muy cruel	is a very cruel animal
se traga el oro metal	it swallows gold metal
y caga puro papel.	and shits pure paper.

¿Qué nos diga el General?	What do you say to us, General?
¿Con que dinero nos paga?	With what money will you pay us?
Si con el oro metal	With gold metal
o con lo que el águila caga.	or with eagle shit.

(Bolio López 1983, 42)

Mayan speakers are, apparently, no less prone to sarcasm; as Norman McQuown points out (personal communication, 1994), the Yucatec Mayan term for money, *tak'in*, is best understood as a compound noun containing the morphemes for "excrement" (*ta'*) and "gold" (*k'in*).[4] In any case, if Way Kot is really a tale about commerce, it only makes sense that the protagonist doubles as money.

But who, then, is Way Pop? Michel Boccara, who likewise notes the tendency of storytellers to use both names, suggests that the term "pop"—a type of reed or mat (DMC 666)—designates the material from which a more technologically astute witch constructs his wings. From Boccara's perspective, the myth of Way Pop/Way Kot is undergoing a transformation parallel to the evolution of technology in Yucatán, and the term "pop" represents the extension of the **waye** (witch) from a malevolent being in animal form to a malevolent technician or to technology itself (see Boccara 1985). However, the only evidence provided in support of this interpretation comes from a brief description of Way Pop manufacturing his wings from a soft wood. No attempt is made to demonstrate that this wood is actually the reed known in Yucatec Maya as *pop*. Furthermore, Redfield, who also noted the tendency to substitute one name for another, claims that it was actually older people, not young ones, who used the term "Way Pop" (Redfield and Villa Rojas 1990 [1934], 179). A more plausible explanation, in my view, is that the name derives from an analogy between this myth and folktales about genies on flying mats that were brought to Yucatán by Lebanese immigrants in the early 1900s. Maya myths, as Allan Burns has noted (1983, 31), have been profoundly influenced by European tales, and Domingo Dzul Poot, a well-known translator, has specifically noted the imprint of Arab tales on local forms of storytelling (personal communication, June 1989).

As both oral and written sources attest (Ramírez Carrillo 1994), Lebanese immigrants began arriving in Yucatán in the late nineteenth century and got their start as itinerant merchants. Stories abound of Arab merchants traveling the back roads of Yucatán with unusual consumer goods. Although few were able to speak more than a few words of Spanish or Mayan, they were persistent salesmen and would gesture or draw diagrams in the dirt in order to sell an article. In addition to developing a reputation for being stubborn (*terco*), they were known for their frugality. In fact, older residents still affectionately refer to Lebanese merchants by the Mayan-Spanish hybrid *haant cebolla* (onion eater) since this was, reportedly, the only thing they needed to sustain themselves.

By the mid-1920s several Lebanese families had established clothing shops or dry goods stores around the central plaza in Maxcanú. Judging by the number of marriages between children of wealthy Lebanese merchants and established Yucatecan families, it appears that the more prosperous ones were easily assimilated into the town's upper class; however, they were also sometimes suspected of being **wayes** (witches). Not only is the merchant in some versions of Way Kot an Arab, but when Don Román began discussing who in Maxcanú were actually wayes, one of the two names that came up was that of Don Jorge, a Lebanese merchant who owned a lucrative business in the center of town. In short, then, one might say that the name "Way Pop" shows a certain deference to the knowledge of the Lebanese merchant/villain himself. But, then, as the young girl who quizzed me in Ticul recognized, who would know better than one who has flown the coop?[5]

Does this mean that the tale of Way Pop/Way Kot first came to life in the 1920s or the early 1930s when commercialization came to the town? Maybe, maybe not. One can certainly find earlier references to Way Kot; for example, Brinton's *The Folk-lore of Yucatán,* published in 1883, contains a reference to this character; however, the way kot found there is a mischievous bird that hides in the exterior walls of a house and throws rocks at pedestrians. It is not clear if the ill-mannered bird is an eagle. In fact, it's not clear whether the Mayan term *kot* refers to this devilish creature at all, since it also means "wall or stone fence" (DCM 1980, 338). Could the way kot have been the "witch of the wall" originally?[6] If so, is this really the same way kot? Could the intensification of commerce in the 1930s have led to a slippage in the referent (i.e., from wall to eagle)?

Similarly, one can consider Boccara's claim that the tale goes back to 1829 if not earlier because Don Claudio, a merchant named in Version 4, was known to have lived in Yaxcaba at that time. But what if the merchant's name was inserted after the fact? In addition to examining how different versions of Way Kot mythologize history, it is important to consider the ways in which different narrators historicize myth. It is, after all, an "historia." In my view, determining the origin of this tale is a little like trying to figure out when English writers began to lament the decline of rural life (Williams 1973). Infinite regress is clearly possible, especially if we allow for slippage between referents. Not only have witch tales served as an idiom for discussing social life for many years, both stories and social life have, undoubtedly, undergone numerous transformations in the last century.

Therefore, instead of pursuing an elusive starting point,[7] I prefer to focus on what's being said. In other words, if Don Román heard the tale as a young man (ca. 1935) as he claims, what was happening at the time that contributes to our understanding of the story? What is the nature of the relationship between narrative and social life or narrative and history? And, finally, what animates the continual retelling of this story?

Commodity Aesthetics, Sex, and History: Chan Kom and Beyond

As it turns out the Lebanese weren't the only ones trying to make money. Between 1931 and 1948, the period covered in Redfield's re-study of Chan Kom (1950), commerce expanded significantly, individual rights in property became far more commonplace, money gained greater currency, and work became increasingly specialized. In 1931 house lots were considered a type of usufruct that would revert to the village, the eminent domain, if the resident moved away; however, by 1948 individual ownership of house lots was common, and properties were routinely bought and sold. Agricultural land and all the things that went with it (e.g., fruit trees, wells) were also being privatized. In fact, notwithstanding dissention on the part of some residents (Goldkind 1965), even sections of the ejido were effectively privatized. Most importantly, perhaps, the ethos of Chan Kom had changed. Not only was Don Eus, Redfield's chief informant, furtively scribbling comments about the "*importancia de dinero*" (1950, 158) in the margins of his books, but monetary transactions had become part of everyday life. "In these seventeen years the people have received many visitors and have come to take it as a matter of course that serving a meal will bring money and that house rent be paid by one who is given lodging" (Redfield 1950, 65). In any case, by 1948 Chan Kom had four well-stocked general stores whereas in 1931 it only had one, and, as Redfield himself notes, the "uayes [ways] were ... real" (1950, 125), meaning that the growth of commerce was transforming social life.

Not surprisingly, perhaps, the state and its various dependencies were behind many of these activities. As Ben Fallow notes, Yucatán's socialist governor, Bartolomé Garcia Correa (1930–33), was intent on modernizing the Maya by spreading "western models of labor, consumption, and recreation" (2004, 558). In addition to promoting baseball and good hygiene and the consumer items that went along with it (e.g., shoes, new clothing), the Garcia Correa administration held female beauty pageants and male strong man contests "to reward the most 'hardworking' and 'progressive' males; winners were crowned 'India bonita' and 'Indio robusto'" (2004, 558). As noted in Chapter 1 (see p. 27), a similar proposal was put forth by Humberto Peniche

Vallado, a prominent Yucatecan educator, on the eve of the Cárdenas agrarian reform in 1935. For agrarian reform to succeed, the Maya villager would first have to be transformed into a subject of irrepressible desires:

> The problem—to my understanding—does not lie precisely in learning how to read or acquiring a certain level of knowledge. The problem lies in elevating [the Indian's] standard of living, in making sure that he enjoys the well-being that civilization has brought, and in creating bodily needs (*necesidades*) for him. (Peninche Vallado 1987 [1937], 95; translated by author)

More importantly, though, it was the responsibility of the rural educator to make modernity enchant by embedding the consumption of new commodities in community events where emotions ran high. In particular, Peniche Vallado recommended that teachers induce villagers to construct a hygienic, cinderblock house with all the latest amenities—running water, a cement floor, etc.—and, in an opportune moment invested with all the pomp and gaiety of the annual fiesta, to raffle off the exemplary construction. Similarly, patriotic holidays and the emerging courtship ritual provided excellent opportunities to help students form an affection for good clothes. While Peniche Vallado was against imposing western dress on young students, the demands of courtship combined with the "capricious" nature of women would, in his view, make the introduction of modern apparel much easier. In short, through rituals old and new—what Sydney Mintz (1985, 122) refers to as "rituals of intensification"—the elementary schoolteacher would gradually develop the student's aesthetic sensitivity and self-discipline, qualities that would not only induce the Maya to covet personal property but that were considered the building blocks of civilization itself.

However, if the ability to purchase new consumer items provided an opportunity to shed signs of servility and was eagerly embraced in some places (see Ownby 1999; Cohen 1990; Miller 1994),[8] Yucatán was not one of them. New forms of consumption required new forms of seduction and, in some cases, new forms of coercion. In fact, as Redfield notes in his famous re-study of Chan Kom, girls adopted western dress only because their teacher demanded it and abandoned the new fashion as soon as they left school (1950, 41).

In my view, then, Way Kot is best understood as part of a more general reluctance to embrace the market and its charms. By equating commerce with witchcraft and the consumption of processed meats with cannibalism, Way Kot provides a rhetorical counterpoint to Peniche Vallado and other educators (including Villa Rojas) who were lavishing the Maya with icons of modernity. While one can reasonably argue that Way Kot is more about profiting off the blood and sweat of Maya workers (i.e., coercion) than about the dangers of seduction, the clothing store the Way Kot operated was, according to Don Román, "*un comercio de pura lozania*" (a luxury goods business) where one could purchase items impossible to find anywhere else.

This does not suggest that the simple lencería was filled with expensive jewelry and silk scarves; lingerie and certain dry goods would have been considered luxuries in their own right. It does, however, emphasize the seductive nature of such an enterprise. And here we should remember that it was seductive or illicit sexual acts that often raised suspicion of witchcraft in the first place. In an unusually candid account of Mayan verbal "intercourse," Paul Sullivan notes that sexual escapades are not only "favorite conversational topics among Maya men in their gatherings" (1989, 110) but highlight the connection between witchcraft and illicit sexual performances in local gossip. Describing how the wife of San (a master shaman) died, Sullivan writes: "Some say San's late wife was a *way*, a transforming witch, killed while in the form of a black dog, the guise she habitually assumed for nightly sexual assaults against a certain young man in the neighboring village. The man would wake up night after night to find himself completely naked, his penis swollen and raw, so one night, the story goes, he lay in wait and shot the witch-dog as she approached" (1989, 201). Similarly, as Redfield noted long ago, "[t]he *uay xib* (male witch) is described as using its tongue as its instrument of lubricity" (Redfield and Villa Rojas 1990, 179).[9]

Interpreting Way Kot as a rhetorical counterpoint to a new ethos of consumption is also strengthened by the behavior and rhetoric of other social classes. In fact, when Don Eus, Chan Kom's wealthiest and most progressive citizen, was not informing Redfield about the need for technological improvement, he was complaining about the buying habits of young people the way some parents now speak about the dangers of marijuana or other "gateway" recreational drugs. "Shoes and dresses mean being advanced, the young people say. But I say, then beds follow, and different foods. . . . If you go *catrín* [become a social climber] you can't carry a load on your back and you aren't content with chayote or squash. And I say it costs too much money" (Redfield 1950, 41).[10]

Similarly, I would argue that even members of the peninsular elite had serious reservations about the growth of consumer culture, a view they expressed through their ridicule of upwardly mobile residents (the catríns). Although many anthropologists have treated the term "catrín" as a neutral ethnic category (Redfield and Villa Rojas 1990 [1934]; Redfield 1964; Thompson 1974; Goldkind 1965; Press 1975) or a term of unknown origin (Hansen and Bastarrachea Manzano 1984, 158), it is actually an insult, equivalent to "dandy" or "fop," and is directed against anyone who dares to dress beyond his supposed station in life. As we have seen in Chapter 3 (p. 66) the term, just coming into popular use in the 1920s,[11] comes from the nineteenth-century novel *Don Catrín de la Fachenda* (The Pretentious Don Catrín), by the Mexican satirist José Joaquin Fernández de Lizardi. Despite his many failings, Don Catrín always manages to wear the latest fashion; and because in his view clothes make the man, he is surprised when, on the verge of poverty, his old friends abandon him.

In short, threatened by the decline of sumptuary regulation *de vestido* (of the dress) and other, more traditional methods of demonstrating status, the cream of Yucatecan society fashioned their own critique of consumer culture and those who sought to advance through it. And, like the Maya, they made ample use of allegory, if of a different sort.

The Riddle of Money

Let me now go out on a limb. Having penetrated the "veil of Way Kot," and discovered its commodity form (i.e., money), it now becomes possible to see the second problem: the enigmatic relationship between commodities, labor, and money, a puzzle the myth attempts to solve as it follows the trail of the disappearing Maya. In the first chapter of *Capital* (1939), Marx painstakingly demonstrates the equivalence or commensurability of labor power, commodities, and money as distinct types of value. Whereas the former creates value, and is sometimes referred to as "value-substance," the latter are considered to be different expressions of "value-form." In turn, commodities and money are distinguished by the fact that, in the former, "value-form" is inseparable from a particular use value or material satisfaction, while in the latter it is not. It is independent and can go where it chooses.

At the same time, however, Marx points out that the relationship between these synchronically ordered elements of value are gradually obscured by the development of money. In the case of direct barter, the social character of value is relatively transparent. But with the emergence of a general equivalent, that is, of a commodity such as gold that becomes the measure of other commodities, value appears to be inherent in the commodity itself:

> What appears to happen is not that gold becomes money in consequence of all other commodities expressing their values in it, but on the contrary, that all other commodities universally express their values in gold because it is money. The intermediate steps of the process vanish in the result and leave no trace behind. . . . We have seen [how]the progressive development of a society of commodity producers stamps one privileged commodity with the character of money. *Hence the riddle presented by money is but the riddle presented by commodities; only it now strikes us in its most glaring form.* (Marx 1939: 65; emphasis added)

The value-relation is obscured even further by the eventual substitution of paper money or tokens for commodity-money, an event that accompanies an increase in the circulation of commodities. As gold, money still contains value, the magnitude of which is rendered directly in terms of its weight. However, as commodity exchange becomes increasingly commonplace, the nominal weight (or price) of money not only deviates from its actual weight (or value) as a result of wear and tear but begins to take its place, a process that highlights the increasing importance of money as a medium of exchange as opposed to a simple measure of value. With the substitution of paper for precious metal, this function becomes pre-eminent: "Its functional existence absorbs, so to say, its material existence" (Marx 1939, 105). In this way value is replaced by its symbol, a move that not only severs the link between labor as a source of value and its expression (i.e., value-form), but leads to the most imaginative fantasies (i.e., commodity fetishism). In short, then, the world from which Way Kot draws its imagery, the world of incipient commodity exchange, is a world of fragmentary, inchoate forms, a world in which things are endowed with inalienable powers and the social relations among producers are obscured by the products of their own labor.

In order to resolve the conundrums of commodity exchange and explain the power of money, Way Kot must first render sensuous experience concretely; that is, it must reduce its object, the contradictory nature of "things" to a few palpable images or, in the words of Adorno, an "exact fantasy." While on the one hand token money, the valueless value-form, is brought to life on the wings of the Way Kot (an image that, perhaps, represents the "independence" of the value-form), humanity is reduced to a passive inert form, first as a helpless, footless prisoner, then as a commodity, ham.

Having depicted the appearance world in terms of its more notable attributes, Way Kot then illustrates the transformation of value into its various constituent forms as it follows Maya labor through the Diaspora. In the opening episode, Way Kot confronts his prisoner—in the plaintive language of political economy, labor comes face-to-face with its value-form. It is a coercive encounter in which value triumphs and labor is forced to go abroad; however, Way Kot does not transgress the limits of his function as a medium of exchange. In a drama in which the equivalence between different items is rendered "metamorphically," either through consumption or through transformation (e.g., the foreman becomes a large eagle), Way Kot and his prisoner remain distinct. Way kot does not consume the prisoner, as one might expect, but simply mediates the transformation of living labor-power into the commodity form. In other words, by ignoring the Way Kot's natural identity as a bird of prey, the myth foregrounds his other identity as money, thus pushing the economic logic of the narrative to the surface.

Indeed, the laborers Way Kot steals are not consumed until after they enter the realm of production, that is, until after the second transaction in which he sells his prisoner to the factory owner. Thus, the myth not only expresses the rural villager's antipathy toward industrial wage labor and, perhaps, a latent xenophobia (Sullivan 1989) but reveals the essence of the commodity as congealed laborers, an image that would surely be the envy of Dalí or Miró. Nevertheless, Way Kot is not unlike many passages of *Capital,* which are so littered with imaginary subjects like Mr. Moneybags that Marx felt compelled to warn his readers that "the characters who appear on the economic stage are but the personifications of the economic relations which exist between them" (1939, 57). The circuit is then completed when way kot returns from abroad with canned goods, sewing machines, and other foreign products (see especially texts 6 and 30 in Boccara 1997, 55 and 124).[12]

The encounter between way kot and his Maya victims can also be seen as a condensed history of productive relations in Yucatán, or what Walter Benjamin sometimes referred to as a "configuration" or "monad", an arresting moment in which the narrator grasps the connection "which his own era has formed with a definite earlier one" (1977, 263). If, as Boccara suggests, the tale of Way Kot goes back to the early nineteenth century, the central drama can be viewed as a highly cathected image of the notorious sale of Maya slaves to Cuba in the 1840s, the expropriation of Maya villagers by henequén producers in the late 1800s, the intensification of commerce in the 1930s, the migration of *braceros* (farmworkers, literally "arms") to the US in the 1940s, and the ongoing necessity of workers to go abroad. In fact, one thing Boccara demonstrates quite effectively through his dialogue with Don Mario, an elder informant, is that Way Kot continues to evolve, incorporating newer, more ingenious methods of capturing labor as well as more talented evil-doers (e.g., engineers, intellectuals).

Indeed, in a story reminiscent of the question posed by the inquisitive six-year-old I met in Ticul, Don Mario remarks:

> Everyone who has completed advanced studies has researched ways . . . to exploit the people. If they weren't able to exploit the women, they have sought to exploit the strength of the peasant. But there are people who . . . are nearly the same as the way kot. There are many cases like this. They steal the infant and they carry him away. There are times where they find the person responsible, but sometimes the child is lost. One time, I don't know who discovered it, but there was a little child who had been taken to another country. And when he was grown up, well . . . they injected ampoules into his arms so that he would become clumsy (one-armed), so that he could get handouts, so he could ask for charity. Each day, the child went out, and when he returned to where the chief who had taken him lived, he gave him the money, and thus he [the chief] lived on the back of the little child. . . . Well, I also think that the way kot are like this, lazy people who don't want to work and that make money with studies, with their ideas. (Boccara 1997, 157; translated by author)

Commerce and Witchcraft

Another vexing issue emerges when we attempt to analyze the relationship between the kidnapper-merchant and his chief antagonist. At first the relationship appears to be nothing other than a classic confrontation between good and evil. While the kidnapper-merchant profits by stealing hacienda workers and selling them for merchandise, his counterpart uses his magical powers to aid in their rescue, all for no apparent reward. While one is surreptitious and operates in the dead of night, the other is law-abiding and conducts his activities in broad daylight.

Upon closer examination, however, the structural polarities of the myth give way to affinity and likeness. For example, the so-called hero of Version 1 turns out to be a merchant himself, a nameless character identified simply as "another one who knows how to convert himself into way pop." In fact, when I asked Don Román the name of the second way pop following his recitation, he treated the question as an historical inquiry and responded: "I think his name was Juan Martín."[13]

Similarly, in Version 3 of the myth, merchants themselves become the victims of Way Kot:

> ... thus every night he took a drunk to Columbia and left him there in a shoe factory. The priest chose the most expensive shoes and returned to Yucatán. The following night he took another person to another factory in another country, left him there, and grabbed the best, most expensive liquor which he sold in his store for less than the factory. Well then, the people paid attention and began to spy. One day he fell into the trap. All the merchants rebelled against the priest because nobody was buying their merchandise. (Manuel Dzib Palominos, personal communication; translated by author)

What should we make of all this? Does it mean that Way Kot is not the critical commentary it appeared to be at the outset? Is the criticism of commerce misplaced?[14] I think not, although it might be safer to say that criticism is being directed against certain business practices or certain businessmen, rather than commerce itself. To put things in perspective, it's helpful to think once more about the merchant's peculiar co-referent, the witch or spiritist, and the public discourse that envelops such individuals. While residents of Maxcanú recognize that it is sometimes necessary to consult a spiritist in order to discover the origin of an illness or to counteract its negative effects, the spiritist's knowledge and power make him or her an object of enduring suspicion, a necessary evil.[15] Therefore, if merchants are truly analogous to witches as Way Kot suggests, it's not surprising that they are thought of as good, or at least necessary, in one instant, and evil or dangerous in the next.

Indeed, the idea that way kot can be either good or bad (or was originally good but turned bad) is presented in a brief summary of the tale in Boccara's encyclopedia (1997, Vol. 6, 89). Appropriately titled "*Le fils du Way Pop ou le bon et le mauvais Way Pop*" (The child of Way Pop or the good and evil Way Pop), the story presents the way pop as an honorable merchant who helps the poor. His son, however, is evil incarnate. The latter not only demands huge sums of money from his father, bringing the elder merchant near ruin, but abuses his adoptive sister.

Such ambiguity is hardly surprising. As myths from ancient Greece to Hollywood (e.g., *Star Wars*) reveal, evil and good often originate from the same source. Still, acknowledging this draws attention to the fact that the way kot himself is a self-contained contradiction or, to borrow once more from Adorno, is one of those images that becomes more paradoxical the "more insistently it is observed".

Conclusion

Like Lévi-Strauss (1963, 230), I believe that myths—at least some myths—contain their own incisive logic. These stories offer a creative way of exploring conundrums that are seldom obvious to outsiders. At the same time, however, I think it would be wrong to reduce myth to a methodology for solving arcane puzzles. Speaking of commerce in the idiom of witchcraft suggests that there is more at stake than cracking unsolved mysteries or explaining the opaque nature of capitalist exchange. It suggests that a judgment is being cast upon the morality of the marketplace and those who participate in it. Whereas institutions of bourgeois society attempt to make commodities enchant, the story of Way Kot presents commodity consumption as a form of cannibalism in which the rich eat the poor or, worse, in which unsuspecting Maya eat their brethren. As the narrator in Version 1 comments, the goods brought back by way kot are "*pura lozas*" (luxury goods), a devilish seduction that leads Maya villagers to participate in their own destruction. Indeed, by characterizing the tale as an historia, the narrator indicates his awareness of its rhetorical/didactic function, not the veracity of every image or trope. Historias, as Sullivan notes, are "colorful and exciting, but they may contain truth, as well—lessons for present or future generations of . . . common people" (Sullivan 1989, 186).

The interpretation of Way Kot as a form of rhetoric—a counterpoint to the commodity aesthetics of the era—is strengthened by the concerns that other classes, including the peninsular elite, expressed about the growth of commerce. Protests from this quarter might appear ironic since the Yucatecan elite apparently had much to gain from the new economy; however, as Appadurai notes (1988, 33), "whereas merchants tend to be social representatives of unfettered equivalence, new commodities, and strange tastes, political elites tend to be the custodians of restricted exchange, fixed commodity systems, established tastes, and sumptuary customs."

Finally, I would argue that the reason Marx's writing provides an effective vehicle for analyzing Way Kot is not because the Maya are in some sense proto-Marxists, or that peasant thought is governed by dialectical reason, but because Marxism itself is part of a rhetorical tradition—stretching from Aristotle to St. Thomas Aquinas and somewhat beyond—that not only emphasizes the importance of labor but questions the value of the merchant and the moneylender alike. As Parry and Bloch note, it "was essentially this idea of material production ... which prompted Tawney to remark that Marx was the last of the true schoolmen" (1989, 3).

CHAPTER SIX

CAUGHT IN THE SPIRIT
Possession, Prophecy, and Resistance

Two things stand out in the recent literature on spirit possession. The first is that it appears to be increasing on a global scale. Although one might expect a reporting bias in the ethnographic literature reflecting the growth of transcultural psychiatry and medical anthropology in recent decades, Erika Bourguignon (2004) insists that anthropological interest is easily matched by a changing reality on the ground. The growth of spirit possession has been fostered not only by the emergence of new religions such as New Age spirituality and the renewal of mystical traditions within older religions (e.g., exorcism) but also by the movement of medico-religious ideas and practices in somewhat unpredictable ways. While the spread of Kardecian spiritism throughout Latin America (discussed below) can be seen as the dissemination and adaptation of an elite discourse, a movement from core to periphery, Bourguignon points out that the opposite can occur as well: as a reaffirmation of their ethnic identity, educated transplants in the industrialized world become involved with possession cults originating in their homeland. This idea is well articulated in the work of Karen McCarthy Brown (1991) on Vodou priestesses in Brooklyn, New York and their followers (including Brown herself).

The other point, almost a tacit assumption by now, is that therapies involving spirit possession or spirit mediums are not directed simply at physical or medically defined bodies but at the social and political bodies in which disease or affliction is experienced (Comaroff 1985; Certeau 2000).[1] Indeed, efficacy studies such as Kaja Finkler's *Spiritualist Healers in Mexico* (1977) have given way to studies that examine possession cults as thinly veiled protest movements (Lewis 1989) or as vehicles for commenting on oppression and inequality. In the *Possessed and the Dispossessed,* for example, Leslie Sharp emphasizes the ways in which Tromba mediums help urban workers cope with life in a plantation economy through their "critiques of community life and its tensions, the meaning of work ... and the dynamics of local power relations over time" (1993, 3). In short, as Michael Lambek argues (1989), the anthropological interest in spirit possession has followed a gradual but inexorable movement from "disease to discourse."

In Yucatán, as opposed to Africa and certain parts of Latin America, interest in spirit possession has been relatively restrained. While there is no shortage of research on "folk medicine" or the much-celebrated Maya shaman, little has been written about the female spiritist who has come to stand in his place. Much of this, I believe, has to do with our concern about the authenticity of traditions of "recent vintage." Shamans, though greatly disparaged at the beginning of the twentieth century, are now seen as the remnants of a long and glorious past in which they served as healers, ritual specialists, and community leaders. They are also noteworthy symbols of cultural and political resistance. As the Argentine anthropologist Miguel Bartolomé writes: "all the rebellions and insurrections, including those following Independence, were led by priests and shamans" (1988, 33). Spiritists, in contrast, seem to exist beyond the pale of regional history. If some concept of them exists, it is as charlatans, inscrutable and unscrupulous individuals who take advantage of poor, ignorant, and desperately sick individuals. From Robert Redfield's perspective, spiritism was little more than a source of "corruption" or "confusion" (1941, 244, 323) and in the words of Donald Stoll, it encouraged "amoral clientalistic relations with a plethora of deities" (quoted in Goodman 2001, 6).[2] In short, seen faintly and from a distance, spiritism is most notable in terms of its differences with shamanism. It is the shadowy side of well-worn oppositions between male and female, genuine and spurious, past and present, good and evil.

This raises an interesting question. If shamans are now greatly revered (at least by anthropologists), and spiritists are highly despised, what accounts for the growing popularity of spiritism at the moment when shamanism, at least in western Yucatán, appears to be in irreversible decline? And in what way, if any, are these two phenomena connected? By 1990, as I noted in the Preface to this book, finding a shaman or observing an *u hanli kol* ceremony, the milpa ceremony described by Redfield and Villa Rojas, was not an easy task. On the other hand, it was not difficult to find a spiritist who was willing to conduct a ritual cleansing (santiguaár) or affect magical cures.

In my view, there is no simple solution to this question. Gender, economy, and medicine are all implicated in this transformation; nevertheless, it seems safe to say that the growth of spiritism has little to do with medical efficacy, at least in any obvious or direct way. Spiritism's appeal, I believe, has more to do with the ability of the spiritist to incorporate herself and her clients within a highly valorized prophetic tradition, a narrative form that is at once critical of modernity and enthralled by its ineffable power. Efficacy, to the extent that it exists, must be sought within the narrative and its somewhat ambiguous signs. Therefore, if anthropologists and members of the regional intelligentsia have tended to emphasize discontinuity between "folk medicine" and modern medicine, spiritists have gained popularity by emphasizing continuity with shamanism in the most bodily way.

In The Spirit of the Times

While residents of Maxcanú tend to view spiritism as an outgrowth and, in some cases, a degeneration of traditional Maya medicine, the roots of contemporary spiritism extend back to late-nineteenth-century Europe, specifically the metaphysical healing tradition associated with Allan Kardec of France. And like other staples of rural life—the jarana, beer, and baseball—spiritism entered the peninsula via Mérida's upper class. The earliest and, to my knowledge, the only historical source on nineteenth-century spiritism in the peninsula is the *La ley de amor* (The Law of Love; volumes cited below are from this journal and are indicated by LA and number in the text; translations are my own). This was a journal published by the Círculo Espirista de Mérida in the 1870s and rediscovered in the 1930s by Asael Hansen, a colleague of Robert Redfield who was writing an ethnography of Mérida at the time.[3]

Established in 1874 "under the name of its protector spirit, the humble Peralta" the circle was composed "in large part by studious youths and illustrious individuals" (LA 1, 1); the first issue of their journal was published in 1876. From the beginning, members of the Peralta Circle viewed spiritism as a philosophy rather than an assortment of healing techniques and hoped that its growth would help resuscitate the authentic spirit of Christianity, a

FIGURE 6.1 Mérida in the 1930s. Courtesy of the University of Yucatán

spirit buried by the Catholic Church and its rigid dogmas. In an editorial published on February 28, 1877, the editor asks rhetorically whether spiritism should be considered a religion and answers:

> Yes, if by religion one simply means the love of God and his neighbor ... but not in the sense that is generally attributed to the word.... What virtue can there be in blindly, or mechanically following, making oneself believe, in repeating what one was taught as a child, submitting oneself unconsciously to passive obedience, or ignoring the sacred flame of intelligence that God has placed in front of him. (LA 2, 25)

In place of Catholic priests, spiritists substituted mediums capable of receiving advice from prominent, recently deceased individuals. In fact, prior to beginning publication of *La ley de amor*, W.G. Canton, the medium of the Mérida circle, asked the spirit Peralta what he thought about launching the new journal. Speaking in perfect Castilian, an indication of his prominent pedigree, Peralta warned that the new venture would invite hatred and persecution: "You shall bring on hatred, persecution, and much ill will in weak and backward spirits. You shall cause great discord in many families. You ... will suffer" (LA 1, 1). However, in spite of this dire warning Peralto final gave W.G. Canton the go-ahead.

While participants in the Mérida circle believed that spiritism would gain adherents by force of the better argument and the use of good examples, they sought to avoid rancor and acrimonious debate. "We detest disputes," wrote a member in the first issue, "because it is the mother of error and the child of ... vanity, but we love tranquil and sustained discussion because from this emerges light" (LA 1, 3). Spiritists of this era also had great faith in science and labored diligently to convince the scientific community to accept their ideas about medicine and the human body. In particular, they believed that the body contained magnetic fluids in greater or lesser quantities that could help mitigate the suffering of ailing humanity (LA 1, 96). Unfortunately, in the 800-plus pages published between 1876 and 1878 accounts of healing involving the use of magnetic fluids are few and far between. From the little that is written on this topic one can assume that touch, or the placement of the practitioner's hands on the patient's body, was of central importance, but it would be difficult to say more. Apparently, the medical aspect of spiritism was of little importance during the early years.

As noted above, the Peralta Circle consisted of the cream of Yucatecan society; however, it wasn't long before other groups were formed, including a spiritist circle in a barrio of Campeche. This new circle was "composed mostly of artisans and villagers [*personas del pueblo*]," and the medium was a simple shoemaker (LA 1, 95). Around the same time, two exclusively female circles were formed, one composed of six of the most notable and distinguished women of Ciudad Victoria in Tamaulipas, and the other in San Juan Bautista, Tabasco. As for Yucatán, the journal mentions that by April 1877 spiritist circles had been established in many of the principal towns but avoided naming them in order to protect their members from the "evil of religious fanaticism that still exists in many of them" (LA 2, 56).

The formation of spiritist circles in Yucatán may also have been influenced by the spiritualist movement founded by Roque Rojas in Mexico in 1861 and described by various writers (Finkler 1985; Quezada 1989; Anzures y Bolaños 1983). According to his biography, "[the founder's] body was bathed in a luminous light at birth," and between the ages of five and 12 he had a "gift for discovering the location of lost items." He joined a seminary but had to leave for financial reasons; then, on June 23, 1861, an angel visited him and informed him that he was "elected to be the Strong Rock of Israel ... to repair, clean, and level the road to the new city of Israel" (Anzures y Bolaños 1983, 124–25). Although several writers, including Kaja Finkler (1985), make a point of distinguishing spiritism from spiritualism—which developed in the US and spread south—both movements, at least in their Mexican phase, can be considered products of La Reforma, a new era of religious tolerance, individual rights, and progress ushered in by President Benito Juárez in 1855. Perhaps as a reflection of their mid-nineteenth-century origins, both doctrines incorporate the concept of evolution in order to distinguish spirits who are well developed from primitive or backward ones. Both also profess a belief in adhering to simple Christian values, although neither "observes or recognizes the Roman rite" (Anzures y Bolaños 1983, 121). And, finally, like spiritists, the majority of spiritualists are women who are knowledgeable of herbs and act as mediums for the spirits of deceased healers.

Spiritism of the 1930s

The only other primary source on spiritism in the peninsula that I have found is Asael Hansen's fieldnotes, compiled in the 1930s and edited and published in 1984 by Juan Bastarrachea Manzano. In the 1930s Hansen was still able to find members of Mérida's upper class who identified themselves as spiritists and who viewed spiritism as an alternative religious or philosophical system. His notes even contain the street address of a veteran medium who ran a training program and channeled the most illustrious spirits: "Erudite people penetrated her body and expounded on philosophical and moral topics" (Hansen and Bastarrachea Manzano 1984, 285). This was a "good spiritist center," but centers such as this were few and far between. According to Hansen's more educated informants, spiritism had not only become a working-class vocation, it had lost its philosophical focus. The spiritism of the 1930s no longer emphasized scientific experiments, brotherly love, or dispassionate debate but centered on magical cures, retrieving errant spouses, and punishing adulterers. In his journal entry for the fall of 1934, Hansen writes:

> For every person who considers himself a spiritist and who views spiritism as a religious institution, there are hundreds of others that simply consider it another technique for connecting to the supernatural. For them it is simply a procedure for curing illnesses, locating something that has been lost or stolen or punishing personal enemies. With spiritism it is possible to do anything that you can do with other types of magic. (Hansen and Bastarrachea Manzano 1984, 286)

The nature of spiritist practice was also transformed by the assimilation of shamanic concepts and black magic. Contemporary spiritists still spoke of magnetic fluids, but they were now easily confused with the evil winds (*malos vientos*) of the Maya shaman. While the nineteenth-century spiritist thought that magnetic fluids could be mobilized to alleviate suffering, the twentieth-century spiritist considered them evil or dangerous and sought their removal.

As spiritism made its way from the parlor room to the popular quarters of Mérida, the sessions took on the character of the marketplace. They not only brought together men, women, and people of different ages but individuals from different ethnic groups and different social classes, not to mention foreign-born anthropologists. Moreover, while communication between the living and the dead had been conducted in Castilian in the 1870s with an air of solemnity, a cacophony of different voices spoken in different languages could now be heard. Talented physicians from Mérida and the US still made their appearance in spirit, but they now had to compete with *yerbateros* (herbalists) from rural communities like Chichimila and spoke a more colloquial brand of Spanish. In short, the sessions had become more animated, more multilingual, and less predictable.

The spirits, as Hansen and Bastarrachea Manzano note (1984, 285), had also become rather "capricious." In the session Hansen observed on January 4, 1933, all the protocols were carefully observed. The medium, Doña Victoria, washed her hands with *ruda* (a special herb) and made sure that all the participants removed their jewelry. The vestibule was treated with smoke in order to expel malevolent spirits, and the table was carefully set with a washbasin, a large bottle, and a glass, all filled with water. As prescribed, Doña Victoria sat with her eyes closed and breathing deeply as two long prayers were read from an unnamed volume of spiritist devotions. From the very beginning, however, there were problems. The first spirit, a North American named Dr. Hyman, not only lied about his identity—referring to himself as Pascual Rodríguez—but refused to work because there weren't any flowers on the table. As Hansen later learned from Doña Concha, one of the participants, Dr. Hyman not only refused to work without flowers but frequently insisted that they be white and placed in an attractive vase. In fact, on a previous occasion he became so enraged about the clay vase Doña Concha had placed on the table in her house that he grabbed it and smashed in on the floor (Hansen and Bastarrachea Manzano 1984, 287).

Following Dr. Hyman's departure, things calmed down for a short time. A more agreeable physician, Leonardo Contreras, took possession of Doña Victoria and began to instruct her. The first patient was her nephew. While her brother held the young child, Doña Victoria treated him for an unknown, or at least unnoted, illness. After washing her hands once more in the herbs, she rubbed the child's body several times, shaking her hands violently following each pass in order to remove excess magnetic fluid. She then massaged the child's front and back, pulled on his fingers and toes, and concluded the treatment by pinching his back until he yelled. Following two similar treatments, Dr. Contreras departed and was replaced by Máximo Cen, a yerbatero during the earthly phase of his existence.

Máximo Cen instructed Doña Victoria in the treatment of Doña Concha, who had been very sick. After washing once more with *ruda,* the spiritist passed her hands over the face and neck of the sick woman, then made large sweeping gestures over the lower part of her body until she reached the ground. Doña Concha was then instructed to sit down so her knees and feet could be treated. Following this, Máximo Cen dictated an identical treatment for Lupe, a woman of about 20 who was reluctant to participate "because she didn't like being cured and wasn't sick" (Hansen and Bastarrachea Manzano 1984, 284). The famous yerbatero then departed without incident.

During the final episode, however, things began to get out of hand once more. After a violent coughing episode that almost caused Doña Victoria to vomit—presumably the ill effect of ingesting too much magnetic fluid— María May, a yerbatera from Chichimila, made her appearance. Like Dr. Hyman, María turned out to be rather intransigent. Although considered a magnificent healer, the young yerbatera had a reputation for causing mischief and, according to one participant, had killed her own mother. She also insisted on speaking Yucatec Mayan. One of the "brothers" at the January 4 session tried to persuade her to speak Spanish since some of the participants didn't understand Mayan, but María refused. In fact, after chatting casually in Mayan with Doña Concha for some time, she invited Hansen to ask a question in English in order to demonstrate that spirits understand all the languages, but then refused to answer him. Hansen was later informed that María May only spoke English when she was drunk, apparently a rather common occurrence. Indeed, during a *kex* ceremony—a traditional Maya curing ritual—hosted by Doña Concha, María became so drunk from inhaling liquor that she berated the host's husband for not following her instructions regarding the offering and spit a mouthful of rum and anis liquor in the poor man's face (Hansen and Bastarrachea Manzano 1984, 286).

If spiritism had infiltrated working-class Mérida neighborhoods by 1935, it was yet to make a significant appearance in the countryside, at least judging from classical ethnographies like Redfield's *Chan Kom* and *The Folk Culture of Yucatán*. Describing the marginal individuals who lived in Dzitás—a railroad town in the interior of the state where his wife, Margaret Park Redfield, was conducting fieldwork—Redfield refers to a woman from Guadalajara as "the sole exponent of spiritualism . . . and [one] who is looked on by many of her neighbors as a dabbler in witchcraft" (1941, 151).

By 1985, however, the situation had changed considerably. Spiritists were now commonplace and shamans were increasingly difficult to find, at least in the western part of the state. In fact, in an admittedly vain attempt at humor for *The Hunter-Gatherer* (the University of Chicago student newsletter), I described my ill-fated attempt to locate a shaman during my first summer in Yucatán (see Preface). A couple of years later, I did get the opportunity to observe an u hanli kol conducted by an entertaining shaman from Kopoma, but events like this, as the shaman and several onlookers noted, were increasingly rare. On the other hand, by the late 1980s there were at least six female spiritists in Maxcanú, women who not only continued certain shamanic rituals but had introduced healing practices of non-native origin. In addition to receiving a santiguaár or *barrida* (literally, sweeping), I was treated for *tip'te* (stomach pain), a malady that results from the dislocation of a ball that, according to the Maya conception of human anatomy, is located just behind the navel. If the ball is pushed up for some reason—perhaps as a result of heavy physical labor—it can cause respiratory difficulties. If it is pushed down, it can lead to gastrointestinal problems. According to other accounts, tip'te is caused when an object resembling a ball of yarn unravels and the yarn-like strands begin to move into different parts of the body. Consequently, one way to cure the condition, as I learned the hard way, is to place the tip of a towel in one's navel and twist it tighter and tighter, metaphorically if not physically rewinding the ball. Other, less traditional aspects of the spiritist repertoire included invisible surgery, fortune telling with tarot cards, the preparation of talismans, recitation of prayers to attract a loved one or to counteract witchcraft, and channeling spirits of deceased healers.

Why has spiritism become so popular? In my view, there is no simple explanation; a variety of factors that have converged to limit or undermine shamanism are apparently less detrimental to spiritism and may even promote its growth. First, it should be recalled that Maxcanú is located within the perimeter of the old henequén zone, an historical circumstance that has limited the autonomy of community life as well as the importance of milpa agriculture and maize production. Given the close association of shamanism and maize production, it is not difficult to understand how the decline of the latter would affect the former. On the other hand, spiritist discourse and practice is virtually, if not entirely, disconnected from milpa agriculture, so it has not been affected by the decline of milpa production. As noted above, spiritism was originally an urban phenomenon and is still connected to the city through various specialty shops.[4] In addition to the disparate services they provide, spiritists serve as intermediaries between their clients and businesses in Mérida that sell amulets, religious icons, magic powders, and other items used in healing sessions. In short, they are mediums in more than one sense of the term, and their sales of such objects probably contribute significantly to their household income.

Secondly, given the fact that shamanism was and is a predominantly male sphere of action, and spiritism an exclusively female domain, one should consider the manner in which modernization has influenced—and been influenced by—gender relations. With the advent of new products and foreign styles adopted by men, women have increasingly come to represent the "traditional" pole of regional social life. They are not only far more likely to be monolingual Mayan speakers than their husbands, but they are more likely to retain elements of the traditional folk costume of Yucatán. Women, as even casual observers will note, are also far more likely to attend the Catholic mass, an activity that, due to the growth of Protestantism (Goodman 2001), is increasingly viewed as a symbol of regional tradition in its own right. Consequently, it can be argued that the substitution of spiritists for shamans as the new "conservators of traditional medicine," or Maya medicine, is a transformation that makes sense within the broader logic of gender relations in Yucatán, not to mention other parts of Mesoamerica (Hendrickson 1995). This, of course, is not intended to suggest that tradition or what is classified as "traditional" is unchanging—quite the contrary, as the example of Catholicism shows—but simply that as the opposition between tradition and modernity is redefined, it is increasingly female practitioners who serve to define the "traditional."

Gender is important in other ways as well. Given the fact that most physicians—whether in private practice or in the social security clinic—are male, it is hardly surprising that the advent of western medicine has had a greater impact on shamans than on spiritists. Modern medicine involves many invasive procedures. Physicians not only probe and prod female genitalia but routinely ask questions or perform physical examinations that violate local conceptions of modesty. Spiritism, in contrast, provides a venue in which embarrassing situations can be avoided and in which women can speak to other women about medical or spiritual issues.

It would be wrong to romanticize spiritism or to overlook the negative stereotypes that surround it. Spiritists are not only roundly condemned by the churches and the medical profession but by other spiritists who resent unwanted competition in a tight market. However, the attraction of spiritism can partly be explained by the effect of the negative stories—sometimes tragic, often comical—about the impersonal nature of modern scientific medicine, and about modernity more generally, that abound in Maxcanú. For example, one story that received wide circulation recounts the travails of a resident who went to visit his wife at the social security hospital in Mérida where she had just given birth. After speaking with his wife, the husband approached an attendant in the nursery and asked which child belonged to him. Her curt response, according to the story, was "who knows, just take one." Doctors at the local social security clinic are also viewed with suspicion because of their association with the federal government and because they are fulfilling a year of public service required for licensure. Even the most dedicated physicians are referred to as *practicantes* (practicing physicians), a not so subtle way of comparing a clinical visit to a clinical experiment. Less talented or less popular physicians are sometimes referred to as *matasanos* (literally, people who kill the healthy), a form of censure reserved for those whose lack of experience or virtue could result in the death of an otherwise healthy individual.

In contrast, those who visit spiritists are assured of a qualified doctor or shaman since the client herself can select the healing spirit. The only requirement is that the person called upon has already died. In fact, it is this tendency to keep things personal that explains why Hansen was warned to "ask the spirit where he exercised his profession" if nobody present recognized the name of the individual invoked (Hansen and Bastarrachea Manzano 1984, 286). This practice also, of course, suggests that the biography or reputation of the spirit is an essential feature of the treatment narrative. Indeed, while Bastarrachea Manzano and, perhaps, Hansen himself felt obligated to change the names of living individuals discussed in the Mérida monograph, Hansen felt it was important to discuss the names and reputation of the spirits who attended the pseudonymous Doña Victoria's seances.

Who, then, do spiritists in Maxcanú invoke, and why? While a variety of spirits, including those of western doctors, may be summoned, one of the more popular spirits, I was told, is that of Máximo Cen, who coincidentally had "appeared" at Doña Victoria's home in 1931. According to Maxcanú residents who know of him through stories their parents or grandparents tell, Máximo Cen was a famous prophet and shaman who lived sometime during the nineteenth century inside Satsunsat, a labyrinth located within the pre-classic Maya site of Oxkintok. Referring to this labyrinth in 1843 as "La cueva de Maxcanú" (The Cave of Maxcanú), the intrepid John Stephens described it as a place that "had a marvelous and mystical reputation" and that instilled great fear: the eight men Stephens had recruited to enter the labyrinth refused to follow him in. Only after threatening to withhold their pay did they agree to follow Stephens who, a bit apprehensive himself, entered with a "candle in one hand and a pistol in the other" (1963, Vol. 1, 139–40).[5]

Similarly, describing contemporary perceptions, Amador Naranjo notes that it is difficult to find anyone who hasn't experienced at least one unusual event while passing by these ruins: "Prodigious and mysterious events occur when one walks through an archaeological city or passes by a mound; especially at noontime or at midnight individuals are likely to hear voices, sounds, music, and may even have spiritual visions" (1987, 68).

Like other archaeological sites, the power and mystery of Satsunsat is enhanced by the presence of *alux,* mischievous beings made of clay or ceramics that periodically come to life. Referring to a small clay head he found in a milpa near Chan Kom, Redfield recounts that a villager immediately identified it as an alux and pointed to a hole in the back of the head where the soul entered and brought it to life. Redfield's informant then went on to mention that he "saw one of these beings, animated, a few years ago in Ticimul and [told] of the experience in some detail" (1964, 147). Though small, I was told that alux can pack a powerful punch; consequently, people who visit archaeological sites are warned not to disturb their surroundings and to leave small offerings, such as burning cigarettes, for the alux to enjoy. More importantly, it is the alux who grant shamans and sorcerers their powers (Naranjo 1989, 68).

Máximo Cen's powers were reportedly so great that, unlike followers of Alain Kardec, he did not have to lay hands on an afflicted individual to restore him to good health. Simply being in the shaman's presence was enough to relieve the afflicted person of pain or illness. Máximo Cen was able to predict when the rains would come and when drought would occur; in addition, he foretold the arrival of a day when brother would kill brother.

Memories of Máximo Cen also intersect with stories about his brother Jacinto Cen, who not only lived in the famous labyrinth but who predicted the arrival of many twentieth-century inventions. According to a somewhat cryptic account penned by Don Rogelio, a local guide who explored the labyrinth as a youth:[6]

Jacinto Cen was a prophet. He predicted the days that remained before the appearance of certain vehicles, *ho huacax kak* [car; literally, motorized cow or fire cow], as well as the airplane, *pepen kak* [literally, motorized butterfly], and the telephone wire, *anicab* [literally, vines]. With these wires foreigners will communicate with their families [using] the telephone. Foreigners will marry Indian women. Before the year 2000 Oxkintok will be restored with the help of foreigners and they will make hot tortillas. The prophet Jacinto Cen wrote at night with the plume of a bird using hieroglyphs, like the Chinese letters of today. Nobody understood them. He never associated with the wealthy, only with the peasants, and when he left Santa Cruz he said goodbye to a woman. Jacinto Cen was a very tall man, two meters, and [had] brown straight hair, white clothing without buttons, and short pants (*pantalon xort*). Everything Don Jacinto, the man of Oxkintok, said is already coming to pass. This is what my grandmother told me.

In short, then, while spiritism is surely many things—a form of therapy, a way of making money, even a way of killing time—I argue that it is, above all, a poorly understood narrative form, a verbal performance that not only brings the sick and the weak together with the strong (individuals with great prognostic as well as diagnostic powers) but associates the suffering of the former with that of the latter. By hosting or channeling prophets of great renown, spiritism incorporates both the spiritist and her client within a prophetic discourse in which symbols of Maya identity and the past—dress, language, writing, even physiognomy—hold great importance.

Rogelio's reference to *pantalon xort* provides one interesting example of this connection. At first it confused me since it is mostly tourists and middle-class youth who wear shorts; however, after some discussion it turned out that *xort* was intended as the "Spanish" translation for the Yucatec Mayan *ex,* an early twentieth-century garment similar to an Indian dhoti; it was made out of rough-hewn cotton and wrapped around the legs and groin. Therefore, mention of *pantalon xort* recalls a different, dimly remembered time when Maya villagers had not yet adopted western dress and could be readily distinguished from their oppressors. It is interesting to note that the garment is sometimes viewed as a sign of servility or subordination.[7] Like other artifacts of early twentieth-century dress, it evokes memories of the epoch of slavery, especially in more historically conceived narratives; however, as Paul Sullivan notes, to abandon the clothing of one's ancestors for manufactured clothing is viewed as a sign of capitulation and a cause of pain and suffering in prophetic discourse:

> There will come the hour of your clothing
> yourselves with the clothes of the foreigner.
> It will number three layers, your clothes . . .
> There will be passed by the door of your homes
> everything proclaimed for you to buy.
> But just for a short time, not for all the year.
> When that has happened like that, it will get painful.
> It will get somewhat difficult for us.
> (Sullivan 1989, 174)

The use of clothing to index class differences or the opposition between native and foreigner is also underscored by Rogelio's statement that "he [Jacinto Cen] never associated with the wealthy, only with peasants." Indeed, what seems to unify somewhat diverse stories about Máximo and Jacinto

Cen, as well as other famous prophets such as Lauriano Ojeda and Enoch, is their rejection of both the upper class and the modern world.

Taken in this light, Rogelio's reference to the grand inventions of the twentieth century—the car, the airplane, and the telephone—not only serves as an affirmation of the prognostic ability of the prophet (and by extension the diagnostic capabilities of the spiritist) but as an index of social disintegration since such inventions invariably accompany fratricide, miscegenation, and domination by foreigners, as described below. Rogelio's narrative, in fact, resembles in content, if not in poetic form, the prophecies of Maya leaders such as Florentino Cituk who governed rebel Maya living in the jungles of Quintana Roo during the first decades of the twentieth century:[8]

> There will be the passing of running-fire [motor-vehicles]
> There will be the passing of bird-fire [airplanes]
> There will be running by wound-around-vines [bicycles]
> There will be tautly planted the roots of the anikab[9] vine in my
>   blessed town.
> He [Cituk] did not say what these things are that he spoke of thus,
> but he knew that they would be.
> (Sullivan 1989, 167)

Rogelio's description of Jacinto Cen as a "night writer" also points directly to Florentino Cituk, as do the themes of prophecy and resistance. During the first part of the twentieth century, Florentino Cituk, "undertook night-long vigils praying to Our Lord True God in the main church of the sacred village called Chun Pom" and, as a reward for his pious behavior, was blessed "with the knowledge of 'night writing'—prophecy," although he was otherwise illiterate (Sullivan 1989, 4). In a community where literacy is the prized possession of a relatively small group, reading or writing even in the daytime may be considered a magical art or a source of unusual power,[10] since they are, after all, another way of communicating with dead people. But writing at night is even more mysterious because this is the time when witchcraft, sorcery, and other unusual occurrences take place.

The ability to write in hieroglyphics with the simplest of technologies, the plume of a bird, can also be understood as an attempt to valorize the Maya past and, perhaps, lay claim to a type of knowledge that is not only being appropriated by outsiders (e.g., epigraphers, archaeologists) but is sometimes attributed to them as well. Throughout much of colonial and post-colonial history, visitors as well as homebred intellectuals have repeatedly questioned whether the Maya built the resplendent cities that dot the Yucatán peninsula. Did native builders construct Chichén Itzá and Uxmal, or were these the vestiges of ancient Egyptian architects? In his 1847 account, *Incidents of Travel in the Yucatán,* a sequel of sorts to the earlier *Incidents of Travel in the Near East,* John Stephens weighed in on the side of native builders if in a rather unflattering way. Recalling the grandeur of the tombs of Thebes, Stephens asserted that the rude construction at Uxmal could not have been done by Egyptian craftsmen: "It was on their tombs that the Egyptians lavished their skill, industry, and wealth, and no people, brought up in Egyptian schools, descended from Egyptians, or deriving their lessons from them would ever have constructed in so conspicuous a place so rude a sepulchre" (Stephens 1963 [1843], 165). Other writers, however, were not persuaded and the search for external sources of civilization continued throughout the nineteenth century. In this light, the prophecies of Jacinto Cen can be seen as an attempt to reconnect the present to a past that had become detached or dissociated from it through skepticism and racism.

Following this line of interpretation it seems safe to assume that the "Santa Cruz" Rogelio refers to near the end of his narrative is Santa Cruz de Bravo in Quintana Roo, the capital established by rebel Maya following the Caste War of 1848. Or is it? The first time I went over Rogelio's account, I thought he was naming a small agricultural community near the recently restored archaeological site of Oxkintok where the labyrinth in which the prophet lived is situated, a site halfway between Calcehtok and Maxcanú. Only after I learned more about Jacinto Cen and began to note parallels between him and prophets such as Florentino Cituk, did I begin to think about the other Santa Cruz, the sacred center of Maya sovereignty during the late nineteenth century. Ambiguity, however, often leads to new insights, and it now seems clear that the narrative occurs in both places, Santa Cruz de Bravo and Oxkintok. In other words, given the sacred character of Santa Cruz de Bravo, I believe it is best to think of Oxkintok as the "localization of theophany" to borrow Mirced Eliade's famous phrase, that is, an attempt to inscribe the narrator's place of residence within the larger prophetic landscape.

Understanding the place of "foreigners" in prophetic discourse also raises some thorny interpretative problems. As both Paul Sullivan and Allan Burns have noted, rebel Maya often viewed foreigners, particularly Britons or North Americans, as allies or potential allies in their fight against the federal government. Sullivan (1989) describes numerous attempts by rebel Maya to secure arms and ammunition from Sylvanus Morley and other archaeologists working in Yucatán during the early decades of the twentieth century. Similarly, Burns (1977) notes that he was regularly asked for money, ammunition, and material aid to fight Mexicans on "Maya territory" long after pacification of the region had been officially completed.

In the present case, however, foreigners are neither US nor British citizens but an old nemesis, the Spaniard. As Jacinto Cen had predicted, the restoration of Oxkintok was just beginning "with the help of foreigners," when Rogelio first told me the story in 1985. In fact, it would probably be more

accurate to say that the restoration of Oxkintok had been undertaken by foreigners with the help of local residents, since the operation was actually being
coordinated by a group of archaeologists from the Universidad Complutense
de Madrid who would excavate during the day and tap dance in the back of a
pick-up truck at night. From my vantage point, "los Españoles," as they were
always described, made a concerted effort to build a good relationship with
the community. They produced a colorful Spanish-language publication each
year that highlighted their discoveries and explained their work-in-progress.
Thanks to the resident ethnographer, *Oxkintok 1*, as it was plainly titled,
included a picturesque description of Maxcanú and featured the portraits
and words of prominent local residents. The work on the site also provided
much-needed employment for local residents; one was hired to teach the
"Spaniards" how to speak Yucatec Mayan. However, in spite of these efforts,
or, perhaps simply because the visiting mission was Spanish, residents of
Maxcanú were quick to find fault with them. Simple phonological differences
between Yucatecan and continental Spanish—such as pronunciation of the
theta (i.e., the "th" sound)—were seen as evidence of Spanish arrogance,
and more than a few individuals began to mock the speech of the visitors
by pronouncing the Spanish theta in a very exaggerated way. Some residents
referred to the archaeological excavation as the first episode in the reconquest
of Mexico and joked that the Spaniards had come back to search for the gold
that had eluded them during the original conquest. The fact that the head of
the Spanish archaeological mission was named Miguel Dorado (Golden or
Gilded) didn't help. In any event, during the summer of 1989 rumors spread
throughout the town that the archaeologists had uncovered priceless artifacts
from Oxkintok, including a solid gold frog, and were storing them in the
large two-story house they had rented from a local businessman.

Rogelio's reference to a time when "foreigners will marry Indian women"
also points to a fear of foreign domination, not to mention a certain ambivalence about being mestizo, a product of Spanish and Indian ancestry. While
the mestizo or mestizaje is a potent symbol of unity invoked by regional
and national elites, at the local level, or in less public venues, the mestizo is
commonly viewed as the bastard child of an Indian woman and hacienda
owner, an illegitimate mixing to say the least. In recounting the oral history
of Pustunich in the 1970s, for example, Irwin Press includes a not uncommon story about marriage in the epoch of slavery:

> There once was the Holy Inquisition, which says to the parents that a
> woman who marries must wait eighteen days before the mass can be per-
> formed. So [they took the bride off and] at the passage of eighteen days the
> bride was delivered to the groom and the priests said, "She is now crossed
> with Spanish blood," for they had lain with her, "and all your children
> will be Spanish." All are mixed, all. The bishops were first to get the girl

during these eighteen days, and then she was passed on to the lower-ranking priests. . . . Such were the times. I had not been born yet. My grandfather told me about this. (Press 1975, 285–86)

Other elements of Rogelio's narrative, however, are more difficult to understand. How do we interpret Jacinto Cen's prediction, bland to the point of bewilderment, that people would begin to eat hot tortillas? And what do we make of his prodigious size? Was he really two meters tall? If he were, he would certainly be taller than any Mayan speaker I've met. Is the prophet's large stature simply another way of suggesting that the Maya of earlier times, Maya untrammeled by the ravages of the modern world, were healthier and more robust than they are today? Perhaps. I can think of at least a half-dozen conversations in which elderly Maya men, reclining in their hammocks, would point to a bare light bulb dangling from the ceiling or to a bottle of soda and assert that this was the reason that people were weak or unable to work a full day in the fields. In the end, though, certain pieces of the puzzle simply elude explanation.

Conclusion

Anthropologists (Sahlins 1985) and literary critics (Williams 1983) have often noted, generally with wry skepticism, that the past is always better than the present. Such a statement not only serves as a testament to the power of nostalgia and tradition, something we all presumably know before we enter the field, but also serves to remind us just how easy it is to collect stories about disenchantment with modern life in the poor, out-of-the-way places anthropologists perennially inhabit. And it is. Upon closer examination, we invariably begin to see the gray tones; elements of narrative that we initially considered either positive or negative turn out to be highly ambiguous. The *ex,* a symbol of difference or non-conformity if not outright resistance to modernity, can also be viewed as a symbol of subordination or slavery, not to mention senescence when worn by an elderly resident.

Similarly, artifacts of modernity—syringes and medicines such as penicillin, as well as the foreigners who bring them—are evocative of both hope and fear. Among residents of Maxcanú, the syringe not only calls to mind the malevolent power of the *chin ki'ix,*[11] a sorcerer whose signature is a thorn with a red thread lodged in the rib cage of his victim, but finds its way into stories about Yucatecans who dare to wander the streets of major US cities. "Would I be stabbed by a syringe," I was asked, "if I looked for a job in Chicago?" As noted in the tale of Way Kot, the syringe is part of a new imperious technology used by astute, educated foreigners to enslave naïve Yucatecans. For my informant Lencho and others, however, an injection of penicillin is also a minimal requirement of good medical care (see the Preface). One may surmise that the syringe has become more acceptable because it is seen as a metonym for the "wonder drug," yet it is clear that Mérida residents already had an "inexplicable faith" in injections during Hansen's time, long before penicillin was available. One woman, according to Hansen's notes, had such difficulty convincing doctors of her need for injections that she finally bought her own box of syringes and convinced a neighbor to give them to her. Therefore, if spiritism is undeniably oriented toward the past, privileging the advice of dead people over living ones, it has a complex relationship with modernity. It not only vacillates between alterity and mimesis, identity and difference, but occupies a liminal space between purportedly pure "male" discursive forms, that is, shamanism on the one hand and biomedicine on the other.

By channeling the spirits of well-known shamans or prophets, spiritists not only forge a bond between modernity and tradition, men and women, the living and dead, but continue a long-standing discursive practice—a prophetic ventriloquism—in which simple, profane, and despised individuals provide a voice for the sacred. During the Caste War, prophecies and communiqués of various types were issued through a talking cross. In some instances, it is unclear who actually spoke, whistled, or issued written missives in the name of the cross, a mystery that has occupied historians for many years. Yet, as Nelson Reed points out, at other times it appears that the "organ of the divine" was neither shrouded in secrecy nor a person of great political importance. In the mid-1850s it was a young man named Braulio Puc who "crouched in the pit, projecting his voice into the sound chamber of a sunken barrel" (Reed 2001, 199). What is important is that young Braulio was possessed by the spirit of Jesus Christ.

Nelson goes on to note the functional and semantic similarities between the "organ of the divine" and the pre-Columbian *chilan*—translated as interpreter or intercessor (DMC 99)—suggesting that this oracular tradition is, perhaps, older than we suspect. Consequently, it might be said that spiritism not only maintains continuity with the past through the content of its narrative but also through, in Hayden White's terms (1987), "the content of the form."

CONCLUSION
Linkages in the Global Economy

As I write the conclusion to this long story at California State University, the state continues to slide further into the abyss. Funding for education is being slashed, faculty and staff are being furloughed and laid off, there are no office supplies in the workroom, and it won't be long before our phones are shut off or removed from our offices. The crisis deepens my empathy for the people I lived with during my fieldwork (beginning in 1985) who were hit first by the neoliberal reforms ushered in during the De La Madrid administration (1982–88) and then by the agrarian reforms pushed through by Salinas de Gortari (1988–94). While the first round of reforms reduced state subsidies for basic commodities and government programs for the poor, the second brought an end to the Mexican ejido, the agricultural safety net.

All economic transformations, whether in Yucatán, the US, or Canada, are connected to changes in the way people are urged to think about themselves. When I began teaching at California State University three years ago, I entered with a virtual promise that the teaching load would be reduced by 25 per cent and that the university was becoming more research oriented. We were supposed to remain good teachers, but we were expected to be excellent researchers. Along with the new identity came a new provost, renewed attention to post-tenure review to see if anyone was sleeping at the wheel, a new tenure and promotion document, and the expectation that people who wanted the golden fleece—tenure—would publish more than their predecessors. In short, a new coercive apparatus was put in place in order to reinforce the new identity.

Then the earth moved—not the long-awaited shift in the San Andreas fault but the economy. Almost overnight we were teachers again. In fact, we were told that we had always been teachers. Sabbaticals began to disappear, release time vanished, the deans told us we would have to spend more time in the classroom, and the new provost vanished as quickly as she had appeared. More importantly, normally erudite faculty members began to use simpler language and began to communicate across disciplinary boundaries. They also began to take up the "Weapons of the Weak," as James Scott discusses in his 1987 classic by that name on peasant resistance in Malaysia. Rather than wait for the opportunity to vote on furloughs or layoffs, faculty members and students began to take action, discussing how to slow down or even shut down the university. They not only talked about the chancellor's incompetence, but satirical posters showing that he earned more than the US President quickly surfaced on the Internet. And his palatial office on Golden Drive became the hot spot for holding vigils and showing off the latest political artwork. It was a k'ub pol American-style.

It is too early to write the California story since it is still unfolding. My point is simply to emphasize some of the similarities that are beginning to emerge between anthropologists and the people they study as the pace of globalization increases and we all, increasingly, fall under the control of capital, political corruption, and diminishing state support for social and educational programs.

I am not a postmodernist. I have a hard time understanding a lot of the work that is written in this mode, and most of what I do understand sounds a lot like the writings of early twentieth-century surrealists such as André Breton. I do, however, think that ethnographies are produced through the interaction and dialogue that occurs between ethnographers and the people they live with. What ultimately gets written is greatly influenced by the historical and cultural moment in which it is produced. If this ethnography was published fresh from the "field" in the early 1990s, an era of relative affluence and hope, especially in the US, it would have been a quite different book.

To be sure, the emphasis on coercive assimilation, the key point of Part I, would not have been excluded or diminished. The attempt by religious groups—both Catholic and Protestant—to Christianize the Maya is well documented in previous ethnographies and historical accounts. This continues today as well-funded evangelical groups from the US—Mormon to Bahai—continue to proselytize both in rural villages and large cities. Likewise, efforts by the federal and state governments to re-clothe the Maya in western dress, to drag them (in most cases unwillingly) into the consumer market, and to encourage them to forsake Mayan for Spanish needs no further demonstration. I will never forget Don Asunción's description of being forced to kneel on a bed of pebbles in the hot sun for an hour just because he dared to speak Yucatec Mayan in primary school. While many of the goals of the Lázaro Cárdenas administration (1934–40) were quite laudable (e.g., literacy, land reform, etc.), the overarching aim was to reorient the Maya as "workers" or "peasants" within a modern corporatist state.

As I suggested earlier, the emphasis on assimilation has diminished thanks to charges of cultural genocide made in the 1970s; however, I think it could also be argued that the growth of neoliberalism is quite compatible with the new emphasis on multiculturalism or cultural pluralism so assimilation is no longer needed. Indeed, Charles Hale's description of the Arzú Irigoyen government (1996–2000) in Guatemala, is not, in my view, that different from the recent Vicente Fox administration in Mexico:

> Consistent with this contrast, the administration of Álvaro Arzú Irigoyen (1996–2000) combined an orthodox neoliberal approach to management of the economy—over hostility to labor organizing; full backing of the interests of capital; development through investment in infrastructure and public works; scaling back of state commitments to social welfare and so on—and a *progressive stance on Maya cultural rights*. Ostensibly in contradiction, these two strands of state ideology meld to yield a new mode of governance on the rise throughout Latin America. (Hale 2006, 75; emphasis added)

In fact, such reasoning could help explain why the Center for Indigenous Development (CDI), which in its previous incarnation as the National Indigenous Institute (INI) was a prime mover for cultural assimilation, is now leading efforts to promote teaching Mayan in public elementary schools. Indeed, it could be argued that the new "controlled populism" within the government sector is actually a correlate to decidedly unpopular economic policies being carried out in the private sector.[1]

Hopefully, this book also provides a much better understanding of the way that religion, as seen through gremios or voluntary Catholic associations, and popular performances, such as the jarana, contribute to hierarchy and the maintenance of invidious distinctions between groups. In short, following in Gramsci's footsteps, I believe that control is always much more effective when it is achieved through consent or through tradition rather than through coercion or force.

The emphasis on cultural resistance, the key point of Part II, is, of course, not entirely new. Other ethnographers (Re Cruz 1996; Hervik 1999) have written about the k'ub pol and the tale of Way Kot. However, the subversive logic of either the ritual or the myth has not been explored in such great depth previously. While the former, in particular, has been described as a humorous or profane event, an important distinction has to be made between humor and parody. One is sheer entertainment and is, thus, frivolous; the other is politics "not as usual." Indeed, in my view, better ethnographic writing about Yucatán requires a rediscovery of irony and satire.

There is also still no detailed analysis of contemporary spiritism. Does this have to do with the fact that female spiritists are held in very low regard compared to the highly revered male shamans? Does this represent a male bias within ethnographic studies? Or does it reflect the difficulty inherent in studying a group of individuals who often don't want to be identified by a particular label? I don't know; however, I think the emergence of spiritism, with its link to the prophetic tradition, provides one of the most potent critiques of modernity at the local level. Hopefully, more research on this topic will be forthcoming.

Had I written this book 15 years ago, I probably would have talked more about "invented traditions" and the essentialism inherent in contemporary accounts of the Maya or within what is often referred to as "rescate cultural" (preservation but certainly also reinvention). In 1992, Eric Hobsbawm and Terrance Ranger published *The Invention of Tradition* in which they argued that many practices considered to be traditions of long standing were actually rituals of recent invention, often serving political or commercial interests. For example, the lead chapter in the book, written by Hugh Trevor Roper, pointed out how the "traditional" tartan, used to distinguish one highland Scottish community from another, was developed by the British textile industry and, thus, was not really Scottish at all. Similarly, in Yucatán, many anthropologists have taken great pains to demonstrate that the term "Maya" is a colonial or post-colonial construct rather than a form of self-ascription and point out that even native Mayan speakers tend to refer to themselves as mestizos or Yucatecans (Casteñada 2004; Restall 2004). There is, no doubt, a certain truth to this claim. I was frequently told during my fieldwork that if I wanted to see real Maya I should either visit the Lacandon in Chiapas or venture into the jungles of Quintana Roo where people still spoke legitimate Mayan. Indeed, I would argue that lack of ethnographic writing on spiritism relative to shamanism reflects a deep-seated preference for describing a romantic tradition on the verge of extinction rather than accounting for the fascinating phenomenon that has increasingly come to replace it.

Therefore, while the critique of essentialism represents a necessary corrective to anthropology's emphasis on writing in the "ethnographic present"—a timeless, idealized view of the past prior to western contact—it seems that the discussion of invented traditions not only serves the hegemonic interests of non-indigenous groups, when it comes to land claims, federal recognition, etc., but often undermines anti-colonial indigenous organizations (Clifford 1988; Haunani-Kay 1991; Fischer 1999; Hale 1999; Warren 1998; Loewe 2007). In *Mas que un indio* (More Than an Indian), for example, Charles Hale (2006) points out that ladino, or non-indigenous Guatemalans, love to use the critique of essentialism to undermine the cultural and political aspirations of indigenous groups who have once again come to see themselves as Maya.

The point is this: all traditions are invented. The Israeli folkdances I learned as a child were invented sometime after 1948, and much of the ritual surrounding the British royalty and Buckingham Palace were invented in the early part of the twentieth century. However, indigenous, subaltern, or marginalized groups are, in my view, more likely to suffer negative consequences of this ideology. For this reason, I like Gayatri Spivak's explanation of "strategic

essentialism," a political compromise that allows for "a provisional recupera-
tion and construction of cohesive identities in response to pressures from
without to assimilate to dominant cultural paradigms" (in Underiner 2004, 10).

Or we could return to Harold Gans's felicitous phrase "symbolic ethnicity" (1979), which was originally used to refer to second- or third-generation
Americans who felt a need to celebrate the non-stigmatizing aspects of their
heritage. I could be wrong, but I don't remember hearing much criticism of
third-generation Irish who enrolled in community colleges in Chicago in the
1980s to study Gaelic or of second- and third-generation Jews who decided
to take up Yiddish. Yet, Mayas interested in reviving their heritage are often
accused of essentialism or of inventing traditions. In any case, it is important to recognize the tremendous resurgence of Mayan language, literature,
theatre, and identity that has occurred throughout Mesoamerica in the last
15 to 20 years. A host of writers—among them, Víctor Montejo (1991 and
2001), Gaspar Pedro González (1995), and Humberto Ak'abal (2001)—are
creating a new Mayan literature, and a new generation of teachers, some
trained by foreign linguists, are promoting spoken Mayan. And while the
revitalization movement is not spread evenly throughout Mesoamerica—it
appears more vigorous in Chiapas and Guatemala than in Yucatán—Tamara
Underiner (2004) has written eloquently about the rebirth of Mayan theatre in Yucatán, specifically in regard to Feliciano Sánchez Chan and the
Peninsular Maya Language Theatre Festival. Unlike *teatro costumbrista* (folk
theatre), which might be accused of recreating stereotypic images of village
life (i.e., essentialism), Sánchez Chan's work focuses on problems of everyday
life and presents them back to the community, an approach reminiscent of
the educational circles run by Paulo Friere (1970) in Brazil a generation ago
or the work of Bertolt Brecht.

For example, in *Las langostas* (The Locusts), the young playwright compares a devastating locust plague that occurred in the 1940s to the health
plague that has been brought on by the arrival of junk food in recent years.
In the opening scene, aural and visual effects are used to recount the mythical history of Yucatán, beginning with prophecies contained in the *Popol
Vuh* (a pre-Columbian book of Maya lore and prophecy), and ending with
a battle between man and locust. The action, however, quickly moves into
the present when the locust takes on human dimensions and invades the
dream world of a sleeping child. When the child wakes up, he refuses to eat
the traditional beans and rice and demands money from his mother so he
can buy junk food. The seductiveness of this diet is revealed by a neighbor
who acknowledges that she gives in to the demands of her child because
junk food is less expensive than good food, allows her to avoid strenuous
gardening, and serving it instead of cooking enables her to watch her favorite
soap operas. As the play reaches its conclusion, the husband finds himself in
a life-and-death struggle with the modern locust—dressed in soda cans and

junk food—a fight that finally rallies the community. The locust is driven out of town; however, as Underiner (2004, 116) points out, he runs away laughing and making crude gestures, an ambiguous ending that leaves the audience wondering if or when he will return.

A resurgent interest in cultural identity and politics can also be found in the Maya Diaspora, and this is where the second linkage comes in. Compared to 15 or 20 years ago, there are not only more Maya living in the US (Adler 2004; Burns 1993; Fink 2003; Loucky and Moors 2000), but they are better organized and much more visible than in the past. For example, in *The Maya of Morganton: Work and Community in the Nuevo New South* (2003), Leon Fink attempts to analyze what motivates a group of Mayan-speaking immigrants, with dubious legal status, to attempt to unionize their company, Case Farms Chicken, in a right-to-work state where previous attempts at unionization have failed. Fink at first assumes that the leadership of the union certification campaign is composed of hardened revolutionaries, veterans of Guatemala's failed revolution, but he quickly realizes that the central figures come from all points on the political spectrum—ex-soldiers, leftists, evangelists, etc. And while Fink, in my opinion, never quite answers his own question, the book contains an intriguing chapter, "How the Dead Organized the Living," which shows how the traditional cofradía, a Catholic mutual aid society that raises money for burials, created a feeling of solidarity across political, religious, and linguistic lines that invigorated the union drive. In addition, Fink discusses the cultural labors of Justo Germán Castro Lux and his wife Tránsita Gutiérrez Solíz Castrón, who not only sponsored a cultural group featuring marimba music and poetry but were drawing up plans to promote the four major Mayan languages spoken in Morganton, North Carolina: Q'anjob'al, Awakateko, K'ich'e, and Mam. To show their commitment to Maya tradition, the couple "chose names for their four children—Tojil, Canil, Ixchel, and Chilam—from the pantheon of Maya literature, [and] Tránsita wore her native *traje* (traditional clothes), even while working in a local convenience store" (Fink 2003, 142).

Similarly, in September 2007, I was invited to attend the annual fiesta of San Miguel Acatán in central Los Angeles, an event that featured the performance of a centuries-old folk dance (The Dance of the Deer), an eight-man marimba band, and the coronation of the new queen of San Miguel Acatán. In addition to the Acatano ex-patriots, many of whom were fluent in English, Spanish, and Q'anjob'al, ex-patriots from other towns in the Cuchumatán region of Guatemala sent representatives, all elegantly dressed in *huiples* (blouses) and *cortes* (skirts), to pay homage to the queen. As I noted in a previous article (Loewe 2009, 2), one of the highlights of the night was a medley of Mexican *rancheros* (cowboy songs) sung by a very talented 15-year-old girl; hardly typical of Maya village life, but the goal of the event was to bring the community together for a good time, not to create an Ur-Maya spectacle for aging anthropologists.

In 2007, according to a newsletter issued by the Federación de Clubes Yucatecos, there were 48 Yucatec/Maya hometown associations in the US, the majority of which are located in the states of California, Texas, Washington, Oregon, and Nevada. Within the Los Angeles area, the first club—Club Yucatán de California—was formed in October 2002 in response to the devastation wrought by Hurricane Isidore on September 29 of that year. Shortly afterward, two additional clubs were formed, leading to the creation of a federation of Yucatecan clubs. While these clubs share many of the objectives of Guatemalan immigrant organizations—providing legal help to recent immigrants; raising money to repatriate the dead; offering classes in Mayan; preserving regional food, dress, and folklore; and providing accessible health care for club members and their families[2]—I have seen nothing comparable to the political activism found among Guatemalan ex-patriots in the struggle to unionize the poultry industry. The one event I attended in Los Angeles was a rather anodyne affair in which Yucatecans joined with other Mexican nationals to celebrate the selection of Chichén Itzá as one of the seven wonders of the world.

While a better understanding of Diaspora politics and culture will require additional research, my initial sense is that the differences between Guatemalans and Yucatecans living in the US is linked to differences in the intensity of the revitalization movements in their respective homelands and the events that led them to emigrate in the first place. First and foremost, the political situation in Yucatán is less like the colonial settings that, according to Wallace (1956) and Worsely (1986 [1968]), spawn revitalization or regeneration movements. While the Cárdenas administration (1934–40) did belatedly attempt to fulfill the promise of the Mexican Revolution in Yucatán by expropriating large henequén plantations and breaking the back of the landed oligarchy, the progressive land reforms attempted by the Arbenz administration in Guatemala in the 1950s were brought to a quick end by a US-backed coup in 1954, an event that ushered in four decades of violent repression. The politics of indigeneity, therefore, can be seen as an accompaniment to, or even a substitute for, the overt military struggles that have occurred in Guatemala beginning in the 1970s. While political violence in Chiapas and Guatemala has been high, Yucatán has remained relatively peaceful. Political struggle on the peninsula appears to be contained within the trade union movement and the electoral sphere.

Secondly, if the politics of revitalization is motivated by the threat of language loss, Yucatán is much less at risk than Chiapas or Guatemala. The number of Yukatec speakers, estimated at 700,000, is increasing, and there are many communities where the primary language is Mayan. In Guatemala in contrast, Itzaj, Tiko, and Mopán are nearly extinct, and four other languages—Awakartik, Uspantele, S'pakapense, and Sakapultek—are limited to one administrative district (Loewe 2006, 256–57).

Finally, if the always bothersome presence of ethnographers and linguists serves as a catalyst to self-reflection and revitalization, it is clear that Chiapas and Guatemala have had more than their fair share of these researchers. Thanks in part to the Harvard Chiapas Project, village ethnographies have been a growth industry in southern Mexico and Guatemala since the 1950s, whereas studies of Yucatán have been relatively sparse. Indeed, the old joke that a Latin American family is made up of a father, a mother, three children, and an anthropologist is undoubtedly truer in Chiapas and Guatemala than Yucatán or, perhaps, anywhere else.

APPENDIX
The Tale of Way Kot: *(Four Versions)*

Note: Version 1 can be found in Chapter 5, pp. 110–111.

Version 2

The Mayan text is taken from Ligorred Perramón 1990; the translation is my own.

> I uet lakileex: ici tzicba teex u historia letee cyaala uay
> My friends: I will tell you all the story that is called Way
>
> popilee, tumen toone ohlilee tuux existido pero casualidad
> Pop, because we know, incidentally, where he existed.
>
> u yaalaa tii ten tumen tenee i uohl uppiti u historiaee letiee
> It was told to me because I know a little of this story
>
> cyaala uay popiloo; tuux u camah le tiee u ment kaz umen utz bin
> called Way Pop; where he learned to do bad and do good
>
> u tyaa india ua u raza india letiee c uuyeex yaalaaloo, pues
> for Indians or the Indian race as we hear it said, [how]
>
> tu canah uppit umen kaz umen utz tii tulaca u yet lakiloo.
> he learned to do a little bad and good for all his companions.
>
> Entonces letiee pues mases kaz tu canee tumen le can kazcunt u ba
> However, he learned more evil because he becomes evil
>
> de noche yetel e kakaz xiuoo cyaalaa. Le dia yan u viajar cyaal
> at night with dangerous herbs they say. They say he must travel
>
> uppe viernes tee cyaalaa kakaz kinoo letiee es . . .
> on Friday, this they say is an evil day . . .

u escogermaalob bueno u tetmoo u tiaa u kazcunc u baoo tumen tyaa
He selects well, it's selected so he can transform himself because

de viernes ua tyaa de martesoo cichintcee xiuoo pero u kabee
on Friday or Tuesday he bathes himself with herbs, but he hand

cu yachhtcee yete uppit u haail letiee cyaalaa ua a kaholeex yan
grinds them with a little water as they say. As you all may know

tii actun letiee yohlee kazoo u tiaal u kazcunc ua maac le
in the caves they know evil. In order to transform a man

haa letiee cu chhaa letiee cu kaxa tac behlas letiee tiempo
they collect water, they still look for it today, until this time

aneloonaa tumen letiee cyaalaa chhac xix cu dzic gotasoo
we're in, because this is called distilled water, it drips.

icel u yachhc e xiuoo u tyaal u yichintce, u tyaal u kalcuntc u
With it he mixes herbs in order to bathe, in order to transform

ba pero letiee cu escogerce, cu tetce diasoo mas kazoo, yohee,
himself, but this one selects, he chooses the worst days he knows,

tia le viernesoò. Entonces le ca dzooc u yutzcintce u yichince le
the Fridays. Then after he arranges things, he bathes [using]

has yetele kakas xiuoo entonces cu volar pero yete de noche, cu
water and evil herbs, then he flies but at night. He

volar, maa yete kine tumen ua yete kinee cu mentah loo xan tii,
flies, not in the day because in daylight it is harmful also.

cu dzoonoo yetele thohbileex le dzon cyaalaa uchben dzonoo,
They hunt and aim the rifle at you, the old rifle they call

uch ciz kaak entonces le oolaa tunoo u escogermae le kakaz dia u
old fart fire, then [the desirable thing] he chooses the evil day

tial u kazcuntc. U tial u biz ua tyilah humppe persona de noche
and becomes evil. In order to carry a person at night, he's seen

u nacxiktic yet u xik, letii u dzamaa
holding him under his body with his wing, the thing he puts

u tyaal u xiko letiee pop cyaala ua tumen a kaholeex; ua maa u
on his wings is called mat as you all may know, or if you don't

kahooleexee letiee baaloo cuadrado u hiiti yete u lee xano letii
all know, this rectangular thing is woven with palm leaves. This

mentbi tii kakaz dia xan beyoo u meyahma u tial u bin u ment e
is done [on] the evil day also since he does [it] in order to go and do

kazoo. Pues yan umppe parte yan umppe kin lailee maalobee tumen
evil. Well there's a place, there's a day that's still good since

tac mercancia tac baaloo cu chhic tee nachilie maa nadz tu
he gathers merchandise and things from far away, not from places

cahaloob tu tac. Le cen zazahcee yan le baaloo tu tazoo yan,
near his town. When the sun rises the stuff he brought is there,

pero chen ba tunee le uay tu chhaab utu chan baal, utu chan
but just like that the witch grabs little things, a little

chhupaa, ua tu chan xipalo, lee icil u alimentarc u ba
girl or a little boy, with which he feeds himself.

le betic le cu kaztah uten ten tzicbatce historia texaa, tumen
That's how he wastes them. I tell this story to you all, because

utenee binoon dzoon yet u utul i laak, i uet xipaalii xan humppe
I went hunting with another person, a young man also, one

noche te kaax tuux binoo dzone letiee cehoo dzooce uuyc u tale
night in the forest where we hunt deer. We heard a deer coming

cehoo pero chen baalmee maa tun kam u tal letiee pero leitee maa
but the only thing is he didn't come fast, but he didn't

caba cu tal i sino que caana, yan lo menos u coochi pakte yet u
come on the ground but from the sky. At a minimum, his wing span

xike yan lo menos cuatro metros a dos metros, caappe metro yan
was at least four meters by two meters, two meters was the

tii caduppel u xik tu lugar u kaa. U nacxikma baaloob
length of each wing in place of his arm. Under his wings he

baaloob yax tuux, yax maane icnal in primo
carried things. First he was [there], first he passed my cousin's house.

bey xan letii, dzu yuubic ance tumen peehtah letiie ceh binaan
He also heard the sound because the deer circled around. He went

dzonoo pero tumen chha zahac yetee u taloo hum e baal tee
to shoot, but he became frightened by the noise coming from

caanaloo. Le u lak i uet xibpaali xanoo como le orayo palatacon
the sky. My other young companion, since now we were several

beyoo chha zahci. Cux tun cu chhuyum, cux tun,
youths, was also scared. What if he picks [us] up? What then?

tenee ti uooti dzon xan yetel ix cizkaako, pero penahi
I also wanted to shoot with "fart fire," but unfortunately

i uol xan beyoo tumen yax ti tuclah beyoo kazi baal
I was excited too. Because, first I thought it was an evil thing

baax ten bucaahoo mex uten i uilee bey tun xan ilac xanoo
because of its size. Not once have I seen anything like it.

yax tzicnah letii yax maani.
First time he covered the house, first time he passed.

Pues tu dzah toone xahcil le orayoo. Maa t uakah dzon yoko beyoo
Well he scared us at this moment. I didn't fire the rifle above

tumen ua t uak dzon, ua maa t tzayic tii cinzic toon cun u nacxik
because if I shoot, if it doesn't happen to kill him he'll carry

toon yet u xik, cenza tuux cun u bizoon
us off with his wing. Who knows where he will take us?

mixmaac yohel pues letiee uuyic cyaalaa cyaalaa uay popiloo,
Nobody knows. Well they called him, called him Way Pop,

tumen yan utu xan cyaalaa uey, cah tuux anoona yan xan
because there is also one called way in the town we're in too.

bin uto Peto xanee humppel letiee cyaalaa arabe ca bin a kaat
He goes to Peto also, one they call the Arab. If you ask for

humppe baa tienda inaanee cu machce cu haatcee le hunoou
something that's not in the store he grabs, he takes some paper

yetel u kuumee xcax tumen le orahe cuxaan le maacoo pues
and a chicken spine because when he lived, well, there

minaan lapiz he bixe yan behlaa yete tun u han tok u kiikelee
weren't pens like there are today and then he draws blood quickly.

cu dziba e hunoob cu lathc e nuhoob baax e inaan
He writes on the paper, holding it in his palm, what's missing

tee tu tienda cen zazace cen xiicech
from his store. When you wake up, just what you went

a kaat tiee yan, tulac le baal cu mentic faltaoo; tuux cu chhic
to ask for is there, all the things one needs. Where did he get

si le epocaso mix e baal cyaala le letiee maquina c aacee
it if in this epoch there weren't what they call fire machines,

u treniloo, tockak, toc zii, letiee cyaalaa le trenoo iciloo u,
trains, burn fire, burn wood, they call them? The train which

u putah baal le behlaa cachoo inaan
carries things now, before there weren't any.

mix c cyaalaa letiee chhiichh cu maan caana
Not even what they call this bird that passes through the sky,

letiee cyaalaa beoraa u clasesi yan avion iclu bizah gente tac
now this kind of thing called an airplane, that takes people to

tyaa extranjeroso cachee inaan eloo, ua maa yoo letyee balcheeoo
foreign countries, didn't exist before. If not for those animals

cuatro yoc yet u nehoo, icil cinzcob e xyaaxcachhoo maa tu
with four feet and a tail that kills [and] flies, nothing would have

kuchu mexbaal uay tuux anoonexoo. Chen le i kaat i tzicba u
arrived here where we are. This is all I wanted to discuss, the

historialee uay pop ca uuyceex yaalaaloo, i uet lakeleex, i uet
story of Way Pop which you all heard spoken my friends, my

uincileex, tee nacenoo.
fellow humans, is finished.

Version 3

This version was written by Manuel Dzib in Maxcanú; the translation is
my own.

un saserdote extranjero llegó a Yucatán en el siglo XIX
A foreign priest arrived in Yucatán in the nineteenth century.

era un año muy canijo quería conquistar a un pueblo rebelde
It was a very rough year. He hoped to pacify a rebellious town.

hace llamada a la gente en campanada y la gente no se prestaba,
He rang the church bell to call the people, but they didn't show

ni le interesaba la doctrina de dios.
nor were they interested in the word of God.

el saserdote se enejó contra de la gente del pueblo,
The priest became angry with the people of the town.

no encontraba la solución. entonces consiguió un sacristán
He couldn't find the solution. Then he found an altar boy.

!que podemos hacer con la gente sacristán?
"What are we going to do with these people, altar boy?"

El sacristán respondió tienes que cambiar tu idea
The altar boy responded, "You have to change how you think."

Entonces reacionó así que no quieren servir a dios Jesucristo
Then he added that they didn't want to serve Jesus Christ.

Voy a servir al diáblo.
"I am going to serve the devil," [said the priest].

llamó uno de los brujos un dia y el brujo se presentó en
He called one of the witches one day and the witch appeared in

la capilla y el saserdote le dijó al brujo, enséñame como podría
the chapel and the priest said to the witch, "Show me how you

bolar así vivo. entonces el brujo le dijó pero tienes que
fly so well." Then the witch told him, "But you must

abandonar a tu dios. Porque con 2 dioses así no vas a aprender
abandon your god. Because with two gods like that you won't learn

nunca. Pues así que no quiere la gente mi enseñansa pues
ever." "Well, since the people don't want my teachings

de una ves. ya estoy muy aburrido yo te sequire, eres mi
any longer, I am very bored. I will follow you, you're my

amigo desde la hora." "Entonces vas a obedecir mis mandamientos.
friend from now on." "Then" [said the witch], "you must obey my orders.

Pues si puedes dar 9 bolantines al derecho y 9
If you can, turn 9 times to the right and 9 times in

al reves y se lo mostraron. ya después empezó la oración de Satan
reverse," and they showed him. Then he began a prayer to Satan.

después de la oración se sintió muy poderoso. y el brujo le dijó
After the prayer he felt very powerful. And the witch told

al saserdote aquí tienes tus alas puedes bolar sobre la ciudad
the priest, "Here are your wings, you can fly over the city

sercana ahora ya son las 12 de la noche, que oiga entonces Bolo
nearby, it's twelve midnight now." He listened then he flew.

se fue y los 30 minutos volvió. así que ya puedes.
He left and returned 30 minutes later. "Like that, now you know."

has lo que quieras. y tuvó una idea buena, voy a
"Do what you like." And he had a good idea: I'm going to

recoger a los borachos para que la gente tengan una Lección y así
gather up the drunks so that the people learn a lesson, and thus

lo hisó cada noche agarra una mujer en la calle no un Borracho
every night he grabs a woman in the street, not a drunk, and

lo transporta en columbia, cada dia hay un desaparecido
transports her to Colombia. Each day there was one disappearance

y desaparicieron mas de 50 personas, y entonces empesó la furia
and more than 50 people disappeared, and then a fury arose

de la gente solitos fueran con el saserdote y le plantearon lo
among the widowers. They went to the priest and they explained

que sucedía no lo que está ocurriendo entonces respondió a la
what happened, not what's occurring. Then the priest told the

gente lo que deberian de hacer es asístir en la misa en la
people what they should do is attend mass in the church of the

iglecia de dios vivo, para que así se finalise las desapariciones
the living god in order that the disappearances come to an end

porque si no es así va ser peor cada dia.
because if it's not this way, it's going to get worse each day.

el Sacerdote cambio de idea entonces planteó una tienda de
The priest changed his mind then and opened a store stocked

mercancía de viveres y mudansa entonces llevaba un Borracho en
with food and new clothing. Then he took a drunk

columbia cada noche en una fabrica de calzado allí deja al
to a shoe factory in Colombia each night. There he left the

borracho el Sacerdote escogía los Sapatos mas caros en esa
drunk. The priest selected the most expensive shoes in this

fabrica y regresa aca en Yucatán siguiente noche lleva
factory and returns here to Yucatán the next night and takes

otro en otro Pais en otro Fabrica
another person to another factory in another country

y allí lo deja lo que transportó y agarra de los mejores
and left what he transported there and grabbed the best,

aguardientes mas caros y lo vende en su tienda menos precio que
most expensive liquors and sold them for less than the

en la Fabrica las mercancias meno entonces la gente se fijó
cheapest merchandise in the factory. Then people noticed things

y lo empesaron a espiar un dia cayó en la trampa todos los
and they began to spy on him. One day he fell in the trap. All

comerciantes se rebelaron contra el saserdote porque ellos nadie
the merchants rebelled against the priest because nobody

compraba sus mercancias empesaron a murmurar preguntaban entre
bought their merchandise. They began to whisper. They asked among

ambos, dónde agarra mercancía ese saserdote quien
themselves, "Where did this priest get his goods [and] who

lo transporta! Una ocasíon el sacristán espioyó.
transported it?" On one occasíon the altar boy spied him.

El saserdote le dijó al Sacristán, yo boy a mi cama y si alguien
The priest told the altar boy, "I'm going to bed and if someone

pregunta de mi, le dises que me fui de biaje, boy a descansar
asks about me, tell him that I went on a trip. I'm going to rest

en la azotea. y el Primer dia de espiación, cuando el Sacristán
on the roof." And the first day of espionage, when the altar boy

subió en la azotea, a llamar al Sasérdote. se imprecionó,
climbed up on the roof to call the priest, he was surprised,

porque no estaba. Encontro no mas la cama. y el Sacristán
because he wasn't there. The bed was empty. And the altar boy was

asustado. dónde se fue, dónde se bajo, por dónde se abra
frightened. Where did he go? How did he get down? Where could

metido, empesó la busqueda. Estaba el Sacristán desesperado,
he have gone? He began the search. The altar boy had given up

cuando escuchó un biento raro y cuando vio con sus
when he heard an unusual wind and when he saw with his

propios ojos. bajaba una sombra, y el Sacristán resó una
own eyes a shadow falling. And the altar boy recited a

oración. Y se fue el miedo, cuando bajó el Sacerdote con sus
prayer. And the fear left him, then the priest landed with his

tremendas alas. un pájaro gigante de 2 metros de largo después de
tremendous wings, a giant bird two meters in length. After he

recobrar su cuerpo, abló el sacerdote, le dijó al sacristán si
recovered his body, the priest spoke. He said to the altar boy,

ya me vistes quien soy, mucho cuidado con la boca porque si
"Now you see who I am, be very careful what you say, because if

no morirás.
you aren't, you will die."

Version 4

This version is from Boccara 1985, 86–87; the translation is my own.

En una época muy antigua, el palacio municipal de Yaxcaba
In an epoch long ago the municipal palace of Yaxcaba

era custodiado todas las noches por un guardia. El Way Kot es muy
was patrolled every night by a guard. Way Kot is very

bandido y tiene conocimientos de otros lugares para comerciar con
sly and is familiar with other places where he can do business

otras personas ... Después de rezar para adormecer al guardia
with others.... After reciting a hex to make the guard sleepy,

regresaba a medianoche al palacio para estar seguro que el
he returned to the palace around midnight in order to be sure

vigilante estaba dormido. Después escondía al hombre dentro de un
the guard was asleep. Next, he hid the man inside a

gran saco fabricado con las hojas del coco (que en Maya es
big sack made out of coconut leaves (which in Mayan is

llamado *kop*). Se lo llevaba en seguida a su casa, subía
called *kop*). He immediately took him to his house, he climbed

al techo a rezar de nuevo; "sacaba sus alas" y se echaba a volar
the roof to pray again; pulled out his wings and began to fly,

llevando su presa. Al cabo de una semana las personas del pueblo
carrying his prisoner. After a week the people of the town

comenzaban a inquietarse por la desaparición de los guardias. . . .
began to get concerned about the disappearance of the guards. . . .

Cierto día, una persona llamada, Hets Kool, más chingón y más
One day, a person named Hets Kool, craftier and more

estudiado que el Way Kot, decidió hacer la guardia del palacio
prepared than Way Kot, decided to guard the palace

para descubrir lo que sucedía.
in order to figure out what was happening.

El Hets Kool hizó tambien sus rezos para que no le pasará nada y
Hets Kool also said prayers so nothing would happen to him and

se pusó a esperar. El Way Kot llegó la medianoche, despúes de
prepared to wait. Way Kot arrived at midnight, after

asegurarse del sueño del Hets Kool,
assuring himself that Hets Kool was asleep,

quien fingía dormir. Se apoderó de él como de los otros y
who was pretending. He overpowered him like the others and

voló llevándolo sobre sus alas. A mitad del trayecto se posó
flew off carrying him on his wings. At the midpoint he rested

sobre un árbol, a la orilla del mar y por fin llegó a una torre
on a tree, at the edge of the sea, and finally arrived at a tower

dónde se vendía a las personas. Fue recibido con la siguiente
where they sell the people. He was received with the following

exclamación: "El que hoy nos trae está bien gordo; yo creo
exclamation: "The one you brought us today is very fat; I think

que muy pronto podriámos venderlo nuevamente."
that we can sell him again very shortly."

El Hets Kool escuchó contar las monedas equivalentes a lo que
Hets Kool heard them count out the equivalent in cash of

costaba su persona. Se le transportó a una pieza dónde se
his person. They then transported him to a place where

encontró con otras gentes de Yaxcaba. Había una persona entera,
he met with other people from Yaxcaba. There was a whole person,

pero la mayoría tenían los brazos y piernas cortados. El Hets
but the majority of them had their arms and legs cut off. Hets

Kool anunció a su compañero válido que hoy mismo regresarían
Kool announced to the healthy one that they would return that day

a Yaxcaba para atestiguar lo que el Way Kot había hecho.
to Yaxcaba to testify about what Way Kot had done.

Poco después el Hets Kool se hizó al vuelo llevando también a una
A little later Hets Kool flew off carrying in addition this

persona sobre sus alas. A medio camino el Hets Kool, en lugar de
person on his wings. At the midpoint, Hets Kool, instead of

posar como el Way Kot, subió aún más alto y continuó
resting like the Way Kot, climbed even higher and continued

su vuelo a fin de llegar primero a Yaxcaba. El Hets Kool
his flight in order to arrive in Yaxcaba first. Hets Kool

regresó a su lugar dentro del cuartel del palacio mientras que el
returned to his place in a room of the town hall while

Way Kot volvió tranquilamente a su casa sin sospechar nada.
Way Kot quietly returned home not suspecting a thing.

A la mañana siguiente el Hets Kool le contó todo al presidente
The next morning Hets Kool told everything to the municipal

municipal, a la autoridad, lo que había sucedido:
president, to the authority, what had occurred:

—Y bien señor, acerca de los guardias que siempre desaparecen,
—And your honor, about the guards that always disappear,

—Es el Way Kot quien los vende.
—It's Way Kot who sells them.

—Y tu, cómo lo sabes?
—And you, how do you know?

—Yo trajé a un testigo. . . .
—I brought a witness. . . .

Entonces el presidente envió a buscar al testigo y éste
Then the president sent someone to look for the witness and he

confirmó las declaraciónes del Hets Kool.
confirmed the declarations of Hets Kool.

Una vez vendidos, les cortan las piernas y los brazos para
"Once they are sold, they cut off their legs and arms to

engordarlos para hacer la comida de allá, que sirve de alimento
fatten them in order to make food from them, to serve as food

a otras personas. El presidente mandó buscar al Way Kot, éste
for other people." The president sent for Way Kot, he

comenzó por negarse, pero fue confundido y se declaró culpable.
began denying it, but became confused and admitted his guilt.

Se le pidió devolver el dinero de la venta de las personas.
They asked him to return the money from the sale of people.

El Way Kot regresó a su casa, pero en lugar
Way Kot returned to his house, but instead

de devolverlo fue a echarlo al cenote.
of returning it [the money], he threw it in the well.

"Si tu sales a tirar el dinero al cenote vas a morir en
"If you throw the money in the well, you're going to die

seguida, si no, pues pasa a la comisaría," le ordenó
right away, if not, then go to the jail," ordered the

el presidente. Como el Way Kot no salía de su casa,
president. Since Way Kot didn't leave his house, they

forzaron su puerta y vieron que se había ahorcado. Se había
forced open his door and saw that he had hung himself. He had

matado, no quisó que alguien más lo fusilara, prefirió
killed himself, he didn't want anyone to shoot him, he preferred

él mismo quitarse la vida. Así termina la historia del Way Kot,
to take his own life. That's how the story of Way Kot ends.

que se aprovechó de muchas personas y finalmente terminó su
He took advantage of many people and finally ended his

existencia ahorcándose.
existence by hanging himself.

Version 5

This excerpt is taken from Rosado Vega (1957, 168–75); the translation is
my own.

El way pach es un ser demoniaco que rapta jovencitas y niños.
Way Pach is a demonic being who kidnaps young women and children.

Su cuerpo fue amasado año tras año por seres infernales,
His body was worked over year after year by infernal beings,

dejándolo largo y delgado para que pudiera escurrirse hasta por
leaving it long and slender so he can slither through

la rendija más pequeña. . . . La mirada de sus ojos verdes como la
the smallest fissures. . . . The look in his green eyes like the

piel de la Chaycan se diluye en el alma como un veneno. Lleva en
skin of a snake dissolves in the soul like a poison. He carries

el cuello tres collares de riñones endurecidos, de jabalí.
around his neck three rings of hardened kidneys from a wild pig.

Uno está destinado para ahorcar a la doncella que atrape, el
One is used to strangle the young woman that he traps, the

otro para oprimir al niño que caiga en su poder y
the other to oppress the child that falls under his power, and

el último, que es el mayor, para ahorcarse a si mismo, cuando
the last, which is the largest, is for hanging himself when the

señale el sol la hora en que todos los genios malos desaparecen. . . ."
sun indicates it is the hour in which all evil beings disappear. . . ."

Ahí va por los caminos de los cielos: míralo:
There he goes down the streets of the heavens: watch him:

va cabalgando sobre el Way Kot que es otro engendro monstruoso,
galloping on Way Kot who is another monstrous creation

gavilán de alas enrojecidas—como si estuvieran encendidas—
a vulture with reddened wings—as if they were on fire—and

que son más ligeras que el viento. . . ."
which are lighter than the wind. . . ."

Un día, hace de esto miles de años, una doncella fue arrebatada
One day, thousands of years ago, a young woman was snatched

por el Way Pach. Esto ocurrió la misma noche en que la virgen se
by Way Pach. This occurred the same evening in which the virgin

desposaba. . . . El joven se lanzó a su persecución, después de
was married. . . . The young man went off in pursuit, after

haber consultado a una asamblea de siete adivinos, quienes
having consulted an assembly of seven oracles, who

lo enviaron a asesorarse con una bruja que vivía en un bosque de
sent him to consult with a witch that lived in a forest of

ceibas (arboles sagrados), ubicados a una distancia de nueve
sacred ceiba trees, located at a distance of nine

milpas grandes. La bruja le entregó un mechón de sus cabellos
large farmsteads. The witch gave him a handful of her hair

lleno de poder, ya que numerosas veces había sido enrollado bajo
full of power, since numerous times it had been rolled up under

la luz de la luna llena, indicándole el camino para llegar a
the light of a full moon, indicating the path to follow to get to

su próximo interlocutor: el pájaro de cuerpo negro y alas de
his next interlocutor: the bird with a black body and wings with

verdes plumas. El pájaro, después de haber cantado una estrofa
green feathers. The bird, after having sung a strophe

que termina así: "Yo soy el pájaro que no muere y que
which ended like this: "I am the bird that never dies and that

no vive; yo soy el pájaro de la vida y de la muerte," le indicó
doesn't live: I am the bird of life and death," showed him

dónde encontrar y vencer a la serpiente de nueve cabezas "Bolon
where to find and defeat the nine-headed serpent "Bolon

Tuppel Kancabil" primer guardian del Way Kot.
Tuppel Kancabil," Way Kot's first guard.

El muchacho tenía que tocar el cuerpo de la serpiente con el
The young man had to touch the body of the serpent with the

mechón del cabello de la bruja. La serpiente Bolon sería entonces
lock of hair from the witch. The serpent Bolon would then be

vencida y él extraería la raíz de las nueve cabezas, la
defeated and he would extract the root of the nine heads, the

piedra mágica: el "zaztok." Todo sucedió como se había previsto
magic stone: the "crystal."[1] Everything happened as predicted,

la serpiente Bolon le señaló quien sería su proximo adversario,
the serpent Bolon indicated who his next adversary would be,

"Ek chapat," de numerosos pies; el que vive en una gruta obscura.
"Black Centipede," with many feet; he who lives in a dark cave.

"Ek Chapat" tiene la particularidad de tener los ojos
"Black Centipede" has the peculiar feature of sleeping

abiertos cuando duerme y los ojos cerrados cuando está despierto.
with his eyes open and having his eyes closed when he is awake.

Para tener éxito, el joven debería pegarle con el zaztok. . . .
To be successful, the young man had to hit him with the crystal. . . .

El muchacho encontró al "Ek Chapat" y logró una nueva victoria.
The youth encountered "Black Centipede" and won another victory.

Éste le indico entonces la proxima etapa: encontrar a la mujer
This signaled the next step: to find the woman

con cabeza de bestia en medio de la caverna. Ésta última, sin
with a beast's head in the center of the cave. Without fighting

combatir, le señaló cual era la morada del "way pach,"
this last one showed him the home of "way pach,"

ubicada a la salida de la colina alta. Ella le reveló que su
located at the exit of the high hill. She informed him that his

novia había sido transformada en una pequeña culebra, delgada
fiancée had been transformed into a small snake, skinny

como un hilo que se esconde dentro de las hendiduras de la
as a thread which hides itself in the fissures of the

piedra. El Way Pach espera la conjunción de la luna para
stone. Way Pach awaits the conjunction of the moon to

posarse en ella. "Toma estos cabellos de mi cabeza, esta
place himself in there. "Take these hairs from my head, this

cal y esta ceniza, echa la cal a los ojos del Way Pach
limestone and this ash, toss limestone in the eyes of Way Pach

y del Way Kot y así serán cegados y vencidos. Los cabellos te
and Way Kot and they will be blinded and defeated. The hair will

servirán para atar sus cuerpos y con la ceniza untarás el
serve to tie their bodies and with the ashes you will coat the

cuerpo de la pequeña serpiente; cuando ella haya sentido la
the body of the small serpent; when she has felt the

ceniza, recuperará a tu novia su forma original. . . ."
ash, your lover will regain her original form. . . ."

El muchacho se enfrenta entonces a la última prueba del combate,
The youth then encountered the ultimate test of battle,

venciendo al Way Pach y al Way Kot.
defeating Way Pach and Way Kot.

GLOSSARY

abolengo: Literally "lineage" or "descent." Referring to one's "abolengo" is a way of highlighting his or her status.

alpargata: A traditional sandal worn in Yucatán, notable for having a very thick sole. The thickness of the sole was an indicator of the wearer's social standing.

autochthonous: Something that was formed in the place that it was found. Also used to refer to native or indigenous people.

baile del cochino: Dance of the Pig. This is part of an investiture ceremony in which responsibility for organizing the annual fiesta for the community's patron saint is passed from one confraternity to another. It's often a humorous occasion.

barrio: A neighborhood or a small section of a town or city.

batab (Mayan): The cacique or headman of a village in pre-colonial and early post-colonial times.

bomba: A humorous four-line verse in which the first and third and second and fourth verses rhyme. Bombas or "bombs" are generally shouted out periodically during a *jarana* or on other festive occasions.

cabecera: The head town or capital of a district or region. The distinction between a head town and a rural village parallels the colonial distinction between culture and nature or civilization and primitiveness.

Cabildo: The basic unit of local government in Spain and colonial Latin America.

Cárdenist: Supporter of Lázaro Cárdenas, president of Mexico from 1934 to 1940.

cargador: The person who bears the burden or responsibility for organizing all or part of the village fiesta.

cargo systems: An alternating system of secular and religious offices in which the prestige and the cost increases as the office holders move up the hierarchy. The offices are held by men in rural indigenous communities throughout central and southern Mexico and Central America.

catrín: Derogatory term meaning dandy or fop. It originally referred to individuals of indigenous ancestry who adopted Western dress in order to disguise their lowly standing. The term is taken from a satirical novel entitled *Don Catrín de la Fachenda.*

Chilam Balam: Books of prophecy and lore that were written down around the time of the Conquest. The term translates literally as Jaguar Priest.

chik (Mayan): An individual who plays the joker in the Dance of the Pig's Head or *baile del cochino.*

Códice de Calkini: One of nine manuscripts that make up the *Chilam Balam.* Also known as the Chronicle of Calkini, this is a series of very old manuscripts that narrate the history of the Ah Canul lineage from the destruction of Mayapan to the conquest of the peninsula by Francisco Montejo. It also contains other interesting information about Maya culture.

cofradía: A Catholic brotherhood created to promote special works of Christian charity or piety.

cuch: Ceremony in which responsibility for organizing the village fiesta is passed from one religious group or one generation to another.

cuchteel (Mayan): A neighborhood or the people of a neighborhood under the control of a cacique or local political leader.

cultura regional mestiza: Regional culture of Yucatán consisting of customs and practices that combine Maya and Spanish characteristics such as the *jarana.*

ejemplo: A short tale with a moral.

ejido: Community lands.

ejidatario/a: One who works ejidal lands and has rights of usufruct; such persons were unable to rent or sell the land prior to the neoliberal agrarian reforms of 1992.

encargado: Sometimes used to refer to the organizer of a festival, the term can also refer to someone who manages agricultural production on a rural estate.

essentialism: The theory that basic cultural ideas and skills are innate and universal rather than constructed socially or ideologically.

estancias: Cattle ranches.

exact fantasy: The projection of images in art or myth that contain social contradictions representative of a given time period or mode of production.

federales: The Mexican federal police, a group generally despised by lower-class Mexicans.

fetishism: The attribution of inherent value or power to an object. Commodity fetishism refers to the idea that money or commodities contain human characteristics such as fertility or power.

fino: Literally "fine." Mestizos finos were a separate social category distinguished from other mestizos by their fine clothes.

folklorization: The constitution of a practice or object as an example of folk culture or popular culture by middle-class intellectuals and state institutions for, artistic, commercial, or political purposes.

gremio: Literally "trade union or worker's organization," the term is used to refer to lay religious organizations in Yucatán. It is roughly synonymous with cofrádía.

Guadalupe: The patron saint of Mexico and an incarnation of the Virgin Mary. Guadalupe is thought to have risen in importance following a serious plague in Mexico City in the eighteenth century.

hacendado: The owner of a hacienda.

hacienda: An agricultural estate with workers who live on the premises.

hagiography: The study of saints or highly venerated individuals.

hegemony: Social, cultural, ideological, or economic influence exerted by a dominant group.

henequén: A strong fiber which comes from tropical American agave leaves and is found primarily in Yucatán. It is used in making twine and rope.

hispanicization: The incorporation of characteristics particular to Hispanic society and culture by people of non-Hispanic origin.

huipil: A dress worn by indigenous women that has embroidery around the neckline and the hemline and may denote the woman's village, social status, and personal taste.

indígena: A person of indigenous or aboriginal ancestry.

indígenismo: A political movement in Latin America advocating a more important role for indigenous peoples in the life of the nation.

indío: Indian. The term now generally has a negative connotation in Mexico.

jarana: Popular Yucatecan dance that symbolizes the confluence of Maya and Spanish civilization. Although the dress and choreography derives from the Spanish Jota, some of the instrumentation and themes are clearly of Maya origin. In addition, Yucatecan dancers have added unique stylistic changes to differentiate the jarana from the jota.

jota: A traditional Spanish dance that is performed either in ¾ time or ⁶⁄₈ time. This is considered the Spanish ancestor of the Yucatecan jarana.

k'ub pol (Mayan): Literally "head delivery," this ritual can be either serious or satirical. In either case, it transfers the responsibility of organizing the annual fiesta from one gremio to another.

Ladino: A Westernized, Spanish-speaking Latin American. The term is used widely in Guatemala in reference to non-indigenous people. Aside from Chiapas, the term mestizo is generally used in Mexico.

lencería: A store that sells lingerie, fabrics, and intimate apparel.

lunero: Peon who provided free labor to the hacienda owner on Monday in exchange for access to estate land.

mayorcol: Hacienda official responsible for overseeing corn cultivation. An interesting folk etymology explains that the term derives from the negative particle *ma,* meaning "no," and *okol* meaning to steal, since the mayokol, although a native Mayan speaker, was responsible for making sure that hacienda workers did not steal anything.

mayordomo: The head of a cofradía. This person is usually responsible for maintaining a particular religious image.

Maxcanú: A large town in the western part of the Mexican state of Yucatán.

mecate: A local unit of measurement, the mecate is 20 meters by 20 meters or 400 square meters.

mestizo/mestiza: A man/woman of mixed European and American Indian ancestry.

mestizaje: The admixture of biologically and/or culturally distinct people resulting in a new type.

milpa: Cornfield.

novena: A series of prayers said over a nine-day period.

ok'ostah pol (Mayan): Dance of the Head or Dance of the (Pig's) Head.

ontology: A branch of metaphysics concerned with the nature and relations of being.

patrimony: Property or other legal entitlements passed down by the father. National patrimony generally refers to the cultural traditions of long standing in a nation state.

patron saint: A saint who is thought to be the protector or intercessor of a person, community, or collectivity. The patron saint of Maxcanú is St. Michael the Archangel.

Porfiriato: The period in which Porfirio Díaz ruled Mexico.

Porfirio Díaz: Dictator who ruled Mexico from 1877 to 1880 and again from 1884 to 1911.

pre-Columbian: The time period prior to the arrival of Columbus and European settlers.

quatrain: A stanza or poem composed of four lines in which the alternate lines rhyme.

rescate cultural: Phrase used by government workers to refer to the preservation of cultural practices or customs that are in the process of disappearing.

santiguar: A ritual cleansing or cure performed by "sweeping" an afflicted individual with a sipche branch.

semantic derogation: The derogatory connotation of the female unit in a pair of male/female terms, e.g., master/mistress.

shaman: Someone who acts as an intermediary between the natural and supernatural worlds, using magic to cure illness, foretell the future, and control spiritual forces.

spiritist: Female mediums who communicate with deceased shamans or Western doctors in order to determine a cure for their patients. Spiritism has roots in the teachings of Allan Kardec, a nineteenth-century French healer, but has combined with indigenous and other popular Mexican medical traditions.

terno: A dress worn on festive occasions. It is similar to a huipil, but instead of two rows of embroidery, there are three rows, thanks to an embroidered cloth inlay.

Tonántzin: Mother Earth in Aztec mythology. Possibly a pre-Columbian version of Guadalupe.

***ts'ul* (Mayan):** Non-Maya, foreigner, individual of high social standing, devil.

***u hanli kol* (Mayan):** Literally, "food of the milpa." A harvest celebration in which a Maya shaman propitiates the deities for a bountiful harvest. Offerings of food and drink are prepared and placed on an outdoor altar.

vaquería: A popular dance held on Yucatán's corn and cattle haciendas during the branding season. The term vaquería derives from the term vaquero or cowboy.

vaquero: A cowboy.

vecino: A political designation referring to fully vested citizens of the state. In the colonial period whites and mestizos were considered vecinos, but Indians were not.

way (Mayan): A witch; a human who takes animal form in order to surprise or harm others.

Way Pop: The witch of the mats or the witch of the reeds.

x-tabay (Mayan): A mythical woman who uses her beauty in order to lure men to their deaths. At the moment they embrace her, she turns into a thorny cactus.

yerbatería: The practice of using herbs in healing.

NOTES

Introduction

1   The chronology of the Mexican Revolution in Yucatán is different than in other parts of the nation. It did not really begin in the peninsula until the arrival of General Salvador Alvarado—a supporter of Venustiano Carranza—in 1914, although in other parts of the country the Revolution was in full swing by 1911. It also continued beyond the conventional end date of 1920, due to continued fighting between the landowners and Felipe Carrillo Puerto's Socialist Party of Yucatán.

2   See http://thinkexist.com/quotation/power_concedes_nothing_without_a_demand-it_never/206374.html.

Chapter 1

1   The original foundation bears the influence of the Franciscan order and was begun in the late sixteenth century.

2   It appears that the Ah Canul dynasty did not fare as well as other noble lineages such as the Xiu, Huit, and Cocom following the Conquest. By the late eighteenth century only one Canul is found in high office (in Dzibikal or Uman), and, as Farriss remarks, "one can only guess at direct descent" (1984, 491).

3   In particular, Farriss notes that luneros could substitute service on the estate for the more demanding obligations placed on village residents. "The difference was that the tenant, unlike the hamlet resident, did not have to travel to the pueblo, and was also often protected from *servicio personal*, courier service, road building, and all the other forms of compulsory labor that were the pueblo Indian's lot" (1984, 217).

4   The vecino population increased from 10 to 28.8 per cent of the total population of Yucatán between 1700 and 1780 (Farriss 1984, 370).

5   Such an interpretation is consistent with studies in other parts of Mexico that view the Indian cofradía of the middle to late colonial period as a vehicle for maintaining Indian identity and power in the face of ever-increasing threats (Gibson 1964, 127–32; Bricker 1981).

6   One mecate equals 400 square meters. One hectare equals 20 mecates or 2.41 acres.

7   The plantations in the western part of the state were generally larger because the yields were lower and the quality of the fiber was worse.

8   It is, of course, no accident that Yucatán's henequén plantations quickly became the most highly mechanized plantations in Mexico since the principal purchaser of fiber after 1902, the International Harvester Company, was also a leading exporter of farm machinery and provided

easy terms of purchase. Like other credits provided through the export houses, expensive machines could be paid off in henequén, a condition that allowed small and medium-sized planters to earn tremendous profits during boom years yet kept them perennially in debt to their North American patrons.

9   The key feature of Yucatán's *de facto* slave regimen was a system of debt peonage that effectively tied the hacienda peon to the land. In most cases this obligation was formalized at the time of his marriage, an event that was arranged, sponsored, and paid for by the owner of the hacienda or one of his majordomos. The newlyweds were provided living quarters and certain basic necessities, all of which were, supposedly, calculated in a contract, the notorious *nohoch cuenta* (big bill). In theory, the hacienda peon had the right to see the contract (although he probably couldn't read) and pay off the debt at any time; however, in practice official records were not kept and plantation workers were neither bought nor sold.

10   The source of the information is the *Secretaría de Reforma Agraria* in Mérida.

11   According to the 1983 report cited above, the population of Maxcanú between 1950 and 1983 is as follows:

1950	1960	1970	1980	1983
4,269	5,139	6,505	8,234	8,837

12   According to the *Manual de Estadística Básica del Estado de Yucatán,* the most important crops (by tonnage) produced in Maxcanú in 1982 were: henequén (1,825.61), corn (2,896), oranges (1,198,80), jícama (141) papaya, (136.92), tamarind (127.10), roatan plantains (81.90), and lemons (70.63). The same source provides the following information on livestock production: 14,276 chickens and turkeys, 2,381 pigs, and 355 cattle.

13   See http://www.starwoodhotels.com/luxury/property/overview/index.html?propertyID =1381.

Chapter 2

1   In *Maya Society Under Colonial Rule* (1984), Farriss describes a four-tiered administrative system in which the higher offices in both the **cabildo** (town council) and the cofradía were controlled by the post-Conquest remnants of the native nobility. These, in turn, were subdivided into positions held by members of particular royal or batab lineages and those open to lesser nobility (*principales*). Located in the highest tier were the chief executive (*gobernador*), who was responsible for the community's tax burden, and the patron of the **cofradía** who discharged various ritual and administrative tasks and, presumably, was in charge of the **cofradía** estate. Although nominally distinct, the two offices were, in fact, often held by the same individual. The second tier, the civil, included two aldermen (*alcaldes*), who assisted the governor, and four councilmen (*regidores*), who may have presided over certain subdivisions of the community. These members, in turn, were counterbalanced by six religious officers (two *priostes* and four *mayordomos*), who cared for the saints and helped to organize various cult activities. Again, however, the formal adherence to Spanish principles of bureaucratic organizations did not impede the movement between the civil and religious spheres. On the contrary, the system was characterized by the continual rotation of officers between the two spheres. The third and fourth levels, according to Farris, were made up of commoners who played minor governmental roles and served on the **cofradía** estate.

2   Chance makes a similar point in his discussion of religious cargos in Chiapas: "[I]t would be erroneous to view religious cargo systems in purely expressive terms and deny them a role in village political life ... [even if] a religious hierarchy is likely to be just one of several local groups competing for power" (1990, 38).

3   Victor Turner remarks in *Dramas, Fields, and Metaphors: Symbolic Action in Human Society:* "Structurally, the parish priest has little to do with the guilds. Certainly, he has no jurisdiction over their affairs, for he belongs to none of them.... As in many other aspects of Mexican religious life, the pueblo, both as people and as locality, has a high degree of autonomy from the secular clergy. This seems to be especially true in the pilgrimage domain" (1974, 221).

4 In Maxcanú, the gremio of the third section, one of the town's largest, has a particularly antagonistic relationship with the parish priest. As part of the annual celebration held in honor of San Miguel, this gremio sets up a 20-foot greased pole (*palo encebado*) supporting a net containing food, rum, cash, and prizes on the church lawn, which happens to be located in the third section. As dusk settles, groups of teenagers take turns building human pyramids in an attempt to climb the pole and retrieve the booty while friends and relatives cheer them on. Because the competition coincides with the evening mass, in 1989 several congregants were sent out to quiet the contestants, all to no avail. When the priest appeared in the doorway of the church, displaying an unusually severe expression, the competition stopped momentarily; however, by the time he had returned to the pulpit, the contest was back in full swing.

5 Indeed, I would argue that the overt hostility between several post-revolutionary governments— particularly the Calles and the Cárdenas administrations—has led scholars to overlook the role of religious associations in the formation of a new hegemonic order.

6 Moreover, unlike Spain, where many cofradías provided mutual aid to their members by the late seventeenth century (Graff 1973, 299), cofradías in the New World often did not. Only 3 per cent of the expenditures among New Granada's cofradías went for charitable purposes, and several cofradías contained no charitable provisions at all. In New Spain, the record appears more complicated. While Bazarte Martínez (1989) describes the support that cofradías provided hospitals in the colony, Bechtloff (1996, 182) notes with surprise that charitable or social functions are often not mentioned in cofradía records of Michoacán.

7 Relations between clergymen and cofradías were not always cordial, however. In fact, conflict over the fees owed for spiritual services sometimes went before ecclesiastical tribunals. In 1682, Augustin Pérez, the priest in charge of the sacristy in the parish church of Las Nieves (Bogota), sued the church's cofradía for withholding the fees due to him for his weekly masses. He also argued that the treasurer of the Cofradía of the Blessed Souls of Purgatory, Jacinto García de Gálves and his son, Francisco García, denied him the fee he had set for tolling the bells for the memory of their deceased cofrades (Graff 1973, 217).

8 According to Graff, the Canal del Dique, which provided water transit between the Magdelena River and the Port of Cartagena, listed debts of 25,000 pesos to cofradías and monasteries in 1790 (1973, 251).

9 For example, Carrera Estampa includes the account of an Italian traveler who witnessed a tumultuous struggle for position at a procession on Sacred Thursday of Easter in 1697: " . . . as the procession arrived at the Royal Palace a conflict over precedence emerged between Chinos—natives of the Philippines in the procession of San Francisco—and the brotherhood of the Sanctified Trinity made up of tailors, resulting in a fight with clubs and crosses which left many injured" (1954, 171).

10 It was these repeated expropriations by church and state during the nineteenth century that, according to Duncan Earle (1990) and others, ultimately led to the development of the current system of festival sponsorship in Mesoamerica whereby an individual contributes his personal resources and the wealth he can generate in short order by borrowing from relatives, friends, and others who may owe him a favor.

11 Bazarte Martínez (1989, 59) mentions that Spanish confraternities sometimes limited their membership to 33 in remembrance of Christ's death at this age. Similarly, Bechtloff (1996, 235) notes that some cofradías in Michoacán had 12 officers corresponding to the 12 apostles of Christ. However, neither of these principles was operative in Maxcanú or any Yucatecan confraternities that I know.

12 A similar observation is made by Victor Turner in his synoptic account of the festival of the Three Kings in Tizimin, Yucatán, the site of one of the largest pilgrimages on the peninsula: "The gremio offices may be held more than once . . . at the local level. Sometimes, however, they remain under the control of a single family" (1974, 220).

13 While I was unable to find membership lists for this period, it is clear from oral testimony and property records in *El Registro del Catastro* in Mérida that non-Hispanic merchants did not begin appearing in the town square until the mid-1970s.

14 It is, perhaps, worth noting that Don Uyé attempted to make up for his folly by greeting an emissary from the Vatican during his term as municipal president. Since government officials

are not supposed to consort with church leaders, this was considered a breach of protocol, albeit in the opposite direction.

15   The diversion of cofradía funds into personal accounts apparently has a long history in Mexico. According to Bazarte Martínez (1989), the Mexican National Archives (AGN) are full of cases in which cofradía officials are accused of stealing from the treasury.

16   According to a former gremio president, the *Gremio de Mestizos* was at one time known as the *Gremio de Mestizos Finos* but changed its name when the poverty of its membership became evident to all, and the title began to invite ridicule. The *coup de grâce*, as the president noted, ceremoniously came one day when a long-time member ripped the word "fino" from the association's standards. The son of the gremio's founder, however, maintains that the name *mestizo fino* was really a joke (*chorteo*) from the beginning. According to his account, towns-people began to use the name in jest one year when two of the gremio's standard-bearers, drunk and disheveled, started marching around in the rain. Whether the gremio title actually included the term "fino" is of little consequence since the term "mestizo" itself was used in a more restricted sense in the 1920s and would have conveyed a sense of superiority *vis-á-vis* the indigenous residents of Maxcanú.

17   The mayokol was not only in a class by himself, he was greatly despised by hacienda peons. The antagonism between these two groups is, perhaps, best captured in Santiago Pacheco Cruz's popular drama *Justicia proletaria* (1935), in which hacienda foremen are forced to take refuge in the main house while an angry mob gathers outside.

18   Unlike other occupational groups, Maxcanú's potters were part of an extensive multi-town network in which a variety of social and economic exchanges were transacted. The ostensible purpose of the network was to exchange *hi'*—a transparent, relatively rare stone used in the making of potter's clay—for *k'at,* a porous clay used to manufacture household vessels. However, at the periodic reunions organized between potters of Maxcanú and Hecelchakan, the traders also arranged marriages for their sons and daughters and formalized their mutual obligations by becoming compadres.

19   Although there is evidence to suggest that pre-Columbian towns were divided into four admin-istrative districts (*cuchteel*) (Farriss 1984, 232; Thompson 1978, 315–18), the quadri-partite divi-sion of towns like Maxcanú is probably the result of eighteenth-century civic reforms that attempted to remake colonial towns in the image of Mexico City or Madrid, "frequently in four or more barrios or *cuarteles*" (Gibson 1964, 55). As Farriss herself notes, the pre-Columbian wards—renamed *parcialidades* by the Spaniards—had all but disappeared by the middle of the seventeenth century: "As towns within a town, the colonial *parcialidades* were fossil relics of the hierarchical pre-conquest political organization that the Spanish compressed into the single, homogenous unit, *república de indios*. They did not need to abolish the top and bottom tiers of the structure. They simply failed to acknowledge their existence and by denying them any role in the colonial political system, let them wither away" (1984, 164).

20   Huipils are bulky, white cotton dresses with embroidery at the hemline and around the neck. Although associated with Indian or mestizo women, there is great variability in their quality and style. The prestige of the wearer is indicated by the complexity of the design, the number of colors, and the type of stitch used. The most expensive huipils are hand-embroidered and are known by their Mayan names *xocbil chuy* (cross-stitch) and *xmanikte*. Somewhat less valuable are the machine-embroidered huipils. There are at least six varieties of these: *relleno* (filled), *sombreado* (outlined), *renacimiento* (renaissance), *rejillado* (netting), Richelieu, and *calado*. By far the least expensive is the simple "*huipil de tira*" made by ironing a printed floral strip onto the hemline and the neckline of the garment. A terno (literally three) is a more elegant version of the huipil with an additional band of embroidery sewn onto a cloth inlay.

21   In fiction as well as in history, the mestiza is depicted as an elegant tradition-bound woman of some means but neither as wealthy nor as avaricious as the white upper class. For example, in Eligio Ancona's popular novel *La mestiza* (1929), the protagonist is a beautiful but somewhat naïve woman of mixed ancestry who is seduced and abandoned by a young man from one of Mérida's upper-class families.

22   In *Revolution from Without* (1982), Gilbert Joseph notes that many henequén plantation own-ers teetered on the brink of financial disaster. During boom years fabulous profits could be

made, but to capitalize a henequén plantation required tremendous initial outlays, and most plantation owners were perpetually in debt either to commodity export houses or to North American banks.

23   This is not a specifically Yucatecan linguistic usage but one that is common throughout Mexico. Those familiar with Oscar Lewis's popular "autobiography" of the Sanchez family, *The Children of Sanchez* (1961), may recall that Consuelo, the oldest daughter, refers *only* to her teachers and the wives of her employers as "señoras."

24   Gremio records from the 1960s not only indicate that Doña Socorro was still in control of the mestizas finas, but that Spanish surnames like Rodríguez and Sanchez—what poor residents derisively refer to as beautiful names—predominate among the office holders.

25   This comment was made in response to my statement that Maxcanú's upper-class women (*xunano'ob*) were approaching the town square.

Chapter 3

1   See Stephen Jay Gould (1994) for an interesting discussion of the relationship between Carolus Linnaeus's system of taxonomy and Johann Friedrich Blumenbach's influential classification of human races.

2   As one of the peer reviewers of this book noted, colonial names didn't work well because of the high degree of intermarriage during colonial times, a factor that led to the dissolution of residential segregation in Mérida at early point.

3   Restall notes that the term "Maya" itself was sometimes used in a demeaning fashion: "One usage in this context was by nobles in reference to commoners, with the term seemingly somewhat derogatory. Thus, when applied to Mayas of another region, the term sometimes implied that such people were of lesser status, although at other times the reference seems neutral. . . ." (2004, 68–69).

4   See the discussion of the term "mestizo" as a trope in Mexican nationalist discourse in the introduction, pp. xxx–xxx.

5   In the case of males, the difference between mestizos and catríns is quite subtle; however, one can often judge their standing by the type of clothing their wives wear. It is also important to point out that, with the advent of mass marketing, even the boundary markers between groups have become commoditized. A generation ago the identification of a teenager as a mestizo or a catrín was largely dependent upon the type of footwear he used (sandals being the last remnant of the traditional folk costume). Today the issue is increasingly determined by the brand name of his tennis shoes. To become a catrín, or to *encatrínar*, a teenager will return from a lengthy stay in Mérida with a pair of Adidas tennis shoes, reflecting sunglasses, and an expensive T-shirt with an English phrase emblazoned on it.

6   In some cases one finds rather astounding differences between brothers separated by only a few years. One of my better informants, Manuel, grew up in a household in which Yucatec Mayan was spoken almost exclusively. By the time I met him, he had been granted the right to work in the ejido near Maxcanú. The expectation was that he would remain near his parents and take care of them in their old age. In contrast, Manuel's brother, his junior by just four years, was discouraged from speaking Mayan either in public or private. He was expected to pursue an education, learn Spanish well, and eventually move to Mérida. Similar distinctions are made among daughters in families that make at least part of their income from farm work. For example, in the Rodríguez family the three older daughters were raised as mestizas, and the younger ones were raised as catrínas.

7   Other, less-than-polite references to Indians or Mayas include *malix,* a Yucatec Mayan term defined as "dog without a pedigree" (DMC 490); and *huiro,* presumably from the Spanish *huir* (to flee or escape) and, thus, a possible reference to Indians who fled into the forest during the Caste War.

8   For example, in an article published in *América indígena* in 1942, Sol Tax criticized his contemporaries—ethnographers Morris Siegal and John Gillin—for suggesting that racial difference

was an important aspect of social stratification, arguing that an Indian with the requisite skills would have little difficulty assuming a position of authority in his own society: "It may be said with confidence, therefore, that essentially the difference between Ladino and Indian in Guatemala is not thought of as biological difference.... Once it is clearly understood that the difference between an Indian and a Ladino is not biological, but cultural, it need not seem strange that one of two brothers can be Indian and the other, perhaps, living in the same town, a Ladino" (1942, 46).

9   After explaining that Don Pedro's habit of standing on the front stoop and patting his bald spot was actually a way of emphasizing his Hispanic heritage—Mayas generally don't go bald—Don Pancho, Maxcanú's most unabashedly gay male, added that there were not many *k'olis* (bald men) who weren't also *k'uruch* (gay). Literally "crayfish" in Mayan, the latter term refers to male homosexuals (DMC 424).

10   One example of Cárdenist political culture is *Justicia proletaria* (1936), a drama by Santiago Pacheco Cruz that depicts an angry mob surrounding the house of a hated hacienda foreman. Written during the Cárdenist agrarian reform in Yucatán, this drama was intended to remind villagers of the things about plantation life they most disliked so they would support Cárdenist political initiatives.

11   Although the term "catrín" is clearly not of Mayan origin—Mayan does not use the "tr" consonant cluster—this moniker is also absent from the *Real Academia Española* and other nineteenth-century Spanish dictionaries. Only in dictionaries printed after 1929 does the term appear.

12   Yucatán of the late nineteenth and early twentieth centuries is often depicted as a tripartite political system composed of Indians, mestizos, and whites. Although mestizos, like whites, were considered vecinos (fully vested citizens), they were distinguished from the latter by their dress and, in some cases, their surnames. As Redfield notes, "the word vecino ... a more or less legal or technical term, included in Mérida two groups socially distinguished: whites and mixed bloods wearing the same garb as the Indians" (1950, 375). Tax describes Guatemala in similar terms and notes that race actually was an important criteria of distinction between the top two groups: "The educated people who think of themselves as pure White ... invest in the term all or many of the connotations that it has when used to distinguish Whites from Indians or Negros; they, therefore, strongly tend to set up a tripartite classification of Guatemalans as Indian, Ladino, and White, and define the Ladino as a mestizo" (1942, 46).

13   According to the *Diccionario maya cordemex, wach* is a word of unknown origin. The editors, however, suggest that it may derive from the Mayan *wa-paach,* a term that refers to Aztecs who arrived in Yucatán during the pre-colonial period (DCM 905). According to popular accounts, the term *wach* derives from the Spanish *huarache* (pronounced "warache"), a type of sandal worn in central Mexico that is quite different from the Yucatecan alpargata. Still others contend that the term *wach* is an onomatopoeic expression referring to the squeaky boots worn by soldiers in General Alvarado's army, the force that placed Yucatán under the control of the federal government in 1915.

14   Common lexical hybrids include a regional dish called *mukbipollo,* from the Maya *mukbil,* meaning to bury or cook underground (DMC534), and the Spanish *pollo* (chicken); a game called *ts'opsandia* from the Mayan *ts'op,* meaning to pierce or stab (DMC 890) and the Spanish *sandía* (watermelon); and *chocolomo,* another regional delicacy, from the Mayan *chokó,* meaning hot (DMC 105) and the Spanish *lomo* (meat from the back of an animal). See Suárez (1979, 131) for others.

15   See Fernando Muñoz's *El Teatro Regional de Yucatán* (1987) and earlier works by Alberto Cervera Espejo (1973), John Nomland (1967), and Alejandro Cervera Andrade (1947) for a detailed discussion of regional theatre (*teatro costumbrista*). The study by Muñoz is of particular interest since it contains an index of authors and their works, brief summaries of many "low brow" dramas, and excerpts in Mayan and Spanish from several musicals.

16   An even more derogatory example of this poetic form is the infamous *Purusxon Kawich* (Fatso Cauich). Maya place names and substantives have been placed in italics.

Purusxon Kawich	Fatso Cauich
nacido en *Tahmek*	born in Tahmek

un pobre *winik*	a poor Indian
con cara de *pek*.	with the face of a dog.
Cuando era *dz'iriz*	When just a child
su papa Don Sos	his father Don Sos
lo dejó *k'olis*	left him bald
de tanto *wask'op*.	from so many head swipes.
Ya grande *purux*,	Now grown the fat lunk
quiso hacerle *mek*	wanted to embrace
a la Linda *Xpet*	the beautiful Xpet
de la hacienda *Xt'u'ul*.	from the hacienda Xt'u'ul.
"Ay no!" dijo *Xpet*	"Oh no!" said Xpet
No estoy tan *poch*	I am not so vulgar
para que un *werek*	that a gross Indian
venga hacerme *loch*.	will come hug me (have sex with me).
Si estás tan *poch*	If you're so forward
de hacerle alguien *hich*	to get someone pregnant
vete a tu *wotoch*	go to your house
y abraza a tu *chich*.	and make love to your grandmother.

(Bartolomé 1988, 311; translated by author)

17   The Yucatecan jarana and the Spanish jota are so similar that in 1990 a group of Spanish archaeologists who were excavating the ruins at Oxkintok (a pre-classic site near Maxcanú) could dance the jarana without training.

18   While most Maxcanú residents acknowledge that spoken Yucatec Mayan has forever lost its purity, a few older people view themselves as the conservators of *legítimo Maya* and tout their ability to count to 100 or say things in Mayan that everyone else now says in Spanish. Such was the case with Don Rogelio, one of my best informants. While Don Rogelio gave freely of his time, he always insisted that I replay the tape so he could review the contents and remove any contaminating Castilian elements.

19   Eligio Ancona's tragic novel, *La mestiza* (1929), provides a glimpse of the romanticism surrounding the mestizo/a in Yucatán. Set in San Sebastián, a picturesque barrio in eighteenth-century Mérida, the novel presents the reader with a simple choice between an unscrupulous Creole youth who seduces and then abandons a young mestiza, and a valiant mestizo who saves the young woman and her bastard child from infamy.

20   One step in this direction was the publication of the *Guía para la alfabetización: Población Maya* (Literacy Guide for the Maya Population) by the Secretary of Public Education (SEP). First printed in 1987, the guide contains a brief description of Mayan grammar and phonology; a set of recommendations for teaching literacy; and a curriculum, divided into 15 lessons, that is intended to train students to read and write stories in Yucatec Mayan. Not surprisingly, perhaps, the cover photo shows three women in elegant ternos (and one elderly male) dancing the jarana. For further discussion of the renaissance in spoken Mayan and Maya identity, see Berkely (1998).

Chapter 4

1   See also Bent's more recent study "Three Green-Eyed Monsters: Acting as Applied Criticism in Shakespeares's Othello" (1998).

2   Although it remains a pervasive feature of Mesoamerican ethnography, the idea of a fixed distinction between the sacred and the profane has been widely criticized. For example, in *Of Wonders and Wise Men*, Terry Rugeley argues that it is no "simple matter to pick apart the sacred from the secular. Terms like 'sacred' and 'secular' present a false duality here.... It is not hard to see a joyous worldliness in the pious traditions of old Mexico" (2001b, 96). For a similar analysis see Enrique Gil Calvo (1991).

3   In the San Bernardo performance these were effigies of the hacienda owner and his wife.

4   While the capital-intensive henequén plantation of northwest Yucatán is properly distinguished from the less capital-intensive corn and cattle hacienda of the colonial era (and other regions in the contemporary era), I have used the two terms interchangeably in referring to the Las Palmas hacienda of San Bernardo. Although Las Palmas was most recently a large henequén plantation, locals have always referred to it as a hacienda. Moreover, the term "hacienda" is used to designate the juridical status of a community as well as a type of agricultural enterprise. While *pueblos* and *villas* (villages and towns) are autonomous self-governing units, settlements categorized as haciendas are not. San Bernardo, much to the chagrin of its inhabitants, remains a hacienda in the latter sense.

5   Here I should note that my observation of the San Bernardo k'ub pol was not a chance occurrence. San Bernardo is a mere five kilometers from Maxcanú, my primary field site, and several of the participants, as well as many of the fiesta goers, live or have close relatives in Maxcanú. Therefore, I was made aware of the fiesta early on and discussed the performance with many Maxcanú residents, including some erstwhile performers, before making the trek to San Bernardo. I also visited the San Bernardo museum on at least one occasion prior to attending the k'ub pol. While the k'ub pol is a spectacle worthy of attention in its own right, I was initially drawn to it because of a more general interest in popular religion and the often contentious relationship between the clergy and lay religious organizations (cofradías or gremios). The exchange about my sexual interest in the pig provides a good example of the teasing and joking that surround preparations for the event. It was also, undoubtedly, a test of my linguistic prowess. My reputation as a good Mayan speaker generally preceded my arrival at a new location, and, invariably, someone was curious to know how much I actually knew. In fact, Yucatecans, as other Mexicans, often refer to linguistic competence as the "ability to defend oneself." Moreover, since many of the gringos who roam the backwaters of Yucatán are Christian missionaries, the sexual jest may have been an attempt to figure out what species of gringo I was. The "evangélicos," as they are called, generally don't like to engage in such crass discussions.

6   The practice of inviting a priest to say mass, but limiting his role, has, according to Terry Rugeley, a long tradition in Yucatán: "Peasants occasionally used priests to sanctify the icons, but still succeeded in keeping them at arm's distance.... His role extended no further than saying an hour of mass while the full range of cult activities extended over whole days and nights...." (2001b, 131–32). The clergy, for their part, have been wary of the cuch for more than a century. "The *kuuch* [sic] ceremony was troubling to the religious authorities, both for its excess of drinking and its resistance to elite control.... The cura of Chancenote found *kuuches* particularly bothersome during the constitutional crisis [of 1812?], when Maya peasants shed all inhibitions in the observance of these ceremonies" (Rugeley 2001b, 126).

7   "A *noox* is a smaller fowl put with a larger one to complete the offering. Such a pair often makes up the gift to the gods. Generally *noox* is something supplied to support or complete another larger than itself in order that the other might not fall or fail. A piece of stone or wood set under the leg of a table to keep it from toppling is *noox*.... The Governor does not fail because he has many *noox*" (Redfield and Villa Rojas 1990 [1934], 131).

8   See note 10, Chapter 3.

9   Pacheco Cruz writes: "It ran something as follows. A group of hacienda residents, for example, *which is where the ritual was done*, elected as 'deputies' a patron or matron to appropriately carry out the fiesta; and from the home of the chief deputy, they carried out the head in procession to the main house, i.e., the house of the hacienda's owner" (quoted in Rugeley 2001b, 189; emphasis added).

10   See Irwin Press's study of Pustunich, Yucatán (1977) for more discussion of priestly abuses during the height of the henequén era.

11   In the *Diccionario maya cordemex* the term *che' che'* is defined as "something raw, neither roasted, nor boiled, nor fried, nor stewed" (DMC 86). The adjective is also used to describe fruit that is not fully mature.

12   In a report published by the International Work Group for Indigenous Affairs in November 1973 (Document 15), and later in *Critique of Anthropology* (Spring 1974), Alicia Barrabas and Miguel Bartolomé charged the Mexican government with ethnocide for their role in the

development of a hydroelectric power plant in Oaxaca and the relocation of the Chinantec. In the report, the two Argentine anthropologists write: "The aim of this report is to call attention to a program of ethnocide which is being applied to ethnic minorities in Mexico as part of a policy of capitalist development being carried out by the Mexican government through regional development agencies. It can be shown that ethnocidal policies of these agencies have an intimate relationship with the broad economic and political goals. . . ." (1973, 3). For a different view, see Aguirre Beltrán (1975). In his rejoinder, Beltrán describes the two critics as "happy savage anthropologists" and anarchist revisionists who have carried the concept of "nation" to absurd levels by applying it to the smallest and least viable indigenous communities.

13 In 1987, for example, the National Institute for Adult Education (INEA), a subdivision of SEP, published a colorful, 340-page textbook for teaching reading and writing in Mayan, something that would have been unheard of just a generation ago. Similarly, in recent years, INI has made a concerted effort to revalidate indigenous medicine, especially herbal cures, despite strong opposition from certain sectors of the medical profession. In addition to setting up an herb garden in front of the INI outpost near Maxcanú, the local office organized a forum in which healers were encouraged to present their most effective herbal remedies. To emphasize its official character, a panel of dignitaries, which included Governor Manzanilla Schafer, municipal presidents from several nearby towns, and a number of high ranking INI officials, were invited to address the audience, and doctors from all the nearby social security clinics were obligated to attend.

14 In *Mayan People Within and Beyond Boundaries,* Peter Hervik provides a similar example of how the k'ub pol or *ok'ostah pol* has been appropriated and recontextualized by the local bourgeoisie. While there are many different enactments of the k'ub pol in Oxkutzcab, the performance Hervik describes has been controlled for decades by one patron, the widow of "an extremely powerful businessman and . . . one of the richest people in Oxkutzcab" (1999, 141). In fact, according to Hervik, poor residents of Oxkutzcab now feel excluded from this event: "Several poor families told me that they participated in the past . . . but the Okosta Pol now carried on by Doña María is perceived to be exclusively for those who have money, or who are her personal friends and family. Moreover, these families argue that the fact that the image of the child Jesus is adorned with golden jewelry and that the participants wait until the next day before they eat the pigs' heads are signs that show an exclusive celebration of rich people and this has altered the nature of the celebration to the point that they no longer care to participate" (1999, 143–44). More importantly, though, like Don Ponso of Maxcanú, Dzul Ek, a school principle from Mani and the son-in-law of the patron, has helped transform the k'ub pol from a ritual performance to a theatrical production worthy of Oxkutzcab's middle-class social clubs. As Hervik writes: "I first experienced this decontextualization at the annual party of one of Oxkutzcab's social clubs, the Bella Época. On this occasion, Dzul Ek mobilized part of the local Maya theatre group to perform a small portion of the *Okosta Pol* to a large audience. It took place in a confined area of the park and, thus, was open to spectators while sheltering club members. . . . In all these cases, however, the *Okosta Pol* is no longer a traditional practice as it is separated from its original context and recreated in a condensed version in theatrical productions. . . ." (1999, 148–49).

15 In their study of the annual fiesta of Hunucma, Fernandez Repetto and Negroe Sierra (1977) make a similar observation about the incorporation of nationalist icons in popular religious observances. In addition to noting the presence of colored flags that reproduce the colors and the disposition of the Mexican flag, they cite the presence of the ubiquitous mariachi band and, ironically perhaps, locals decked out in Aztec dress. Having contemporary Maya dress up like pre-Columbian Aztecs may seem like an odd way of bolstering the modern nation-state, yet it makes sense if one remembers that the Aztecs inhabited the center of political power while the Maya have subsisted at the periphery of a succession of pre-colonial, colonial, and post-colonial states. For a discussion of the mariachi band as a national symbol, see Napolitano (2002).

16 Rugeley notes that one of the *gigantones* was the heretic Ecolompadio, a Swiss theologian named Johann Hausschien, 1482–1531, who spoke out of both sides of his mouth. When speaking with Catholics he led them to think he was Catholic, and when dealing with Protestants he pretended he was one of them (2001b, 90).

Chapter 5

1   For example, Michael Taussig explains the significance of the devil pact in Colombia's Cauca Valley in terms of the alienation peasants experience upon becoming wage laborers for the first time. Unlike their fully proletarianized co-workers, who have become accustomed to the logic or illogic of the market, the newly proletarianized plantation workers are caught between two opposing production systems and, therefore, experience firsthand the disappearance of a more satisfying life, one in which "work, organically connects soul with hand" (Taussig 1980, 11). In an attempt to illustrate the nature of peasant consciousness, Taussig presents a tale (presumably one of many) in which money acquires supernatural power through an illicit baptism ritual. By concealing a peso in his hand, an unscrupulous godparent is able to capture the blessing intended for his godchild. Endowed with heavenly grace, the baptized peso returns to its owner each time it is spent and enriches him at the expense of his godchild who loses any chance of eternal salvation. However, the status of this literary fragment is never directly discussed. While the story might reasonably be considered an allegory, Taussig views it as a précis on peasant thought in general, an example of an inflexible mode of reasoning that simultaneously "reflects" and "distorts" the reality of pre-capitalist exchange. In other words, the "peasantariet" cannot decipher the mysteries of commodity production because it does not decipher it at all, it simply "thrust[s] into prominence the salient contrasts of the structures that enclose them ..." (1980, 103–04). For a sample of the large and growing number of writers who question the value of sharply contrasting gift and commodity exchange, or pre-capitalist and capitalist modes of production, see Bayly (1986), Comaroff (1985), Hart (1986), and Kopytoff (1986).

2   In *Of Wonders and Wise Men,* Terry Rugeley points out that the priest and the hacienda owner were often one and the same, living fat off the labor of Maya workers. He also includes some rather colorful complaints about priestly excess, including one alleging that Raymundo Pérez, the priest of Mascuspana, forced his parishioners to hunt alligators that were so ferocious "they will eat a Christian" (2001b, 44). While Rugeley views this complaint as an example of rhetoric rather than historical fact, it points to a tradition of discussing priests in unflattering ways. For another account of abusive priests in the peninsula, see Irwin Press's study of Pustunich, Yucatán (1977). Mayan folk literature also contains a healthy share of dumb priest stories. See, for example, "A Story about a Trickster and a Priest" in Burns (1983, 152–57).

3   The terms *pach* and *pach'* open up a variety of interpretive possibilities. According to the *Diccionario maya cordemex,* the term *pach'* not only refers to an object striking the ground, but to an object or animal that hangs limply like a piece of wet rope. Since several versions of the tale conclude with the evil witch hanging himself in his prison cell, this referent is particularly apt. Indeed, death by hanging is considered an act of redemption in Maya mythology. The term *pach* also leads in an interesting, if somewhat different, direction. In its nominal form it describes a measure of cloth, the spine of an animal, or the plumage of a bird (DMC 615). In its verbal form it means: 1) to appropriate or take possession, or 2) to augment or multiply. Both of these make sense if the Way Kot is an anthropomorphic image of gold or token money (DMC 615–16).

4   The equation between feces and money has, of course, been noted in other contexts. Not only does the Thompson motif index (Thompson 1955–58) have a place for donkeys that defecate ducats, but as Alan Dundes notes, this association is "well attested in contemporary folkspeech: filthy lucre, to be filthy or stinking rich, to be rolling in it, to have money up the ass, and so forth.... Still other illustrative slang terms are 'paydirt' and 'shitload'" (2002, 101). However, contra Dundes, I see no reason to view money or accumulation as a sublimated form of infantile pleasures (e.g., the desire to play with one's feces) or as evidence of anal-erotic tendencies. I prefer a more direct approach: monetary accumulation is filthy because it is inherently anti-social and undermines established forms of reciprocity. In any case, readers who are interested in further examples of money as feces should refer to Margaret Redfield's tale of Don Juan Conejo, a trickster who sells the same corn to several different animals and then buries the money in the ground. Later he decides to dig it up and divide it among his friends, but it has turned to shit so he plays with it, "throwing it up as if they were balls" (1937, 35).

5   A recent article by John Tofik Karim (2004) allows for an interesting comparison between Lebanese immigrants in Yucatán and the Sirio-Lebanese population of Brazil. Like their

counterparts in Yucatán, Brazilians of Lebanese ancestry got their start as peddlers, selling cheap goods in a cash-poor economy. Like the former, they were also depicted as parasites "who traded goods but failed to 'produce' real wealth" (2004, 321). As Karim points out, Middle Eastern merchants were even disparaged by leading statesmen like Roquette-Pinto: " ... *turcos* peddle in all parts. They entrench themselves, seeking clients in all corners. From the thousands of them that Brazil annually receives, there is not even a hundred [agricultural] producers ..." (2004, 330; bracketed material in the original).

6   Redfield and Villa Rojas (1990 [1934], 179) interpret Way Kot as the "stone-wall witch."

7   Those interested in discovering the origin of Mesoamerican tales should heed the warning Robert Laughlin provides in *Tales of the Bat:* "'What's Man Like?'—a tale with undoubted European influence—had one scene that was absent from any of the collections I had reviewed.... [A] woman's 'pestiferous wound' seemed so typical of Zinacantec imagination that I concluded it must be a local innovation. But this product of Zinacantec genius, I learned entirely by chance, had been forecast almost literally by none other than François Rabelais in his *Second Book of Pantagruel*" (Laughlin and Karasik 1988, 16–17).

8   Ted Ownby argues that African Americans generally, and blues musicians in particular, viewed consumption as an avenue to inclusion in America: "The men and women of the blues appreciated the hope of abundance, saw choice as a substantial freedom unavailable to farm workers, and believed goods could be part of a new dignity available to mobile, urbanized people. Above all, by connecting goods to new women, new men, and new excitement, the blues upheld the romantic possibilities of consumer culture" (1999, 127). Similarly, Lizabeth Cohen argues that "with strict limitations on where blacks could live and work in Chicago, consumption became a major avenue through which they could assert their independence" (quoted in Ownby 1999, 124).

9   Although generally hidden in footnotes or appendices, the association between witchcraft and sexual promiscuity is well documented in the work of Redfield and Villa Rojas. Summarizing a tale told by Tiburcio Coyi in *Chan Kom*, they write: "A certain man, having become suspicious of his wife, made up his mind to spy on her. One night, when they were sleeping together, he saw her get up, perform certain mysterious acts, and turn into a cow. In the street some bulls were waiting for her, and as soon as she appeared they surrounded her and had intercourse with her.... At daybreak he saw that what he had taken for a church was only a *sascabera* [i.e., a cave] and that in the bush there remained not a trace of what he had seen the night before.... When he reached his home, he found his wife grinding corn, apparently quite ignorant of what had happened" (1934, 334). Thanks to Robey Callahan who directed me to this passage and several similar ones.

10   Don Eus, as it turns out, was right. Although based on a multiplicity of factors, social status in Yucatán circa 1930 was clearly encoded in variants of a domestically produced folk costume. While poor mestizos or Indians wore white garments made of *manta cruda* (unrefined cotton) and simple sandals or no footwear at all, the mestizo fino wore a more elegant version of the folk costume and leather alpargatas. Therefore, the adoption of western clothes, which imitated in form if not in quality the fashion of the urban upper class, not only transcended the opposition between poor and fine mestizos resulting in a new social designation, the catrín, but linked the wearer to the market, a fact that insured that all social gains would be short-lived. Unlike the mestizo fino, whose status was rooted in the more stable terrain of family surname and reputation, the catrín functions as a floating signifier in a constantly shifting field of commodity signifieds. If tennis shoes were at one time sufficient to claim this identity, one now needs Nikes, sunglasses, and a nylon gym bag with a team logo.

11   In the *Folk Culture of Yucatan* (1941), Redfield notes that this unusual moniker was just beginning to grace the lips of Dzitas residents during his stay in the peninsula. The term "catrín," in fact, cannot be found in the *Real Academica Española* or other nineteenth-century dictionaries. Only in dictionaries printed after 1929 does it appear.

12   In "L'origine des machines a coudre Singer," a grateful Way Kot leaves a late-model Singer sewing machine for a hunter who spares his life (Boccara 1997, Vol. 6, 55).

13   For the record, a 1925 census of Maxcanú does include a merchant named Juan Martín.

14   For a different perspective on commerce and indigenous life in México circa 1940, see Malinowski and de la Fuente (1982). In what turned out to be his last field study, Malinowski coined the phrase "commercial libido" to describe the Zapotec zeal for commerce. Although the eminent ethnographer was working in central México, he notes that "people in our region are not the only good merchants in the republic" (1982, 62).

15   Here we should note that spiritists, like merchants, are constantly engaged in economic as well as supernatural competition. Criticism of spiritists emanates not only from the church and the medical profession but from other spiritists. Indeed, Asael Hansen's observation (Hansen and Bastarrachea Manzano 1984) that spiritists begin each consultation by criticizing other spiritists the visitor may have seen remains true 70 years later (Loewe 2003).

Chapter 6

1   "Possession trance rituals do not necessarily deal with illness and curing. They may serve to alleviate many different kinds of stress, such as marital or financial problems or concern over school examinations. They may also be experienced as forms of devotion and fulfillment of obligations to the spirits inherited in family lines or revealed to specific individuals" (Bourguignon 2004, 143).

2   From Redfield's perspective, spiritualism or spiritism was a symptom of the general disintegration of urban folk medicine. Quoting a passage from a paper by Asael Hansen on magic in urban Yucatán, Redfield writes: "In this treatment elements were brought together which had probably never been in association before. The medium in charge gave the impression that she was selecting items from her experience which presented themselves at the moment. It is doubtful if she ever recalled them in exactly the same order twice. It is not uncommon for treatments to be recommended in one séance and revised in the next" (1941, 323).

3   Asael Hansen was part of the team assembled by Robert Redfield to study the influence of urban life on rural communities, a study that formed the basis for Redfield's famous writings on the rural-urban continuum. While Villa Rojas collaborated with Redfield on Chan Kom, and later produced Los elegidos de Dios (1987), based on his research in more isolated Maya communities of Quintana Roo, Hansen was in charge of producing a monograph on Mérida. Unfortunately, Hansen's research was not published until 1984 when a Yucatecan ethnographer, Juan Ramon Bastarrachea Manzano, published an edited and annotated version of Hansen's work in Spanish. According to faculty at the University of Alabama who remember him, it was Hansen's fond affection for the other type of "spirits" that prevented him from publishing his work. Copies of the journal La ley de amor can be found in the Biblioteca Carlos R. Menéndez in Mérida.

4   As Redfield tersely comments in The Folk Culture of Yucatan (1941, 325), "The activities of the urban curers are independent of the gods."

5   John Stephens writes: "My retinue consisted of eight men, who considered themselves in my employ.... I tied one end round my left wrist, and told one of the men to light a torch and follow me, but he refused absolutely, and all the rest, one after another did the same.... I terminated the matter abruptly by declaring that I should not pay one of them a medio;... I entered with a candle in one hand and a pistol in the other" (1963, 140).

6   The original Spanish/Mayan version is as follows. I have italicized Yucatec Mayan phrases and have added accent marks in a few places to clarify the tense of the verb. Otherwise the narrative is unchanged.

> Jacinto Cen era un profeta. Profetizó [los] días [que] faltan para conocer algunos vehículos, ho huacax kak, tambien el avión pepen kak, también el alambre anicab. Por medio de los alambres los extranjeros se comunicaron con sus familias, el teléfono. Se casarán los extranjeros con las mujeres indias. Oxkintok antes del año 2000 lo han de restaurar por ayuda de los extranjeros y también se hara choco wah, tortilla caliente. El señor profeta don Jacinto Cen de noche escribe con pluma de ave con sus letras jeroglíficas, como la letra de China ahora. Ninguna persona lo entendía. No se llevaba con los ricos, solamente con los campesinos y cuando salió

en Santa Cruz dijó adios a una mujer. Jacinto Cen era un hombre de altura, dos metros y color café, pelo lacio, vestidura blanca sin botones, pantalón *xort*. Todo ya se esta cumpliendo, las palabras de don Jacinto Cen, el hombre de Oxkintok. Así lo dijó mi abuela.

7 Like other elements of early twentieth-century dress, the *ex* lacked buttons or fasteners of any type and was, thus, easily distinguished from more elegant versions of the folk costume. Consequently, reference to this piece of clothing sets up a contrast between Mayas and mestizos, particularly mestizos finos, as well as between natives and foreigners.

8 Florentino Cituk was a prophet who lived in the sacred village of Chun Pom and served as the Patron of the Cross, or head priest, during the first decades of the twentieth century. According to published sources discussed by Sullivan, Cituk was considered an important political leader and was invited to meet with the Governor of Yucatán in 1914. Though he was given the power to interpret "night writing" ('*akabciib*), he was otherwise illiterate (Sullivan 1989, 224).

9 Sullivan defines *anikab* as a "vine used for lashing and tying together poles" and notes that it appears in other prophetic texts as a metaphor for telegraph or telephone poles or even underground cables (1989, 167).

10 In twentieth-century Yucatán, writing and books were closely linked to slavery through stories of the *nohoch cuenta* (or Big Bill). Since slavery was prohibited by law, control over the plantation work force was based on a system of debt bondage in which all the laborer's "debts" were allegedly written down in a large account book known as the *nohoch cuenta*. Stories about the epoch of slavery, in fact, often contain references to a majordomo, or mayokol, who would scribble things down in a strange or indecipherable script. In reality debts were seldom if ever recorded. In more contemporary times, the power of writing is symbolized by the escribiente (scribe), an officer of the ejido who is responsible for keeping track of the ejidatarios, the tasks they do, and the pay they receive. It is an important political post because the escribiente can reward his friends and punish his enemies through his record-keeping (e.g., by losing their names and records). Although it is an elected post with a maximum three-year term, it is not unusual for the same individual to retain the post for many years. The escribiente of Calcehtok, an ejido near Maxcanú, had been in office for 18 years when I arrived. Similarly, as Hansen and Bastarrachea Manzano note, the ability to write long prescriptions is considered evidence of great medical knowledge (1984, 278).

11 The *Diccionario maya cordemex* defines the term *chin k'iix* as a "sorcerer who inflicts damage through the use of thorns" (DMC 137).

Conclusion

1 See http://www.cdi.gob.mx/index.php?option=com_content&task=view&id=396&Itemid=51).

2 See http://www.yucatecos.org/quiensomos.html.

Appendix

1 In Yucatec Mayan *sas* (or, zaz, in zaztok) can be translated as a clear thing and light, as well as to illuminate or whiten (DMC 718). *Tok's* refers either to flint or a very hard stone that gives off sparks when it is struck by another object (DMC 805).

REFERENCES

Adler, Rachel H. 2004. *Yucatecans in Dallas, Texas: breaking the border, bridging the distance.* Boston: Pearson, Allyn and Bacon.

Adorno, Theodore. 1997. *Aesthetic theory.* Minneapolis: University of Minnesota Press.

Aguirre Beltrán, G. 1975. Etnocidio en México: una denuncia irresponsable. *América Indígena* 35: 403–18.

———. 1992. *Obra polemica.* México City, MX: Instituto Nacional de Antropologia e Historia.

Ak'abal, Humberto. 2001. *Ajkem Tzil/Tejedor de palabras.* Guatemala City, GT: Editorial Cholsamaj.

Alcides Reissner, Raúl. 1983. *El indio en los diccionarios: exegesis lexical de un Estereotipo.* México City, MX: Instituto Nacional Indigenista.

Amador Naranjo, Ascensión. 1989. El origen del mundo en Oxkintok. *Okintok* 2: 157–71.

Amparo Gamboa, Jesús. 1984. *El uayismo en la cultura de Yucatán.* Mérida, MX: Ediciónes de la Universidad de Yucatán.

Ancona, Eligio. 1929. *La mestiza.* Mérida, MX: Biblioteca de la Voz Peninsular.

Annis, Sheldon. 1996. *God and production in a Guatemalan town.* Austin: University of Texas Press.

Anzures y Bolaños, María del Carmen. 1983. *La medicina tradicional en México: proceso histórico, sincretismos y conflictos.* México City, MX: Universidad Nacional Autónoma de México.

Appadurai, Arjun. 1988. Introduction: Commodities and the politics of value. In *The Social life of things: commodities in cultural perspective,* ed. Arjun Appadurai. Cambridge, UK: Cambridge University Press. 3–63.

———, ed. 1988. *The social life of things: commodities in cultural perspective.* Cambridge, UK: Cambridge University Press.

Bakhtin, Mikhail. 1984. *Rabelais and his world.* Bloomington: Indiana University Press.

Barabas, Alicia, and Miguel Bartolomé. 1973. *Hydraulic development and ethnocide: the Mazatec and Chinantec people of Oaxaca, México.* Copenhagen, DK: International Work Group for Indigenous Affairs.

Barrera Vásquez, Alfredo. 1957. *Códice de Calkiní.* Campeche, MX: Biblioteca Campechana.

———. [DMC]. 1980a. *Diccionario Maya cordemex.* Mérida, MX: Ediciones Cordemex.

———. 1986. "Lo Ignoraba U´sted" Produccion Editorial Dante. Mérida, Yucatán, México.

———. 1980b. *Estudios lingüisticos.* Vol. 1. Mérida, MX: Fondo Editorial de Yucatán.

Barthes, Roland. 1972. *Mythologies.* New York: Noonday Press.

Bartolomé, Miguel Alberto. 1988. La dinámica social de los Mayas de Yucatán: pasado y presente de la situación colonial. *Serie de Antropología Social, Número 80.* México City, MX: Instituto Nacional Indigenista.

———, and Alicia Barabas. 1982. Tierra de la palabra: historia y etnografía de los Chatinos de Oaxaca. *Coleccion Cientifica 108.* México City, MX: Instituto Nacional de Antropologia e Historia.

Bauman, Richard. 1996. Transformations of the word in the production of Mexican festival drama. In *Natural histories of discourse,* ed. Michael Silverstein and Greg Urban. Chicago: University of Chicago Press. 301–28.

———, and Charles Briggs. 1990. Poetics and performance as critical perspectives on language and social life. *Annual Review of Anthropology* 19: 59–88.

———, and Joel Sherzer. 1974. *Explorations in the ethnography of speaking.* Cambridge, UK: Cambridge University Press.

Bayly, C.A. 1986. The origins of Swadeshi (home industry): cloth and Indian society, 1700–1930. In Appadurai, *The social life of things,* 295–321.

Bazarte Martínez, Alicia. 1998. *Las cofradías de Espanioles en la Ciudad de Mexico (1526–1869).* Azcapatzalco, MX: Universidad Autonoma Metropolitana.

Beaucage, Pierre. 1998. The third wave of modernization: liberalism, Salinismo, and indigenous peasants in Mexico. In Phillips, *The third wave of modernization,* 3–27.

Bechtloff, Dagmar. 1996. *Las cofradías en Michoacan durante la ipoca de la colonia: la religion y su relacion politica y economica en una sociedad intercultural.* Zinacantepec, MX: El Colegio de Michoacain.

Becker, Marjorie. 1994. Torching La Purísima, dancing at the altar: The construction of revolutionary hegemony in Michoacán, 1934–1940. In *Everyday forms of state formation: revolution and the negotiation of rule in modern Mexico,* ed. Gilbert M. Joseph and Daniel Nugent. Durham: Duke University Press, 247–264.

Beltran, Aguirre. 1975. Etnócidio en México: una denuncia irresponsable. *América Indigena* 35: 403–18.

Benjamin, Walter. 1977. *Illuminations.* New York: Schocken Books.

Bent, Geoffrey. 1991. Chronicles of the time: acting as applied criticism in Hamlet. *Theatre Research International* 16.1: 17–29.

———. 1998. Three green-eyed monsters: acting as applied criticism. *Shakespeare's Othello. Antioch Review* 56.3: 358–73.

Berkley, Anthony R. 1998. *Remembrance and revitalization: the archive of pure Maya.* PhD diss., University of Chicago.

Boccarra, Michel. 1985. El Way Kot (Brujo Águila). *Revista de la Universidad de Yucatán* 155.

———. 1997. *Encyclopédie de la mythologie Maya Yucatèque: les labyrinthes sonores.* 15 vols. Paris: Editions Ductus.

Bolio Lopez, Jésus. 1983. *La historia regional Yucateca en anecdotas picantes.* Mérida, MX: Maldonado Editores.

Bourdieu, Pierre. 1977. *Outline of a theory of practice.* Cambridge, UK: Cambridge University Press.

Bourguignon, Erika. 2004. Possession and trance. In *Encyclopedia of medical anthropology: health and illness in the world's cultures,* ed. Carol Ember and Melvin Ember. New York: Kluwer. 137–44.

Boyer, Pascal, ed. 1990. *Cognitive aspects of religious symbolism.* Cambridge, UK: Cambridge University Press.

Brandes, Stanley. 1988. *Power and persuasion: fiestas and social control in rural Mexico.* Philadelphia: University of Pennsylvania Press.

Bricker, Victoria. 1981. *The Indian Christ, the Indian King: the historical substrate of Maya myth and ritual.* Austin: University of Texas Press.

Briggs, Charles. 1988. *Competence in performance: the creativity of tradition in Mexicano verbal art.* Philadelphia: University of Pennsylvania Press.

Briggs, Jean L. 1970. *Never in Anger: Portrait of an Eskimo Family.* Cambridge, MA: Harvard University Press.

Brinton, Daniel. 1976 [1883]. *El folk-lore de Yucatán.* Mérida, MX: Ediciones del Gobierno del Estado.

Brown, Karen McCarthy. 1991. *Mama Lola: a Vodou priestess in Brooklyn.* Berkeley: University of California Press.

Buck-Morss, Susan. 1977. *The origin of negative dialectics: Theodore Adorno, Walter Benjamin, and the Frankfurt Institute.* Sussex: The Harvester Press.

Burns, Allan. 1977. The Caste War in the 1970's: present day accounts from villages in Quintana Roo. In *Anthropology and history in Yucatan,* ed. Grant D. Jones. Austin: University of Texas Press, 259–27.

———. 1983. *An epoch of miracles: oral literature of the Yucatec Maya.* Austin: University of Texas Press.

———. 1993. *Maya in exile: Guatemalans in Florida.* Philadelphia: Temple University Press.

Cancian, Frank. 1965. *Economics and prestige in a Maya community.* Stanford: Stanford University Press.

Carey, James. 1984. *The Mexican Revolution in Yucatán, 1915–1924.* Boulder: Westview Press.

Carlson, Robert. 1996. *The war for the heart and soul of a highland Maya town.* Austin: University of Texas Press.

Carrera Estampa, Manuel. 1954. *Los gremios Mexicanos: la organizacion gremial en Nueva España, 1521–1867.* México City, MX: EDIAPSA.

Casteñeda, Quetzil. 2004. "We are not Indigenas!": the Maya identity of Yucatán, an introduction. *The Journal of Latin American Anthropology* 9.1: 36–63.

Cervera Andrade, Alejandro. 1947. *El teatro regional de Yucatán.* Mérida, MX: Impresa Guerra.

Cervera Espejo, Alberto. 1973. *Apuntes sobre el teatro de la revolución en Yucatán.* Mérida, MX: Gobierno del Estado de Yucatán.

Chance, John K. 1990. Changes in twentieth-century Meso-American cargo systems. In Stephen and Dow, *Class, politics, and popular religion,* 27–42.

———, and William B. Taylor. 1985. *Cofradías* and cargos: an historical perspective on the Mesoamerican civil-religious hierarchy. *American Ethnologist* 12.1: 1–26.

Chase, Jacquelyn, ed. 2002. *The spaces of neoliberalism: land, place, and family in Latin America.* Bloomfield: Kumarian Press.

Christian, William. 1981. *Local religion in sixteenth-century Spain.* Princeton: Princeton University Press.

Ciudad Real, Antonio de. 1929. *Diccionario de motul Maya-Español.* Mérida, MX: Talleres de la Compañía Tipográfical Yucateca.

———. 1976. *Tratado Curioso y Docto de las Grandezas de la Nueva Espana.* MX: Universidad Nacional Autonoma de Mexico.

———. 1993. Tratado curioso y docto de las grandezas de la Nueva España: Relación breve y verdadera de algunas cosas de las muchas que sucedieron al padre fray Alonso Ponce en las provincias de la Nueva España, siendo comisario general de aquellas partes. México, MX: Universidad Nacional Autónoma de México.

Cline, Howard. 1948. The henequén episode in Yucatan. *Inter-American Economic Affairs* 2.2: 30–51.

Clifford, James, and George E. Marcus, eds. 1986. *Writing Culture: the Poetics and Politics of Ethnography.* Berkeley: University of California Press.

Clifford, James. 1988. *The predicament of culture: twentieth-century ethnography, literature, and art.* Cambridge, MA: Harvard University Press.

Cocom, Juan Castillo. 2004. *Commentary:* lost in Mayaland. *The Journal of Latin American Anthropology* 9.1: 179–86.

Cohen, Lizabeth. 1990. *Making a New Deal: industrial workers in Chicago, 1919–1939.* Cambridge, UK: Cambridge University Press, 1990.

Comaroff, Jean. 1985. *Body of power, spirit of resistance: the culture and history of a South African people.* Chicago: University of Chicago Press.

Cook, Garrett. 2000. *Renewing the Maya world: expressive culture in a highland town.* Austin: University of Texas Press.

de Certeau, Michel. 1984. *The practice of everyday life.* Berkeley: University of California Press.

DeWalt, Billie R. 1975. Changes in the cargo system of Mesoamerica. *Anthropological Quarterly* 48: 87–105.

Dow, James. 1977. Religion in the organization of a Mexican peasant economy. In *Peasant livelihood: studies in economic anthropology and cultural ecology,* ed. Rhoda Halperin and James Dow. New York: St. Martin's Press. 215–26.

Dumont, Louis. 1970. *Homo hierarchicus: the caste system and its implications.* Trans. M. Sainsbury, L. Dumont, and B. Gulati. Chicago: University of Chicago Press.

Dundes, Alan. 2002. *The Shabbat elevator and other sabbath subterfuges: an unorthodox essay on circumventing custom and Jewish character.* Lanham: Rowman and Littlefield Publishers.

Eagleton, Terry. 1983. *Literary theory.* Minneapolis: University of Minnesota Press.

Earle, Duncan. 1990. Appropriating the enemy: Highland Maya religious organization and community survival. In Stephen and Dow, *Class, politics, and popular religion,* 115–39.

Eco, Umberto. 1984. Frames of comic freedom. In *Carnival!,* ed. Thomas Sebeok. New York: Mouton. 1–9.

Elmendorf, Marg Lindsay. 1976. *Nine Ma'yan Women: A Village Faces Change.* New York: Schenkman Publishing Co., John Wiley and Sons.

Fallaw, Ben W. 1998. Bartolocallismo: Calles, García Correa, y los henequeneros de Yucatán. *Boletín del Archivo Plutarco Elías Calles* (Bulletin of the Presidential Archives of Plutarco Elías Calles) 27: 1–32.

Eiss, Paul K. 2004. Deconstructing Indians, reconstructing patria: indigenous education in Yucatán from the Porfiato to the Mexican Revolution. *The Journal of Latin American Anthropology* 9.1: 119–50.

Fallaw, Ben. 1997. Cárdenas and the Caste War that wasn't: land, ethnicity, and state formation in Yucatán, 1847–1937. *The Americas* 53.4: 551–77.

———. 2004. Rethinking Mayan resistance: changing relations between federal teachers and Mayan communities in eastern Yucatán, 1929–1935. *The Journal of Latin American Anthropology* 9.1: 151–78.

Farriss, Nancy. 1984. *Maya society under colonial rule: the collective enterprise of survival.* Princeton: Princeton University Press.

Favre, Henri. 1973. *Cambio y continuidad entre los Mayas de Mexico.* México City, MX: Siglo Veintiuno.

Fernández de Lizardi, José Joaquin. 1944. *Don Catrín de la Fachenda y fragmentos de otras.* México City, MX: Editorial Cultura.

Fernandez Repetto, Francisco, and Genny Negroe Sierra. 1977. Caminando y paseando con la virgen: practicas de la religion popular e identidades sociales en el noroccidente de Yucatan. In *Identidades sociales en Yucatán,* ed. Maria Cecilia Lara Cebada. Mérida, MX: Universidad Autonoma de Yucatan, Facultad de Ciencias Antropologicas. 101–31.

Fink, Leon. 2003. *The Maya of Morganton: work and community in the Nuevo New South.* Chapel Hill: University of North Carolina Press.

Finkler, Kaja. 1985. *Spiritualist healers in Mexico: successes and failures of alternative therapeutics.* Salem: Sheffield Publishing Company,

Fischer, Edward. 1999. Cultural logic and Maya identity: rethinking constructivism and essentialism. *Current Anthropology* 43.4: 473–99.

Fischer, Edward F., and Carol Hendrickson. 2003. *Tecpán, Guatemala: a modern Maya town in global and local context.* Boulder: Westview Press.

Foster, George. 1953. Cofradía and compadrazgo in Spain and Spanish America. *Southwestern Journal of Anthropology* 1: 1–27.

———. 1967. *Tzintzuntzan: Mexican peasants in a changing world.* Boston: Little Brown and Company.

Freire, Paulo. 1970. *Pedagogy of the oppressed.* Trans. Myra Bergmean Rios. New York: Herder and Herder.

Friedlander, Judith. 1975. *Being Indian in Hueyapan: a study of forced identity in contemporary México.* New York: St. Martin's Press.

Fuente, Julio de la. 1951. Ethnic and communal relations. In *Heritage of conquest,* ed. Sol Tax. Glencoe: Free Press, 76–96.

Gabbert, Wolfgang. 2004a. *Becoming Maya: ethnicity and social inequality in Yucatán since 1500.* Tucson: University of Arizona Press.

———. 2004b. Of friends and foes: the caste war and ethnicity in Yucatán. *The Journal of Latin American Anthropology* 9.1: 90–118.

Gal, Susan. 1989. Language and political economy. *Annual Review of Anthropology* 18: 345–67.

Gamio, Manuel. 1916. *Forjando patria.* México City, MX: Librería de Porrua Hermanos.

———. 1926. "The Indian basis of Mexican civilization." In *Aspects of Mexican civilization,* ed. José Vasconcelos and Manuel Gamio. Chicago.

Gans, Harold. 1979. Symbolic ethnicity: the future of ethnic groups and cultures in America. *Ethnic and Racial Studies* 2.1: 1–20.

García Cantón, Alberto. 1965. *Memorias de un ex-haciendado henequenero.* Mérida, MX: Imprenta Diaz Massa.

García Márquez, Gabriel. 1984. *Chronicle of a death foretold.* Trans. Gregory Rabassa. New York: Ballantine Books.

Gibson, Charles. 1964. *The Aztecs under Spanish rule: A history of the Indians of the Valley of Mexico.* Stanford: Stanford University Press.

Gil Calvo, Enrique. 1991. *Estado de fiesta.* Madrid, ESP: Espasa Calpe.

Giménez, Gilberto. 1978. *Cultura popular y religión en el Anahuac.* México City, MX: Centro de Estudios Ecumenicos.

Godelier, Maurice. 1977. *Perspectives in Marxist anthropology.* Cambridge, UK: Cambridge University Press.

Goldkind, Victor. 1965. Social stratification in the peasant community: Redfield's Chan Kom reinterpreted. *American Anthropologist* 67.4: 863–84.

González Navarro, Moisés. 1970. *Raza y tierra.* México City, MX: El Colegio de México.

González, Gaspar Pedro. 1995. *A Mayan life.* Rancho Palo Verdes: Yax Te' Press.

Goodman, Felicitas. 2001. *Maya apocalypse: seventeen years with the women of a Yucatan village.* Bloomington: Indiana University Press.

Gossen, Gary. 1974. *Chamulas in the world of the sun: time and space in a Maya oral tradition.* Cambridge: Harvard University Press.

Gould, Stephen Jay. 1994. The Geometer of race. *Discover.* November: 65–69.

Graeber, David. 2001. *Toward an anthropological theory of value: the false coin of our own dreams.* New York: Palgrave.

Graff, Gary Wendell. 1973. *Cofradías in the New Kingdom of Granada: lay fraternities in a Spanish American frontier society, 1600–1775.* PhD diss., University of Wisconsin, Madison.

Greenberg, James B. 1981. *Santiago's sword: Chatino peasant religion and economics.* Berkeley: University of California Press.

———. 1990. Sanctity and resistance in closed corporate indigenous communities: coffee money, violence, and ritual organization in Chatino communities in Oaxaca. In Stephen and Dow, *Class, politics, and popular religion,* 95–114.

Gutiérrez Estévez, Manuel. 1988. *Mito y ritual en América.* Madrid, ESP: Editorial Alhambra S.A.

Gwynne, Robert N. 1999. Globalization, neoliberalism, and economic change in South America and Mexico. In *Latin America transformed: globalization and modernity,* ed. Robert N. Gwynne and Cristobal Kay. London: Oxford University Press. 68–97.

Hale, Charles. 1999. Travel warning: elite appropriations of hybridity and other progressive sounding discourses in highland Guatemala. *Journal of American Folklore* 112.445: 297–315.

———. 2006. *Más que un indio: racial ambivalence and neoliberal multiculturalism in Guatemala.* Santa Fe: School of American Research.

Hanks, William F. 1990. *Referential practice: language and lived space among the Maya.* Chicago: University of Chicago Press.

Hansen, Asael, and Juan Bastarrachea Manzano. 1984. *Merida: su transformacion de capital colonial naciente metropolis en 1935.* México City, MX: Instituto Nacional de Antropología e Historia.

Harris, Marvin. 1964. *Patterns of race in the Americas.* New York: Wallen.

Hart, K. 1986. *Economics as culture: models and metaphors of livelihood.* London: Routledge and Kegan Paul.

Haunani-Kay, Trask. 1991. Natives and anthropologists: the colonial struggle. *The Contemporary Pacific* (Spring): 159–67.

Haviland, John. 1977. *Gossip, reputation, and knowledge in Zinacantán.* Chicago: University of Chicago Press.

Hendrickson, Carol. 1995. *Weaving identities: construction of dress and self in a highland Guatemala town.* Austin: University of Texas Press.

Hervik, Peter. 1999. *Mayan people within and beyond boundaries: social categories and lived identity in Yucatán.* Amsterdam, NL: Harwood Academic Publishers.

Hewitt de Alcantara, Cynthia. 1984. *Anthropological Perspectives on Rural Mexico.* London: Routledge and Kegan Paul.

Hobsbawm, Eric, and Terrance Ranger, eds. 1992. *The invention of tradition.* Cambridge, UK: Cambridge University Press.

Hostettler, Ueli. 2004. Commentary: rethinking Maya identity in Yucatan, 1500–1940. *The Journal of Latin American Anthropology* 9.1: 179–86.

Jay, Martin. 1973. *The dialectical imagination: a history of the Frankfurt School and the Institute for Social Research, 1923–1950.* Boston: Little, Brown and Company.

Joseph, Gilbert. 1982. *Revolution from without: Yucatán, Mexico, and the United States 1880–1924.* Cambridge, UK: Cambridge University Press.

———. 1994. Rethinking Mexican revolutionary mobilization: Yucatan's seasons of upheaval, 1909–1915. In *Everyday forms of state formation: revolution and the negotiation of rule in modern Mexico,* ed. Gilbert Joseph and Daniel Nugent. Durham: Duke University Press. 135–69.

Karim, John Tofik. 2004. A cultural politics of entrepreneurship in nation-making: Phoenicians, Turks, and the Arab commercial essence in Brazil. *The Journal of Latin American Anthropology* 9.2: 319–51.

Katz, Friedrich. 1962. El sistema de plantacion y la esclavitud. *Revista Mexicana de Ciencias Politicas y Sociales* 8.27: 102–35.

Kopytoff, Igor. 1986. The cultural biography of things: commoditization as process. In Appadurai, *The social life of things,* 64–94.

Lafaye, Jacques. 1976. *Quetzalcóatl and Guadalupe: the formation of Mexican national consciousness, 1531–1813.* Chicago: University of Chicago Press.

Lambek, Michael. 1989. From disease to discourse: remarks on the conceptualization of trance and spirit possession. In *Altered states of consciousness and mental health in cross-cultural perspective,* ed. C.A. Ward. Newbury Park: Sage, 36–61.

Laughlin, Robert M., and Carol Karasik. 1988. *The people of the bat: Maya tales and dreams from Zinacantán.* Washington, DC: Smithsonian Institution Press.

Levine, Lawrence W. 1977. *Black culture and black consciousness: Afro-American thought from slavery to freedom.* London: Oxford University Press.

Lévi-Strauss, Claude. 1963. *Structural anthropology.* Garden City: Anchor Books.

————. 1969. *The savage mind.* Chicago: University of Chicago Press.

Lewis, I.M. 1989. *Religion in Context: Cults and Charisma.* Cambridge University Press.

Lewis, Oscar. 1961. *The children of Sanchez: autobiography of a Mexican family.* New York: Random House.

Ligorred Perramón, Francisco de Asís. 1990. *Consideraciones sobre la literatura oral de los Mayas modernos.* México City, MX: Instituto Nacional de Antropología e Historia.

Limón, José. 1983. Legendry, metafolklore, and performance: a Mexican-American example. *Western Folklore* 43: 191–208.

————. 1989. Carne, carnales and the carnivalesque: Bakhtinian bathos, disorder and narrative discourse. *American Ethnologist* 16: 471–86.

————., and M.J. Young. 1989. Frontier, settlements and development in folklore studies, 1972–1985. *Annual Review of Anthropology* 15: 437–60.

Loewe, Ronald. 1995. *Ambiguity and order: a study of identity and power at the Mexican periphery.* PhD diss., University of Chicago.

————. 2003. Yucatán's dancing pig's head (*Cuch*): icon, carnival, and commodity. *The Journal of American Folklore* 462: 420–43.

————. 2006. Mayan folklore. *Encyclopedia of world folklore and folklife.* Westport: Greenwood Press. 256–68.

————. 2007. Euphemism, parody, insult and innuendo: rhetoric and ethnic identity at the Mexican periphery. *Journal of American Folklore* 120.477: 284–307.

————. 2009. Reviews. *Anthropology* 38: 237–62.

Löfgren, Ovar. 1994. Consuming interests. In *Consumption and identity,* ed. Jonathan Friedman. Chur, Switzerland, CH: Harwood Academic Publishers. 47–70.

Loucky, James, and Marilyn Moors, eds. 2000. *The Maya diaspora: Guatemalan roots, new American lives.* Philadelphia: Temple University Press.

Luna Kan, Francisco, Luis H. Hoyos Villanueva, Carlos A Echánove Trujillo: Comisión éditora de la Enciclopedia Yucatanense. 1977–1981. *Enciclopedia Yucatanense.* Mexico: Gobierno de Yucatán.

Malinowski, Bronislaw, and Julio de la Fuente. 1982. *Malinowski in México: the economics of a Mexican market system,* ed. Susan Drucker-Brown. London: Routledge and Kegan Paul.

Marx, Karl. 1939. *Capital: a critical analysis of capitalist production.* New York: The International Publishers Company.

Medin, Tzvi. 1972. *Ideologia y praxis politica de Lazaro Cardenas.* México City, MX: Siglo Veintiuno Editores.

Menéndez Diaz, Conrado. 1986. *El humorismo en Yucatán.* Mérida, MX: Maldonado Editores.

Miller, Daniel. 1994. Style and ontology. In *Consumption and identity,* ed. Jonathan Friedman. Chur, Switzerland, CH: Harwood Academic Publishers. 71–96.

Mintz, Sydney. 1985. *Sweetness and power: the place of sugar in modern history.* New York: Viking Press.

Molina Enríquez, Andrés. 1909. *Los grandes problemas nacionales.* México City, MX: Ediciones Era.

Montalvo, F., and E. Codina. 2001. Skin color and Latinos in the United States. *Ethnicities* 1: 321–41.

Montejo, Víctor. 1991. *The bird who cleans the world and other Mayan fables.* Willimantic, CT: Curbstone Press.

————. 2001. *El Qanil: man of lightning.* Tucson: University of Arizona Press.

Muñoz, Fernando. 1987. *El teatro regional de Yucatán.* México City, MX: Grupo Editorial Gaceta.

Napolitano, Valentina. 2002. *Migrants, mujercitas, and medicine men: living in urban México.* Berkeley: University of California Press.

Nash, June. 1970. *In the eyes of the ancestors.* New Haven: Yale University Press.

————. 1979. *We eat the mines and the mines eat us: dependency and exploitation in a Bolivian tin mining community.* New York: Columbia University Press.

Nash, Manning. 1958. Political relations in Guatemala. *Social and Economic Studies* 7: 65–75.

Nelson, Diane. 1999. *A finger in the wound: body politics in quincentennial Guatemala*. Berkeley: University of California Press.

Nomland, John B. 1967. *Teatro Mexicano contemporáneo (1900–1950)*. México City, MX: Ed. INBA.

Nugent, Daniel, and Ana Maria Alonso. 1994. Multiple selective traditions in agrarian reform and agrarian struggle: popular culture and state formation in the ejido of Namiquipa, Chihuahua. In *Everyday forms of state formation: revolution and the negotiation of rule in modern Mexico*, ed. Gilbert Joseph and Daniel Nugent. Durham: Duke University Press. 209–46.

Nutini, Hugo G. 1968. *San Bernardino Contla*. Pittsburgh: University of Pittsburgh Press.

O'Gorman, Edmundo. 1981. *Servando Teresa de Mier: Obras Completas*. Mexico: Universidad Autónoma Nacional de Mexico.

Ownby, Ted. 1999. *American dreams in Mississippi: consumers, poverty, and culture, 1830–1998*. Chapel Hill: University of North Carolina Press.

Pacheco Cruz, Santiago. 1936. *Justicia proletaria*. Mérida, MX: Editorial Oriente.

———. 1960. *Usos, costumbres, religión y supersticiones de los Mayas*. Mérida, MX: Imprenta Manlio.

Paredes, Americo. 1966. The Anglo-American in Mexican folklore. In *New voices in American Studies*, ed. R. Brown. Lafayette: Purdue University Press. 113–28.

Parry, Jonathan, and Maurice Bloch, eds. 1989. *Money and the morality of exchange*. Cambridge, UK: Cambridge University Press.

Patch, Robert. 1981. *Maya and Spaniard in Yucatán, 1648–1812*. Stanford: Stanford University Press.

Peninche Vallado, Humberto. 1987 [1937]. La incorporación del Indio a la civilización es la obra complementaria del reparto ejidal. In *Unificación campesina en Yucatán (1938)*, ed. Cetina Sierra, José Adonay, and Luis Alvarado Alonzo. Edición Conmemorativa del Estado de Yucatán. Mérida, MX: Gobierno del Estado de Yucatán.

Pérez Sabido, Luis. 1983. *Bailes y danzas tradicionales de Yucatán*. Mérida, MX: de DIF.

Phillips, Lynne, ed. 1998. *The third wave of modernization in Latin America: cultural perspectives on neoliberalism*. Wilmington: Jaguar Books on Latin America, Number 16.

Pohl, Mary. 1981. Ritual continuity and transformation in Mesoamerica: reconstructing the ancient Maya Cuch ritual. *American Antiquity* 46: 513–29.

Press, Irwin. 1975. *Tradition and adaptation: life in a modern Yucatan Maya village*. Westport: Greenwood Press.

———. 1977. Historical dimensions of orientation to change in a Yucatec peasant community. In *Anthropology and history in Yucatan*, ed. Grant Jones. Austin: University of Texas Press, 275–288.

Quezada, Noemí. 1989. *Enfermedad y maleficia: el curandero en el México colonial*. México City, MX: Universidad Nacional Autónoma de México.

Ramírez Carrillo, Luis A. 1994. *Secretos de familia: Libaneses y élites empresariales en Yucatán*. México City, MX: Consejo Nacional para la Cultura y las Artes.

Re Cruz, Alicia. 1996. *The two milpas of Chan Kom*. Albany: State University of New York Press.

Redfield, Margaret Park. 1937. The folk literature of a Yucatecan town. *Contributions to American Archaeology*, Vol. 3. Washington, DC: Carnegie Institution of Washington.

Redfield, Robert. 1941. *The folk culture of Yucatán*. Chicago: University of Chicago Press.

———. 1950. *A village that chose progress*. Chicago: University of Chicago Press.

———. 1964. *A village that chose progress: Chan Kom revisited*. Chicago: University of Chicago Press.

Redfield, Robert and Alfonso Villa Rojas. 1934. *Chan Kom: a Maya village*. Washington, DC: Carnegie Institution of Washington.

———. 1990 [1934]. *Chan Kom: a Maya village*. Prospect Heights: Waveland Press.

Reed, Nelson. 2001. *The Caste War of Yucatán*. Palo Alto: Stanford University Press.

Reina, Ruben E. 1966. *The law of the saints*. Indianapolis: Bobbs-Merrill.

Restall, Matthew. 1997. *The Maya World: Yucatec Culture and Society, 1550–1850*. Stanford University Press. 308–309.

Rockwell, Elsie. 1994. Schools of the revolution: enacting and contesting state forms in Tlaxcala, 1910–1930. In *Everyday forms of state formation: revolution and the negotiation of rule in modern Mexico*, ed. Gilbert Joseph and Daniel Nugent. Durham: Duke University Press. 170–208.

Rosado Vega, Luis. 1957. *El alma misteriosa del Maya: tradiciones, leyendas y consejas*. México City, MX: Ediciones Botas.

Roys, Ralph. 1957. *The political geography of the Yucatan Maya*. Washington, DC: Carnegie Institution of Washington.

Roys, Ralph L. 1967. *Book of Chilam Balam of Chymayel (civilization of the American Indian)*. 2nd rev. ed. Norman: University of Oklahoma Press.

Rugeley, Terry. 1996. *Yucatán's Maya peasantry and the origins of the caste war*. Austin: University of Texas Press.

———. 2001a. *Maya wars: ethnographic accounts from nineteenth-century Yucatán*. Norman: University of Oklahoma Press.

———. 2001b. *Of wonders and wise men: religion and popular cultures in Southeast Mexico, 1800–1876*. Austin: University of Texas Press.

Rumeu de Armas, Antonio. 1942. *Historia de la previsión social en España*. N.p.

Sahlins, Marshall. 1985. *Islands of history*. Chicago: University of Chicago Press.

Scholes, France V., and Ralph L. Roys. 1968. *The Maya Chontal Indians of Acalan-Tixchel: a contribution to the history and ethnography of the Yucatan Peninsula*. 2nd ed. Norman: University of Oklahoma Press.

Scott, James. 1985. *Weapons of the weak: everyday forms of peasant resistance*. New Haven: Yale University Press.

Sharp, Lesley. 1993. *The possessed and the dispossessed: spirits, identity, and power in a Madagascar migrant town*. Berkeley: University of California Press.

Sherzer, Joel. 1983. *Kuna ways of speaking: an ethnographic perspective*. Austin: University of Texas Press.

Slade, Doreen L. 1973. *The mayordomos of San Mateo: political economy of a religious system*. PhD diss., University of Pittsburgh.

Smith, Waldemar. 1977. *The fiesta system and economic change*. New York: Columbia University Press.

Spell, Jefferson Rea. 1931. *The life and works of José Joaquin Fernández de Lizardi*. Publication of the Series on Romantic Languages and Literature, no. 23. Philadelphia: University of Pennsylvania Press.

Stavenhagen, Rodolfo. 1975. *Social classes in agrarian societies*. Garden City: Anchor Press.

Stephen, Lynn, and James Dow, eds. 1990. *Class, politics, and popular religion in Mexico and Central America*. Washington, DC: Society for Latin American Anthropology Publication Series.

Stephens, John L. 1963 [1843]. *Incidents of travel in Yucatán*. New York: Dover Publications.

Suárez, Víctor M. 1979. *El español que se habla en Yucatán*. Mérida, MX: Ediciones de la Universidad de Yucatán.

Sullivan, Paul. 1989. *Unfinished conversations: Mayas and foreigners between two wars*. New York: Alfred A. Knopf.

———. 2000. The Yucatec Maya. In *Supplement to the Handbook of Middle American Indians*, Vol. 6, ed. John Monaghan and Victoria Bricker. Austin: University of Texas Press. 207–23.

Taussig, Michael. 1980. *The devil and commodity fetishism in South America*. Chapel Hill: University of North Carolina Press.

Tax, Sol. 1937. The municipio of the midwestern highlands of Guatemala. *American Anthropologist* 39: 423–44.

———. 1941. World view and social relations in Indian Guatemala. *American Anthropologist* 39: 423–44.

———. 1942. Ethnic Relations in Guatemala. *America Indigena* 2.4: 43–47.

Tedlock, Barbara. 1982. *Time and the highland Maya*. Albuquerque: University of New Mexico Press.

Thompson, Philip C. 1978. *Tekanto in the eighteenth century.* PhD diss. Tulane University, New Orleans.

Thompson, Richard A. 1974. *The winds of tomorrow.* Chicago: University of Chicago Press.

Thompson, Stith. 1955–58. Motif index of folk-literature. 6 vols. Bloomington: Indiana University Press.

Trask, Haunani-Kay. 1991. "Natives and Anthropologists: The Colonial Struggle," *Contemporary Pacific* Volume 3, No. 1. (Spring): 111–117.

Turner, John Kenneth. 1969 [1911]. *Barbarous Mexico.* Austin: University of Texas Press.

Turner, Victor. 1974. *Dramas, fields, and metaphors: symbolic action in human society.* Ithaca: Cornell University Press.

Underiner, Tamara L. 2004. *Contemporary theatre in Mayan Mexico: death defying acts.* Austin: University of Texas Press.

Vasconcelos, José. 1966. *La raza cósmica: misión de la raza iberoamericana; notas de viajes a la America del Sur.* Barcelona: Agencia Mundial de Librería.

Vazquez Lopez, Effy Luz. 1987. El bracero. *Novedades de Yucatán* 19 July.

Villa Rojas, Alfonso. 1987. *Los elegidos de Dios: etnografía de los Mayas de Quintana Roo.* México City, MX: Instituto Nacional Indigenista.

Villanueva Mukul, Eric. 1984. *Asi tomamos las tierras: Henequén y haciendas en Yucatán durante el Porfiriato.* Yucatán, MX: Maldonado Editores.

Vogt, Evon. 1969. *Zinacantan: a Maya community in the highlands of Chiapas.* Cambridge, MA: Belknap Press of Harvard University Press.

Wallace, Anthony F.C. 1956. Revitalization movements. *American Anthropologist* 58.2: 264–81.

Warren, Kay. 1978. *The symbolism of subordination: Indian identity in a Guatemalan town.* Austin: University of Texas Press.

———. 1998. *Indigenous movements and their critics: pan-Maya activism in Guatemala.* Princeton: Princeton University Press.

Wasserstrom, Robert. 1983. *Class and society in central Chiapas.* Berkeley: University of California Press.

Watanabe, John. 1992. *Maya saints and souls in a changing world.* Austin: University of Texas Press.

Weigle, M. 1978. Women as verbal artists: reclaiming the Sisters of Enheduana. *Frontiers* 3: 1–9.

White, Hayden. 1987. *The content of the form: narrative discourse and historical representation.* Baltimore: The Johns Hopkins University Press.

Williams, Raymond. 1973. *The country and the city.* London: Chatto and Windus.

———. 1983. *The country and the city.* New York: Oxford University Press.

Wilson, Carter. 1974. *Crazy February: death and life in the Maya highlands of Mexico.* Berkeley: University of California Press.

Wolf, Eric. 1957. Closed corporate peasant communities in Meso-America and Central Java. *Southwestern Journal of Anthropology* 13.1: 1–18.

———. 1959. *Sons of the shaking earth.* Chicago: University of Chicago Press.

Worsley, Peter. 1986 [1968]. *The trumpet shall sound: a study of "cargo" cults in Melanesia.* New York: Schocken Books.

Zea, Leopoldo. 1974. *Positivism in Mexico.* Austin: University of Texas Press.

INDEX